Mulattoes
and Race Mixture

Studies in
American History and Culture, No. 4

Other Titles in This Series

Mulattoes
and Race Mixture

American Attitudes and Images, 1865-1918

by
John G. Mencke

RESEARCH PRESS

Library of Congress Cataloging in Publication Data

Mencke, John G   1949-
  Mulattoes and race mixture.

   (Studies in American history and culture ; no. 4)
   Bibliography: p.
   Includes index.
   1. Mulattoes—United States. 2. United States—Race
relations. 3. Afro-Americans in literature. I. Title.
II. Series.

E185.62.M46 1978   301.45'1'0420973   78-27611
ISBN 0-8357-0984-1
ISBN 0-8357-0985-X pbk.

CONTENTS

TABLES

INTRODUCTION

One of the marked peculiarities of the American racial system has been the general failure to distinguish between blacks and mulattoes. With the exception of Canada, the United States is unique in its insistence upon classifying all persons of Negro ancestry as black, regardless of their actual physical appearance. In essence, there are only two qualities in the Americana racial pattern: white and black. An individual is either one or he is the other--there simply is no intermediate position in this country.

A large part of the explanation for this curious fact revolves around the way in which Americans have always identified those who were Negroes. Elsewhere in the hemisphere, the most important considerations involve physical appearance (and, to a lesser extent, economic status). Considerable attention is given to an individual's skin color, facial features, hair texture, etc., in recognition of the possibility of a mixed racial heritage. The result is that the racial system reflects a continuum or spectrum of colors from white to black, with an individual's social status significantly linked to his position on that color continuum (although a high economic position can help to offset a darker skin color). In the United States, however, the most important factor is ancestry. If it is known that an individual is even remotely descended from a black person, he is classified as a Negro, even if he looks and/or acts white. Although words like *mulatto, quadroon,* and *octoroon* have been used on occasion in America, in reality they have little or no social or legal significance. America's racial system recognizes only the dichotomy of black and white, and the mixed-blood is invariably classified as black if his ancestry is known.[1]

At the heart of this attitude is the particular manner in which Americans understand the meaning of race and racial differences, the fundamental concept of which is the notion of "blood." In Western culture, blood has traditionally been regarded as that vital element of the body which carries, and through which is transmitted, the hereditary qualities of a people. As anthropologist M. F. Ashley Montagu explained in 1943

> most people believe that blood is equivalent to heredity, and that blood, therefore, is that part of the organism which determines the

quality of the person. By extension, it is further generally believed that the social as well as the biological status of the person is determined by the blood he has inherited.[2]

Blood thus carries with it a variety of traits--physical and cultural, individual and racial--so that a person is very much the product of his ancestry, including his racial ancestry.

The interaction of this line of thought with basic racial attitudes is most apparent in American perceptions of the mulatto and the question of racial amalgamation. Indeed, it seems to offer an explanation of why Americans have consistently viewed mixed-bloods as blacks. Certainly there is no inherent logic in this attitude. A person whose ancestry is half white and half black could just as easily be defined as white than Negro, yet this has never been the case in the United States. Deeply-rooted beliefs in the permanence and distinctiveness of racial traits have led Americans to see all who possess "black blood" as Negroes, even if that black blood is greatly outweighed by white.

The mulatto has therefore held an anomalous position in American race relations. Sociologists speak of him as a "marginal man," an individual caught between conflicting races and/or cultures whose position lacks concrete definition.[3] Unlike marginal beings in some other societies, the status of the American mulatto is particularly complex due to the dynamics of the racial system. In many societies, the mixed-blood acts as a bridge between the two primary groups; often mixed-blooded status is a first step towards eventual social mobility for one's descendants. In the United States, though, whites have sought to force mulattoes back into the black race by insisting on a two-caste racial system. Such an attitude essentially denies the existence of cultural and economic divisions within the Afro-American population. Yet the Afro-American community has in fact always been characterized by conspicuous social stratification in which color plays a significant although not determinant role in affixing an individual's status. The fact that a light complexion has often been linked to high socioeconomic status among Afro-Americans, however, has inclined Negroes towards perceiving the American racial system more in terms of a three-caste pattern, similar, perhaps, to that of Latin America.

Consequently, the mulatto finds himself in an unsettled position. Pressures from the white majority seek to deny his intermediate status, particularly in regard to biological racial considerations. At the same time, stratification within the Afro-American population promotes at least a culturally intermediate role for those mulattoes of middle- and upper-class status. Culturally, then, many mulattoes lean towards the white side of the racial division, while in racial terms they are pushed back toward the black side. For many mulattoes, the result of these antagonistic pressures has been bitter frustration and mental conflict. The very fact that the mulatto is often closer to the white man in cultural attainments and physical traits renders it all the more difficult for him to accept the extreme color division of the American racial system and the discrimination which accompanies it. The mulatto finds himself unable to enter the white group yet at the same time out of touch with much of the black.

This study seeks to explain how Americans viewed the mulatto and the idea of race mixing in the years between Reconstruction and the First World War. This was a crucial period in American race relations, as both races struggled to adjust to emancipation, changing social and economic patterns, and new ideas about the nature of man and his world. The notions about race which evolved during this half-century found expression in a variety of legal and extra-legal practices which dominated relations between whites and Afro-Americans until the middle of the twentieth century.

Attitudes about mulattoes and racial amalgamation reflect the turmoil inherent in this process of racial readjustment. More significantly, however, they offer insight into how Americans understood race and the meaning of racial differences. Ultimately, it was these ideas which were at the foundation of public policy and social practice. White Americans treated Negroes in accordance with their understanding, conscious and unconscious, of the nature of the black man and his relation to themselves. Since they perceived him, for a variety of reasons, as distinctly inferior, they had few qualms about circumscribing his opportunities or denying him equal rights.

Attitudes about mulattoes go somewhat beyond basic ideas about race, however. Mulattoes were visible evidence of the mixing which had long gone on in the shadows of black/white relations. As such, they were a powerful source of guilt, for they physically contradicted white notions about the crucial importance of maintaining racial purity. In this sense, white attitudes about the mulatto reveal an uneasiness which haunted white self-perceptions. Perhaps, after all, the white man was not really that different from the Negro he so disdained.

Because this study deals with attitudes about color and color differences, I have attempted to be rather precise when speaking of such color differences among Afro-Americans. This effort was hampered by the fact that Americans have traditionally lumped all persons of African descent into a single category. This is itself testimony to how little attention Americans give to color gradations among Afro-Americans, despite the fact that the vast majority of them are of mixed white and black ancestry.[4]

Various words have passed in and out of fashionable use among whites and Afro-Americans for referring to persons of African descent--"Negroes," "colored people" (or the more formal "people of color"), "Afro-Americans," "blacks," etc. Unlike Latin America, however, there have never been widely used words to designate people of mixed ancestry. The word "mulatto" technically refers to the offspring of one white parent and one black parent. However, I have used it in the more general sense to include all those of mixed white and black ancestry, but particularly those who show marked physical signs of white blood, especially in skin color. This is essentially the way in which the word has been used in the United States.[5] I have likewise adopted the popular usage of the word "blood," including employing it in a figurative sense to mean ancestry. Consequently, a "mixed-blood" is any individual whose ancestry includes both blacks and whites, and the term is therefore synonymous with "mulatto." Today the word "black" is generally used in a collective sense to include all persons of African ancestry, regardless of their actual skin color. At times, chiefly for literary purposes, I have also employed the word in this manner, but more often it is used to mean black (or very dark) in color or to designate pure African ancestry rather than a mixed racial background. I trust the variations in these two usages will be evident by the nature of the text. As an inclusive term, I have alternately used "Negro" or "Afro-American" to designate all those persons of African ancestry, whether mixed or not, although "Negro" is also used to refer to the racial grouping as well.

In essence, then, I have accepted the traditional classification of mulattoes as Negro. While there is obviously no logic in this outlook, for purposes of clarity it seemed unavoidable. Perhaps the question to be pondered is why white Americans have always been so intent upon making this classification. Why have they found it so necessary to attempt to disavow their kinship with the mulatto, almost to the point of denying his very existence? What does this attitude reveal about race relations in the United States and about the white man's fundamental understanding of himself?

NOTES

[1]The best discussion of this contrast in basic racial patterns regarding classification of Negroes and its overall consequences for race relations is Carl N. Degler, *Neither Black Nor White: Slavery and Race Relations in Brazil and the United States* (New York: Macmillan Company, 1971), esp. pp.101-112. Degler contends that the mulatto is the key to understanding the nature of race relations in the United States and Brazil.

[2]M. F. Ashley Montagu, "The Myth of Blood," *Psychiatry.* VI, 1 (February, 1943), 17.

[3]See Everett V. Stonequist, "The Problem of the Marginal Man," *American Journal of Sociology,* XLI, 1 (July, 1935), 1-12 and Everett V. Stonequist, *The Marginal Man: A Study in Personality and Culture Conflict* (New York: Charles Scribner's Sons, 1937). The concept of the "marginal man" was originally developed by Robert E. Park, a sociologist at the University of Chicago.

[4]See Thomas F. Pettigrew, *A Profile of the American Negro* (Princeton, N.J.: D. Van Nostrand Company, Inc., 1964). p.68. Pettigrew notes that the estimates of the proportion of Afro-Americans with white ancestry varies from 72 to 83 percent. Perhaps it should be noted that there is no uniformity of color among native Africans, so that estimates from physical appearance are hindered by the basic problem of a lack of a standard of comparison.

[5]On the American use of the word "mulatto" to apply to all persons of mixed blood and other terms which have been employed in the United States and elsewhere to designate persons of mixed racial backgrounds, see Edward Byron Reuter, *The Mulatto in the United States, Including a Study of the Role of Mixed-Blood Races Throughout the World* (Boston: Richard G. Badger, 1918), pp. 11-14; Salme Pekkala, Marian B. Hamilton, and Wiley Alford, "Some Words and Terms Designating, or Relating to, Racially Mixed Persons or Groups," in Edgar T. Thompson and Everett C. Hughes, eds., *Race: Individual and Collective Behavior* (Glencoe, Ill.: The Free Press, 1958), pp. 52-57; Stonequist, *Marginal Man,* pp. 24-27.

CHAPTER I

AN AMERICAN ANOMALY

Few people in American history have held as ambiguous a position as those whose blood mixes that of the white and the black. Racial distinctions, of course, have always been a cornerstone of the American social system. Yet mulattoes clearly confounded all efforts to solidify those distinctions, for logic contradicted their assignment to either the white or black race. They defied the black/white dichotomy whites sought to impose upon race relations in America. At the same time, they represented a striking affront to the very foundation of that dichotomy, because their mixed blood testified to the white man's inability to maintain racial distinctions in the sexual realm. From the earliest English settlement in North America, whites publicly decried the practice of racial mixing. On an individual, private basis, however, whites in all social classes often abandoned their racial scruples to mix with blacks. Perhaps this was inevitable, for as the anthropologist Melville J. Herskovits has noted, "two human groups never meet but they mingle their blood."[1] Yet in America, this mixing produced a highly confusing situation, as whites struggled to come to grips with the presence of a large and ever-increasing mulatto population in their midst--to understand just what the nature and the role of the mulatto were, and what his presence ultimately revealed about the white man himself.

Although race mixing began soon after the first blacks were landed in English American in 1619, it was not until 1850 that extensive, concrete statistics were generated which detailed color as well as racial differences within the American population. Prior to that time, only a few special or local censuses had made such distinctions. In 1755, for instance, a Maryland census showed 8 percent of the colony's Negroes to be mulatto. Out of a total Negro population of 42,764, mulattoes numbered 3,592, of whom 1,460 were free.[2] At that time, Maryland had about one-sixth of the total Negro population in America. Edward Byron Reuter, a sociologist whose career was devoted to the study of the subject of race mixture in America, argued that, taking Maryland as typical of the mainland colonies with regard to racial intermixture, it can be estimated that there were approximately 21,000 mulattoes in the country at that time. By 1790, he suggested, that number might well have reached 120,000.[3]

In 1850, for the first time, federal census enumerators were instructed to designate whether Negroes were black or mulatto by registering a "B" or an "M" in a space on the schedule. Subsequent censuses in 1860, 1870, 1890, 1910, and 1920 also sought to establish the number of mixed-bloods within the overall Negro population. In 1890, in fact, this effort even extended to dividing mixed-bloods into mulattoes (persons having three- to five-eighths black blood), quadroons (those with one-fourth black blood), and octoroons (those having one-eighth or less black blood). The variability of instructions given to enumerators and the fact that ultimately all designations depended on the enumerators' ability to perceive traces of white or black blood together made the specific accuracy of these census figures somewhat dubious.[4] Yet the total numbers do provide a rough picture of basic demographic factors involving the nation's mulatto population. It is possible, for example, to get an idea of the proportion of Negroes who were of mixed blood, as well as of the urban and rural distribution of mulattoes and the age and sex divisions within the mulatto population.

In 1850, the census indicated that there were 405,751 mulattoes out of a total Negro population of 3,638,808 and a white population of 19,553,068. Roughly one in nine Negroes (11.2 percent) was of mixed blood. Ten years later, the number of mulattoes had grown 45 percent to 588,352, so that they were now 13.2 percent of the Negro population.[5] These raw figures, however, belie the complexity of the mulatto's status as it had evolved during the ante-bellum period--a position which was itself to change markedly with the coming of the general emancipation in 1865.

2

Throughout the ante-bellum period, most mulattoes, as well as most blacks, were found in the South. In 1850, only 14 percent of all mulattoes (56,877) lived in the North and West, and in 1860 only 11.9 percent (70,003). Yet outside the South mulattoes composed a much larger proportion of the Negro population than they did for the nation as a whole. In 1850, 28.9 percent of Negroes in the North and West were mulatto, and 1860 the figure was 30.9 percent.[6]

There was little or no inclination among Northern whites to recognize color distinctions within the Negro population. Some whites might prefer hiring mulattoes over blacks, but by and large all Negroes were viewed as a single, inferior group. Nevertheless, within the Negro population itself, there was noticeable social stratification, part of which, at least, mirrored distinctions of skin color.[7] Leon F. Litwack, who studied race relations in the ante-bellum North, has explained that, while a light complexion did not guarantee a Negro's place in the socioeconomic hierarchy, "it often afforded him greater economic opportunities, which, in turn, assured him of a high rank in Negro society."[8] Because they believed mulattoes to be more intelligent and physically attractive than pure blacks (usually because of the former's white ancestry), some whites were more inclined to hire mixed-bloods. As Litwack notes, such preferences invariably led some mulattoes to develop a sense of superiority to blacks. Yet because mulattoes were still excluded from white society and had to suffer the legal proscriptions imposed on blacks, most accepted their position in the Afro-American community and, in many instances, provided much of its militant leadership.[9]

Nevertheless, whites' admiration for Caucasian features among mixed-bloods was mirrored by similar sentiments within the Northern Negro community. With whites generally associating light skin with superior qualities, it was not unnatural for many Afro-Americans consciously or unconsciously to do likewise. Among upper- and middle-class Negroes, there was a marked tendency to envy a light complexion and to accept white standards of beauty. Many sought diligently to alter their own appearances accordingly through processes to lighten the skin or straighten the hair.[10] Color, however, was not the sole criterion of social status. Other factors of importance included occupation, wealth, education, church membership, and family background (including the length of a family's freedom and the status of possible white ancestors).[11]

Similar correlations between color and social status characterized the mulatto population in the South, but there the overall situation, because of the much larger numbers involved, was more complex.

For the most part, ante-bellum Southerners tended to follow the general American practice of lumping all persons of any recognizable African ancestry into a single group, regardless of the number of white progenitors. In this regard, American race relations were radically different from those elsewhere in the Western Hemisphere. In both Latin American and the British West Indies, there arose early in the colonial era a recognized pattern of color differentiation which established mulattoes as a distinct intermediate group between the white minority and the black majority. The explanation of this divergence lies in an intersection of various economic, demographic, and psychological factors.

Donald L. Horowitz has compared the British West Indies to the mainland British colonies in an effort to determine why this color distinction developed in one region and not in the other, although the cultural background of the white settlers was identical. One important factor, he believes, involved the genesis of the mulatto population itself. In the United States, a very large portion of mixed-bloods was descended from poor whites (especially through the mixing of white indentured servants and black slaves early in the colonial period). The social stigma attached to their birth and the economically depressed circumstances into which they were born proved overwhelming forces in insuring the degradation of mulattoes. Whites had no reason to differentiate them from free blacks, for mulattoes generally held the same lowly economic position. Many mulattoes, in fact, remained in slavery. This view was so pervasive that it often extended even to the mulatto progeny of high-status whites. While such offspring might be freed and educated, they had little hope of attaining educational equality with white children and were usually prohibited by law from inheriting their fathers' estates. As Horowitz explains, in the United States,

> Economic condition and social status were related. The prevailing social sentiment inhibited the full expression of paternal sentiment, and the depressed condition of the overwhelming majority of free mulattoes reinforced the prevailing social sentiment.[12]

In the British West Indies, on the other hand, the planter class was actively engaged in racial mixing from the very outset, largely because of a scarcity of white women. Planter concubinage with Negro women was open and pervasive, and it led to the growth of a relatively large class of free mulattoes whose position was recognized by their high-status fathers and by the rest of the society. While not the majority of the free Negro population, the number of these cultured mulattoes was sufficiently large to elevate the status of the entire group. Moreover, their own economic and cultural condition, in combination with their fathers' social standing, provided the necessary basis for the perceptual differentiation of the entire mixed-blood group from the free blacks. Paradoxically, explains Horowitz,

> where the class system was most rigid [i.e., in the British West Indies], the color system tended to be most fluid. . . . In the United States, by contrast, the advantaged mulatto group was so exceptional that the depressed status of the great majority was imputed on a color basis to the group. The differences among the colonies were thus quantitative, but their gravitational pull produced qualitative differences in the ascriptive stratification systems.[13]

Other factors important in the decision by whites to recognize mulattoes as a distinct group included the mixed-bloods' role in the economic system and the relative proportion of whites to blacks in a country's population. In the colonial periods of both the British West Indies and Latin America, whites were vastly outnumbered by their black slaves. The resultant security problem and the white sense of uneasiness led the minority to view the mulattoes as allies. To a degree, this involved military support, both against insurrectionary blacks and foreign enemies, but it also involved general social support for the whites. Security needs, then, could help to reinforce the tendency to distinguish brown from black. In the United States, the generally high ratio of whites to blacks rendered the problem of security less acute, so that from the very beginning whites had little reason to look to the mulatto class for assistance. Indeed, as white apprehension about slave unrest grew in the latter decades of the ante-bellum period, their traditional patterns of racial separation made them insist upon the necessity of further circumscribing the privileges of all free nonwhites, brown as well as black.

Particularly in Latin America, there was also an economic need linked to the demarcation of mulattoes as a distinct class. In Brazil, for instance, mulattoes dominated almost all of the skilled trades, providing an essential service which there simply were no whites to perform. As Brazilian society became more complex in the nineteenth century, mulattoes tended to move into the growing professional ranks of the middle class as well.[14] In the United States, although free Negroes, including mulattoes, did fill certain important interstitial economic positions in the ante-bellum South (particularly in the manual trades), they were never as essential to the survival of the plantation system as was the case in Latin America. Further, the large population of lower-class whites may have acted to inhibit the development of mulattoes as an important intermediate economic class.[15]

The most important contrast between the United States and the nations of Latin America and the West Indies involved the extent of racial mixing and social attitudes toward it. In the British West Indies, the heavy white sexual imbalance early in the islands' history resulted in widespread and socially accepted amalgamation between white men and Negro women. Initially, British settlers may have been a bit more squeamish than their Latin neighbors about the fundamental idea of interracial sexual contact, but demographic pressures overcame these reservations rather quickly. By the eighteenth and nineteenth centuries, planter concubinage was nearly universal in the West Indies, even after the white sex ratio had begun to equalize itself.[16] With racial mixing on an overt, accepted level, there was no pressing reason to attempt to hide its results. Consequently, planter manumissions of mixed-blood offspring were the rule, while those whites who failed to do so suffered considerable social scorn.[17]

Similar forces were at work in Latin America. There too the mulatto population was largely the product of mating between white men and slave women, but once again the practice did not involve significant social opprobrium. The relatively small number of white women, their highly subordinate status, and the presence of masses of Negro women made miscegenation a natural and common practice.[18] Social acceptance of miscegenation also promoted mores which favored manumission of one's mixed-blood children. The process was further eased by the innumerable and simple ways in which a white master could free his children.[19]

The situation differed markedly in the United States. There, in the earliest decades of settlement, when the white sex ratio was heavily weighted in favor of men, Negroes were also few in number, so that the basic opportunities for mixing were less frequent. This was a sharp contrast from conditions in Latin America and the Caribbean, where large numbers of blacks were imported at the very earliest stages of settlement. Later, before the number of Negro women in America began to increase significantly, white settlement patterns shifted toward families, so that white men had less need for women of another race.[20] Carl N. Degler has also emphasized the difference in the status of white women in the two regions. The high status of women in society and in the family in North America (as opposed to their low status in the colonies of Latin nations) tended to prevent men from acknowledging the mulatto offspring they might have spawned under the opportunities provided by slavery. In Latin America and the Caribbean, white planters acknowledged their mixed-blood children, provided for their education, and often left them inheritances. The position of women in the United States, however, allowed them to thwart such social recognition of illicit interracial unions and their mulatto products.[21]

In America, then, miscegenation never received the widespread public acceptance that was characteristic of the other colonial areas of the Western Hemisphere. Indeed, colonial authorities early assumed a strong public stance against race mixing, whether in the form of casual liaisons or interracial marriage. At no time, however, could public pronouncements be entirely effective in eliminating inter-racial sexual contacts. Among the earliest surviving records of colonial Virginia, for example, are documents concerning the punishment of white men convicted of fornicating with Negro women.[22] In 1662, Virginia established a firm law which truly expressed public distaste for the practice of miscegenation. This provision imposed a fine for fornication between whites and blacks which was twice the amount usually level for illicit sexual intercourse. In the same act, Virginia took a major step in clarifying the status of the mulatto offspring of interracial unions. Flatly announcing that mulatto children of Negro slave women would be slaves themselves, the Virginia assembly broke with the English tradition that the status of a child follows that of its father in favor of the Roman rule that a child inherits the status of its mother.[23] In 1691, an act was passed which even enslaved the mulatto offspring of a free white woman and a Negro slave until the child reached the age of thirty.[24] That same year Virginia acted to prohibit interracial marriages, including in the law a banishment from the colony of the white partner in the union.[25]

Virginia's heightened attention to the problem of race mixing in the waning years of the seventeenth century probably reflected pressures arising from the augmented imports of black slaves at that time. However, this sensitivity was not limited to Virginia. As Winthrop Jordan has noted, by the turn of the century English settlers in many of the continental colonies clearly felt genuine revulsion for interracial sexual contact, at least in principle.[26] Several colonies followed Virginia's lead, for instance, in outlawing marriages between whites and blacks.[27]

Ultimately, attitudes about racial amalgamation were linked to the growing importance of slavery and the need to insure white dominance. One means of doing so was to deny the product of uncontrolled white sexual desire. By relegating the mulatto to the status of the pure black, by describing him as "spurious" or "mongrel" (as numerous laws and public statements did in the late seventeenth and early eighteenth centuries), whites could maintain the sharpness of racial distinctions and thereby the power relationships that went with them. It was not so much interracial sex itself that was to be feared (for many whites certainly continued to indulge in the practice), but the challenge which it implicitly raised to the domination and superiority of the white man and the subordination of the black. After all, in the plantation colonies, the entire economy demanded that whites be able to control the labor force completely. Gary B. Nash has summarized the situation in commenting that,

> In the American colonies, the need was for plantation labor and the urge was for occasional sex partners with whom one could act out all one's sexual fantasies, since black women were defined as lascivious by nature. By prohibiting racial intermarriage, winking at interracial sex, and defining all mixed offspring as black, white society found the ideal answer to its labor needs, its extracurricular and inadmissible sexual desires, its compulsion to maintain its culture purebred, and the problem of maintaining, at least in theory, absolute social control.[28]

This is not to say that the status of the mulatto had as yet been concretely defined, for it had not. Yet attitudes about mixed-bloods were inextricably linked to attitudes about miscegenation, and with few exceptions, white Americans condemned that practice. That they continued to indulge in interracial sex inevitably aroused considerable feeling of guilt. Mulattoes became a visible reproach to the white man that he was failing to live up to his basic social and moral precepts, that he could not master his own inner urges. The only ways to resolve this guilt would have been either to recognize mulattoes as somehow a part of the white race, or to ignore them by relegating them to the status of blacks. Since the first alternative would have undermined the racial distinctions upon which the slave system was built, the latter alternative was necessarily the one chosen. As Winthrop Jordan explains, if the white man could not restrain his sexual nature (which obviously he could not),

> he could at least reject its fruits and thus solace himself that he had done no harm. Perhaps he sensed as well that continued racial intermixture would eventually undermine the logic of the racial slavery upon which his society was based. For the separation of slaves from free men depended on a clear demarcation of the races, and the presence of mulattoes blurred this distinction. Accordingly he made every effort to nullify the effects of racial intermixture: by classifying the mulatto as a Negro he was in effect denying that intermixture had occurred at all.[29]

The overall result was that, for the most part, mulattoes were loosely classed as Negroes, with relatively little attention given to the problems inherent in the presence of a people who were in reality not entirely of any one race. Except for Louisiana, there was little inclination to distinguish varying degree of white and black blood among mulattoes, although this was the practice in the Caribbean and Latin America.[30] Indeed, prior to the Revolution only Virginia and North Carolina bothered to define who was a Negro and who was not. Both colonies ruled that an admixture of black blood within the last three generations served to class an individual as a Negro, and at times North Carolina even stretched the limit to four or five generations. These edicts simply codified the common notion that anyone who bore the physical marks of black ancestry or who could recall such ancestors was, for all intents and purposes, as black as a full-blooded Negro.[31] Elsewhere, while this same definition was probably followed in most legal matters, it was not deemed necessary to write it into law, perhaps because the actual number of mulattoes, particularly those who were free, was not very great.

When the free Negro population burgeoned after the Revolution, however, whites became more concerned with insuring the precision of racial demarcations, lest large numbers of mixed-bloods slip into the ranks of pure whites. Within the next several decades, most Southern states acted to define the limits of blackness or whiteness. In 1785, Virginia lawmakers declared that an individual with one black ancestor in the previous two generations was a Negro. This definition was subsequently adopted by other Southern states: Kentucky, Missouri, Arkansas, Florida, North Carolina (except for marriage to a white person), and Mississippi. A stricter law, pushing the line back to three generations was adopted in Georgia, Alabama, Tennessee, Texas, and North Carolina (in case of marriage to a white person).[32] Some Northern states also felt it necessary to establish such definitions. There the line of demarcation was usually the third generation.[33]

It was a paradoxical position that whites had gotten themselves into. If they were too strict in their definitions, some families who had long been living as white might be pushed back into the Negro race.[34] Yet because whites were highly conscious of race and racial differences, they were uneasy about the chance that some Negroes whose black blood was well diluted might be able to slip into the white race surreptitiously. In practice, however, legal definitions were not as important as public attitudes. With few exceptions, if it was publicly known that an individual was descended from a black, regardless of how distantly, he was generally treated as a Negro, even if physically he appeared to be white. This, of course, limited how much legal passing for white actually went on, but it probably had the effect of spurring the rate of clandestine passing. Winthrop Jordan has noted that the practice of passing was a peculiarly American phenomenon, spawned by a racial system which did not recognize any intermediate point between pure white and pure black. It was the existence of this broad chasm which necessitated the sudden leap which passing literally represented.[35] There is no way to determine just how many mixed-bloods have chosen this route, and many, for reasons of affection, family ties, etc., have declined the opportunity. Nevertheless, there can be little doubt that manifold numbers of "white" Americans in fact carry some degree of black blood in their veins, although in most instances, probably unconsciously.

3

Although mulattoes were generally classed as Negroes in the United States, distinctions were drawn between mulattoes and blacks during the ante-bellum period. Probably the most significant differential factor involved freedom--a much larger proportion of the mulatto population was free than was true of the black population. During the colonial period, patterns of manumission seem to have been influenced by the practice of miscegenation, for a high proportion of those who obtained their liberty were either women (black and mulatto) or mulatto children. In South Carolina, for instance, one-third of all recorded colonial manumissions were mulatto children, while three-fourths of all adult manumissions were females.[36] Throughout the colonial period, the free Negro population was heavily mulatto, and although proportions changed dramatically as many blacks were emancipated because of Revolutionary ideology and/or economic pressures in the late 1700s, mulattoes continued to be disproportionately represented in the free population throughout the ante-bellum era. It should be noted, however, that in the United States, social mores never greatly promoted the manumitting of one's mulatto offspring as they did elsewhere in the hemisphere. The practice was certainly common enough, but clearly not universal.   Furthermore, it became less common as legislation increasingly proscribed all emancipations in the last decades of the ante-bellum period.

Ira Berlin has contended that in ante-bellum America, there were in reality two Souths, distinguished by the number of free Negroes and the treatment accorded them. This view seems equally valid with regard to mulattoes and, to a degree, with regard to attitudes about racial mixing itself. The Upper South, composed of North Carolina and the states northward and westward, was characterized by a relatively large mulatto population. Mulattoes had appeared in this region early in the colonial period, especially in the area around the Chesapeake Bay. Usually they were the offspring of poor whites and Negroes. Later, intermarriage among mulattoes and between mulattoes and .blacks augmented this original contingent, while new admixtures of white blood diminished. A considerable portion of Upper South mulattoes were free, but they tended to be rural and relatively poor, just as their white ancestors had been. Most importantly, whites in the Upper South did not usually concern themselves with the mixed-blooded nature of mulattoes, i.e., they made few distinctions about color or ancestry among Negroes. Instead, they treated mulattoes very much as if they were black.

A very different set of circumstances characterized the Lower South. There, race relations evolved in a pattern borrowed from the West Indies, with the result that many whites developed a different perspective about mulattoes (at least those who were free). This attitude was most evident in South Carolina and Louisiana, the earliest areas to be settled, but extended to other parts of the Lower South as well.

Slavery in the Lower South was distinguished by the high proportion of black slaves to the number of whites. Just as in the Caribbean and Latin America, this fact gave rise to considerable miscegenation between white masters and slave women. Indeed, in South Carolina some planters publicly defended the practice of interracial sex.[37] The eventual result was a small but significant number of mulattoes, many of whom benefited from the recognition and largess of their white fathers in becoming free and comfortably established. From the outset of the colonial period, mulattoes composed the bulk of the free Negro population in the lower South, although the free Negro population itself was always much smaller than that in the Upper South. More importantly, free mulattoes in the Lower South were often treated by whites as a third caste, intermediate between whites and blacks, the slave and the free. Because of the overwhelming number of black slaves around them, whites were disposed to view free mulattoes as valuable allies, and consequently accorded them certain privileges and a higher status than free mulattoes possessed elsewhere in America. As Ira Berlin has commented, it was ironic that while slavery in the Lower South was blacker and harsher than elsewhere in the United States, it brought with it greater freedom and higher status for the small minority of Negroes who were free.[38]

The attitudes and demographic patterns developed during the colonial period in the Lower South continued to distinguish that region from the Upper South throughout the ante-bellum period. South Carolina, for instance, never legally prohibited racial intermarriage, nor did it attempt to establish strict definitions about who was white and who was a Negro.[39] Typical of this sort of thinking was a judicial decision rendered by Chancellor William Harper of South Carolina in 1835. Harper refused to rule on the whiteness of a man merely with regard to the proportion of white or black blood in his veins. "We cannot say what admixture . . . will make a colored person," he announced.

> The condition . . . is not to be determined solely by . . . visible mixture . . . but by reputation . . . and it may be . . . proper, that a man of worth . . . should have the rank of a white man, while a vagabond of the same degree of blood should be confined to the inferior caste.[40]

The result of such an attitude, of course, was that many of the lightest and most accomplished mixed-bloods were able to pass over into the white race.

Within the bounds of this three-caste racial system, South Carolina's free mulattoes were able to develop a relatively comfortable lifestyle. By 1850, there were 4,372 free mulattoes in the state, almost 50 percent of the state's total free Negro population. Of these, 2,554 lived in Charleston, where they composed about one-quarter of the city's population.[41] Throughout the Lower South, free mulattoes tended to congregate in urban areas where they filled a variety of artisan positions. The most successful mulattoes were involved in professional or business pursuits. Strong class divisions split Charleston's free Negro population, and as was generally true throughout the Lower South, the top-most echelons were dominated by light-skinned mulattoes. The elite free mulattoes composed a distinct caste unto themselves, highly class-conscious and determined to maintain their privileged position in Charleston society. Although considerations other than color were important in determining an individual's social status among Charleston's free Negro population, there is no question that there was a consciousness of color as well. The city's most elite free Negro organization, for instance, was the Brown Fellowship Society, whose membership was limited to wealthy, light-skinned men.[42] Families like the Noisettes, Kinlochs, and McKinlays, often as rich as their wealthy white neighbors, prided themselves on how closely their lifestyles approximated that of the city's white upper class. Further, because they saw their own interests as closely aligned with those of the elite whites, they were staunch supporters of the slave system and the status quo. Their values were those of the white race, and it was natural that their source of identification would be with the white race as well.[43]

Admittedly this elite group of Charleston mulattoes was but a minority, yet they dominated the free Negro population of the city and helped to shape the impression whites held of free Negroes in general. For the most part, whites were relatively confident of their control of the racial situation, at least prior to the 1850s, so that instead of viewing these mixed-bloods as a threat, they saw them as worthy citizens of the community, performing necessary economic functions. When mulattoes did press too closely, either socially or as economic competitors, this attitude might shift towards viewing them as a presumptuous, arrogant, and insolent people, but whites and mulattoes were usually able to coexist peacefully. There is some evidence, in fact, that this attitude of general acceptance even extended into the countryside. In Edgefield County, for example, some 250 free persons of color were living relatively easily among the county's 22,000 whites in 1850. As with the rest of the Lower South, perhaps the explanation lies in the fact that the county's slave population of 24,000 was held in harsh bondage. In such a situation, whites had no reason to be concerned about such a small free mulatto minority.[44]

The significance of Caribbean and Latin American race relations was even more vividly seen in Louisiana, since the region had once belonged to both France and Spain. The immigration of large numbers of whites and mulattoes from the island of St. Domingue in the 1790s had helped to solidify a pattern of race relations which tolerated miscegenation and recognized color distinctions among Negroes. Overall, the free people of color of Louisiana (as the mulattoes were called) enjoyed the most secure position of any free Negroes in the South. Not only were their rights protected by the treaty which annexed Louisiana to the United States in 1803, but whites in general were inclined to see a significant difference between free mulattoes and slaves (the vast majority of whom were black).

Louisiana's free mulatto population was by far the largest in the Lower South (14,083 in 1850) and was well integrated into the economy of the state. In effect, it was composed of three parts. The most distinctive group was the large slaveholding planters. Although relatively few in number, they were an important economic force, and because of the fact that their wealth was tied to the slave system, they tended to be conservative defenders of the established social and economic order.

Generally located in the southwestern portion of the state, their wealth and white blood usually derived from early French settlers, unless they had brought their wealth with them from St. Domingue. These mulattoes were the wealthiest Negroes in America, some being worth more than $200,000 and owning nearly 100 slaves.[45]

A sizable number of free mulattoes in Louisiana was located in the rural parishes of the state, either in small towns or on farms, interspersed among the slave population. Some held one or two slaves themselves (often a relative), but most were poor, unable to compete with the large white landowners who dominated the rural economy.

The largest segment (57 percent) of Louisiana's free mulatto population was found in New Orleans. There they contributed to the evolution of a racial system which was unique in North America. The most striking feature of race relations in ante-bellum New Orleans, John Blassingame has argued, was "the pervasiveness of miscegenation."[46] Indeed, interracial mixing was so common that it was virtually institutionalized in the city's notorious "quadroon balls." These were elaborate dances where wealthy white men formally courted prospective mulatto mistresses. The arrangement was formalized through an agreement with the girl and her parents. Known as a *placage*, it usually required that the white man agree to maintain the woman in a certain style of life and to provide for any children which might result from the union. These liaisons represented a rather sophisticated form of concubinage, yet because they involved a socially accepted practice neither partner suffered public condemnation.[47]

As an intermediate caste, Louisiana's free mulattoes developed a distinct social system of their own, for despite their light color, they were excluded from membership in the white race. In New Orleans in particular, they maintained their own schools, churches, and cultural life, although there was considerable overlap in the cultural patterns followed by many mulattoes and the state's white Creole families.[48] Mulatto society evidenced class distinctions similar to those in white society, although in the former lightness of complexion was a necessary credential for admittance to higher social positions, while those at the bottom of the social order were always blacker in color. The aristocrats at the top dressed, thought, and acted in much the same manner as their white counterparts. The most significant fact about Louisiana's free mulatto population, though, was the manner in which it was integrated into the economic life of the state. Few mulattoes were able to live in luxury, but most found rewarding employment at some skilled occupation. They monopolized the building trades, catering, the cigar industry, and service positions like barbering and tailoring. Moreover, the rise of New Orleans as a port and urban trade center generated the need for a variety of middle-class employees, a void which the free people of color were quick to fill.[49]

Elsewhere in the Lower South the number of free mulattoes was far less than that in Louisiana and South Carolina, but the same basic characteristics seem to hold true there as well. Free mulattoes tended to congregate in urban areas, to form a majority of the overall free Negro population, and to be recognized by whites as a distinct group separate from the mass of blacks. In Mississippi, for example, there were only 930 free Negroes in 1850, but 68 percent of these were mulatto. Ten years later, the percentage had increased to 78. Most were located in urban areas, especially around Natchez, where gradations of color mirrored socioeconomic class divisions among free Negroes.[50] Creole mulattoes similar to those in Louisiana dominated the small free Negro caste in Alabama. Most were found in and around Mobile, where 91 percent of the free Negroes were of mixed blood. The city's French and Spanish heritage prompted many whites to be rather tolerant of miscegenation and also led them to see mulattoes as different from blacks.[51] Similar patterns were evident in Florida. While the free Negro population there was also small, it was 75 percent mulatto in 1850. A sizable portion was found in Pensacola, where because of their Creole ancestry free mulattoes held a respected place in the community, forming "an active, property-owning class," according to one student. Some were even well-to-do. For the most part, these urban mulattoes constituted a distinct class. Unable to mingle socially with whites of the same cultural and economic position, they themselves disdained contact with the common blacks of the area.[52]

Several significant facts, then, stand out about the mulatto population in the Lower South during the ante-bellum period. In comparison with the Upper South, the free mulatto population, like that of free Negroes in general, was small, but as Table 1 indicates, mixed-bloods formed a disproportionately large segment of the free Negro population in each state. Because of the early influence of France, Spain, and the West Indies in the area, and because of the massive numbers of slaves, mulattoes (at least those who were free) tended to be seen as an intermediate group between blacks and whites. In the Lower South, mulattoness possessed a certain quality or distinctiveness which generated patterns of race relations somewhat different from those in the rest of the United States. As one historian has observed, whites in the Lower South demonstrated a "remarkable ability to resist the Upper South tendency to jumble all Negroes together."[53] Indeed, at times the distinctions were quite sharp. As late as 1856, a judge in Louisiana would declare that "there is . . . all the difference between a free man of color and a slave, that there is between a white man and a slave."[54] Many free mulattoes responded by accepting their status as a separate

TABLE 1.--FREE NEGRO POPULATION IN THE LOWER SOUTH, BLACK AND MULATTO, 1850 AND 1860

1850

State	Total	Mulatto	Black	% Mulatto
South Carolina	8,960	4,372	4,588	48.8
Georgia	2,931	1,528	1,403	52.1
Florida	932	703	229	75.4
Alabama	2,265	1,698	567	75.0
Mississippi	930	635	295	68.3
Louisiana	17,462	14,083	3,379	60.6
Texas	397	257	140	64.7
Arkansas	608	407	201	66.9
Totals	34,485	23,683	10,802	68.7

1860

State	Total	Mulatto	Black	% Mulatto
South Carolina	9,914	7,134	2,780	72.0
Georgia	3,500	2,004	1,496	57.3
Florida	932	643	289	69.0
Alabama	2,690	2,098	592	78.0
Mississippi	773	601	172	77.7
Louisiana	18,647	15,158	3,489	81.3
Texas	355	273	82	76.9
Arkansas	144	87	57	60.4
Totals	36,955	27,998	8,957	75.8

Source: *Negro Population in the United States, 1790-1915* (Washington, D.C.: Government Printing Office, 1918), pp. 220-221.

caste, adopting the outlook and attitudes of the whites, and consciously avoiding interaction with the black masses.[55]   Consequently, whites perceived them as an auxiliary bulwark against rebellious stirrings among the slave population.   According to a South Carolinian writing after the Denmark Vesey affair, free mulattoes represented

> a barrier between our own color and that of the black--and, in cases of insurrection, are more likely to enlist themselves under the banner of the whites.   Most of them are industrious, sober, hardworking mechanics, who have large families and considerable property: and so far as we are acquainted with their temper, and disposition of their feelings, abhor the idea of association with the blacks in any enterprise that may have for its object the revolution of their condition.   It must be recollected, also, that the greater part of them own slaves, and are, therefore so far interested in this species of property as to keep them on the watch, and induce them to disclose any plans that may be injurious to our peace--experience justifies this conclusion [the Vesey plot had been revealed by a free Negro].[56]

Free mulattoes therefore became supporters of the status quo in the Lower South.   By granting them special privileges and thereby winning their loyalty, whites succeeded in isolating free mulattoes from the slave population while still maintaining the integrity of white domination.

4

It is important to recognize one further feature of mulatto life in the Lower South.   As Table 2 makes clear, the privileged free mulattoes were a very small minority.   Most mulattoes in the Lower South remained slaves.   Indeed, between 1850 and 1860 the percentage of mulattoes in the slave population increased.   In 1850, 17 percent of all mulattoes in the Lower South were free, but by 1860, although the absolute number of free mulattoes had increased slightly, the percentage of mulattoes who were free had dropped to 12.   Meanwhile, the number of slave mulattoes in the region had risen sharply during the decade. Slavery was becoming more deeply entrenched in the Lower South in the face of mounting abolitionist pressure and intersectional tensions.   As a result, some who might have earlier gained their freedom because of their mixed blood were now finding such opportunities fading.   A variety of legislative actions made manumission difficult if not impossible, as rising fevers of anxiety in the 1850s led most whites to fear the growth of a free Ngro class, regardless of its color.

South Carolina whites, for instance, had proven rather tolerant of free Negroes after the Denmark Vesey affair in the 1820s and even during the early surge of abolitionist fervor during ther 1830s, but in the 1850s the tide swung in the other direction.   The demand for sharp free and slave demarcations resulted in cries for the ouster of the state's free Negro population.[57] A sizable portion of the free mulatto population of Pensacola, Florida emigrated in 1857 in response to growing pressures against them among local whites.[58]

Even in Louisiana, where free mulattoes had always been well integrated into the overall social and economic order, the 1850s witnessed a rise of agitation against them. Aroused by a fear of abolitionism and

TABLE 2.--SLAVE POPULATION IN THE LOWER SOUTH, BLACK AND MULATTO, 1850 AND 1860

1850

State	Total	Mulatto	Black	% Mulatto
South Carolina	384,984	12,502	372,482	3.2
Georgia	381,682	22,669	359,013	5.9
Florida	39,310	3,022	36,288	7.7
Alabama	342,844	21,605	321,239	6.3
Mississippi	309,878	19,730	290,148	6.7
Louisiana	244,809	19,835	224,974	8.1
Texas	58,161	7,703	50,458	13.2
Arkansas	47,100	6,361	40,739	13.5
Totals	1,808,768	113,427	1,695,341	6.3

1860

State	Total	Mulatto	Black	% Mulatto
South Carolina	402,406	21,180	381,226	5.3
Georgia	462,198	36,900	425,298	8.0
Florida	61,745	5,253	56,492	8.5
Alabama	435,080	34,330	400,750	7.9
Mississippi	436,631	36,618	400,013	8.4
Louisiana	331,726	32,623	299,103	9.8
Texas	182,566	24,987	157,579	13.7
Arkansas	111,115	14,049	97,066	12.6
Totals	2,423,467	205,940	2,217,527	8.5

Source: *Negro Population in the United States, 1790-1915* (Washington, D.C.: Government Printing Office, 1918), pp. 220-221.

slave insurrection, whites began to challenge traditionally permissive attitudes about miscegenation, concubinage, and interracial connections of other sorts. Outright violence erupted in the Attakapas region west of New Orleans, where white vigilantes attempted to drive free Negroes (many of whom were wealthy slaveholders) out of the state and to punish whites and mulattoes involved in illicit interracial unions. The Monroe *Register* caught the spirit of much of the white opposition to the continued presence of free mulattoes when it declared that if "this mongrel race" were not soon expelled from the state, mulattoes would "pollute the name of our fair State with their worthless carcasses and pave the way to indolence, dissipation and vice" among all peoples of Louisiana.[59]

The tendency of Lower South whites to distinguish mulattoes from other Negroes was dissolving amid rising anxieties and fears. In essence, the Lower South was becoming much as the Upper South had been all along. There was no room for those who were not clearly black or white, nor could there be any toleration of the interracial sex which produced them. In words more telling than he himself realized, Henry Hughes of Mississippi evidenced the new outlook against miscegenation in the Lower South in an 1854 statement. "Hybridism is heinous," he argued.

> Impurity of races is against the law of nature. Mulattoes are monsters. The law of nature is the law of God. The same law which forbids consanguinous amalgamation forbids ethnical amalgamation. Both are incestuous. Amalgamation is incest.[60]

The white South was becoming one with regard to the mulatto and its attitudes about miscegenation. As a result, the mulatto's own peculiar status grew even more tenuous.

5

Whites in the Upper South had never been inclined to distinguish mixed-bloods from pure blacks. The free Negro population was much larger than that of the Lower South, and it was also much blacker. Mulattoes still made up a much larger portion of the free Negro population than they did of the Negro population as a whole, but in the Upper South, free mulattoes were still a minority of their class (See Table 3). Mulattoes did tend to constitute the upper strata of free Negro society,[61] but most were poor and lived in rural rather than urban settings. The overall result was that Upper South whites had no reason to see free mulattoes as different from free blacks. The entire free Negro group was viewed as a social sore, a dark, threatening force potentially fomenting rebellion among the slave population.   Ira Berlin has emphasized that many Upper South whites were uneasy enough about the institution of slavery itself. Free Negroes, whether black or brown, only exacerbated their tensions.   Further, Latin American and West

TABLE 3.--FREE NEGRO POPULATION IN THE UPPER SOUTH, BLACK AND MULATTO, 1850 AND 1860

1850

State	Total	Mulatto	Black	% Mulatto
Delaware	18,073	1,648	16,425	9.1
Maryland	74,723	13,614	61,109	18.2
District of Columbia	10,059	3,276	6,783	32.6
Virginia	54,333	35,476	18,857	65.3
North Carolina	27,463	17,205	10,258	62.6
Kentucky	10,011	2,630	7,381	26.3
Tennessee	6,422	3,776	2,646	58.8
Missouri	2,618	931	1,687	35.6
Totals	203,702	78,556	125,146	38.6

1860

State	Total	Mulatto	Black	% Mulatto
Delaware	19,829	2,896	16,933	14.6
Maryland	83,942	16,040	67,902	19.1
District of Columbia	11,131	4,500	6,631	40.4
Virginia	58,042	23,485	34,557	40.5
North Carolina	30,463	21,808	8,655	71.6
Kentucky	10,684	4,077	6,607	38.2
Tennessee	7,300	4,292	3,008	58.8
Missouri	3,572	1,674	1,898	46.9
Totals	224,963	78,772	146,191	35.0

Source: *Negro Population in the United States, 1790-1915* (Washington, D.C.: Government Printing Office, 1918), pp. 220-221.

Indian influences never made themselves felt in the Upper South, so that whites never grew to tolerate miscegenation nor to see any reason for granting special privileges or status to its mixed-blood product.[62]   To whites in the Upper South, a mulatto was a Negro, and a Negro was black.   There was no middle status.

Moreover, as in the Lower South, most mulattoes in the Upper South were slaves.   In 1850, census figures indicated that there were 246,635 slaves of mixed blood.   Of these, 54 percent (133,208) lived in the Upper South (See Table 4), where they composed 63 percent of the total mulatto population.   This percentage was also on the rise, as it was in the Lower South.   By 1860, the mulatto population of the Upper South had risen to 284,411, and the increase was almost entirely in the slave population.   That year, over 72 percent of all mulattoes in the region were in bondage.   The total number of Upper South mulattoes in slavery increased by 72,431, or 54 percent, between 1850 and 1860, compared with an increase of only 62,515 black slaves (up only 5 percent).   It is likely that many free mulattoes either left the Upper South, went underground out of view of white census takers and others who threatened their peaceful existence, or passed over into the white race during this decade, since the period was marked by a rise of proscriptions against the freedom and rights of free Negroes in that region.[63]   Yet the glaring fact is that throughout the South, mulatto slavery was on the rise in the decade before the Civil War.   Slavery as an institution was becoming whiter and whiter, a direct contradiction to the fundamental white notion that slavery was meant for black people.   In 1835, Chancellor Harper of South Carolina had declared that it was "hardly necessary to say that a slave cannot be a white man,"[64] but by the end of the ante-bellum period the facts said otherwise.   Growing numbers of persons with predominantly white blood were being held as slaves.

The only way for white Southerners to resolve this paradox was through a redefinition of whiteness and blackness, and this is precisely the direction in which white thought was moving by the eve of the Civil War.   White meant free, black meant slave.   No middle ground existed for those of both black and white blood.   The white man's solution, in essence, was to say that the latter simply did not exist.   By classifying as black all who had any degree of black blood--by insisting that "one drop" of black blood was enough to make an individual a Negro--whites conveniently did away with the mulatto as an anomaly in their racial schema.   If whiteness meant pure white, then those of mixed blood were, by definition, not white.   Within the increasingly biracial classification system of American race relations, mulattoes thereby were thrust into the black race.   For whites this served a dual purpose: it essentially erased the sin of miscegenation, since they were denying the whiteness of mulattoes; and it dispelled the uneasiness generated by the thought of enslaving people who possessed the blood of the superior race. Mulattoes and blacks were ultimately all the same in white eyes, and would be treated as such.

TABLE 4.--SLAVE POPULATION IN THE UPPER SOUTH, BLACK AND MULATTO, 1850 AND 1860

1850

State	Total	Mulatto	Black	% Mulatto
Delaware	2,290	83	2,207	3.6
Maryland	90,368	7,889	82,479	8.7
District of Columbia	3,687	802	2,885	21.8
Virginia	472,528	44,299	428,229	9.4
North Carolina	288,548	16,815	271,733	5.8
Kentucky	210,981	29,729	181,292	14.1
Tennessee	239,459	20,356	219,103	8.5
Missouri	87,422	13,235	74,187	15.1
Totals	1,395,283	133,208	1,262,075	9.5

1860

State	Total	Mulatto	Black	% Mulatto
Delaware	1,798	83	1,715	4.6
Maryland	87,189	8,873	78,316	10.2
District of Columbia	3,185	933	2,252	29.3
Virginia	490,865	69,979	420,886	14.3
North Carolina	331,059	22,990	308,069	6.9
Kentucky	225,483	43,281	182,202	19.2
Tennessee	275,719	37,586	238,133	13.6
Missouri	114,931	21,914	93,017	19.1
Totals	1,530,229	205,639	1,324,590	13.4

Source: *Negro Population in the United States, 1790-1915* (Washington, D.C.: Government Printing Office, 1918), pp. 220-221.

6

Thus throughout the ante-bellum period, skin color seems to have had an important role in determining the status of individual Negroes. In all parts of the United States, a much larger portion of mulattoes than black was free. Further, among free Afro-Americans, color was one key to high status, as elite free Negroes generally prided themselves on their light complexion and their white ancestors. Those who held the highest socioeconomic positions were usually of mixed blood. Even among the slave population, where most mulattoes still found themselves, there is evidence that there was a certain amount of differentiation involving color. House servants, the privileged members of any plantation's slave contingent, tended to be mulattoes, although this was not an invariable rule. The practice was probably most visible in the Lower South, particularly around New Orleans and Charleston, but was common in most other parts of the South as well.[65] The overall effect was that during the ante-bellum period, many mulattoes, because they constituted the privileged minority among the Afro-American population, stood somewhat aloof from the mass of the race. They were proud of their white blood and of their cultural approximations to white lifestyles, and therefore often resented being treated or thought of by whites as no different from less fortunate blacks.

A marked shift in this attitude, however, seems to have taken place during the Civil War and Reconstruction. Many upper-class mulattoes abandoned their detached posture and freely joined in supporting the Negro and his cause. A survey of prominent Negro leaders in Reconstruction, both at the state and national level, indicates that most were of mixed blood. Indeed, this fact was not only characteristic of politics, but of religion, education, business, and the professions as well.

This shift in attitudes can be explained in part by the altered patterns of white thought and behavior in the 1850s. During that decade mulattoes had lost most of what preferred status they did have in the eyes of whites. Mulattoes were being pushed inexorably towards an alliance with blacks, and the pressures of war, emancipation, and Reconstruction only solidified this trend. Nevertheless, the reorientation did not proceed without some resistance, especially from among elite free mulattoes, nor did it ever successfully eradicate all color and class divisions within the Negro race.

The well-established mixed-blood Creoles of the Lower South evidenced perhaps the greatest struggle in changing their attitudes and allegiances. In New Orleans and Mobile, for instance, mulattoes of French and Spanish ancestry rushed to support the Confederate cause at the outbreak of hostilities, and in both cities were for a time accepted as a part of the armed forces of their respective states. There is no question that many of these light-skinned mulattoes saw their interests as linked to those of their white neighbors. They volunteered their services to protect their property and privileged position in Southern society. Ira Berlin has noted that those who filled the ranks of the Negro militia were almost invariably slaveholding planters and successful tradesmen, "the flower of that description in the State," according to one Louisiana newspaper. Some feared loss of their slave property, some the retribution of the black masses, and some the dissolution of Southern society were the inferior blacks loosed from bondage. John Rapier, a light-skinned Alabama mulatto evidenced such apprehension in 1861 when he wrote of his conviction that "a greater curse could not be imposed upon the United States or any other country than the emancipation of negro slaves." Conditioned by the general belief that blacks were inferior to whites (and to mixed-bloods), mulattoes rued the day when all blacks would be free, especially since it would mean the end of their own special status.[66]

As the tide of the war swung to the Union side, however, mulattoes in the South quickly abandoned the Confederate cause. Yet old class divisions among Negroes were not forgotten, for the distinctions between free mulattoes and black slaves had deeply split the ante-bellum Afro-American community. Charleston's old free Negro elite, for instance, initially refused to associate with the "parvenu free." Disdaining to attend church with the black freedmen, they established their own congregation, hired a white minister, and announced that "no black nigger [was] welcome."[67]

Nevertheless, the fact was that all Negroes were now free, and the old mulatto elites eventually adjusted to the situation. By late 1865, a visitor to Charleston reported that the

> wealthy slaveholding mulatto families of Charleston are fully identified in interest with the mass of the colored people, and are becoming leaders among them, while the old jealousy between blacks and mulattoes is disappearing.[68]

The same proved true throughout the South; mulattoes sprang to the fore in the Negro's struggle to establish his rights. In Alabama, for example, the dominant Negro figures in the state's Reconstruction legislatures and in the 1867 constitutional convention were light-skinned mulattoes from Mobile and the Tennessee Valley (including John Rapier's brother, James T. Rapier).[69] Likewise, in Louisiana the Negro leaders during Reconstruction were of mixed blood.[70] Luther Porter Jackson's study of Negro office-holders in Virginia between 1865 and 1895 indicated that a disproportionately large number, both at the state and local level, was mulatto.[71]   Of the twenty-two Negroes elected to Congress from the South between 1870 and 1901, eighteen were of mixed blood.[72]   In Washington, D.C., itself, members of the pre-war mulatto elite dominated Negro office-holding in the city government.[73]   The background of freedom, education, privilege, and property-holding made members of the mulatto group the natural candidates for leadership positions.   Further, because all of the proscriptive laws whites attempted to enact after the war now applied to elite Negroes as well as to the mass of the race, such individuals were merely protecting their own interests by taking an active role in shaping Reconstruction politics and policies.

In essence, these mulatto leaders, and mixed-bloods in general, affirmed their membership in the Negro race during the difficult years of Reconstruction.   Changing white attitudes were in part responsible for this decision, of course, for once all Afro-Americans were free, whites were even less inclined than they had been earlier to distinguish mulattoes from blacks.   Clearly the reluctance of whites to do so proved costly in a political sense, for it helped to unite the Negro race and to provide it with much able leadership.   At the same time, mulatto leaders recognized that their road to prestige and power lay in supporting the cause of the Negro masses, black as well as brown, for it was the votes of the masses which were the ultimate source of political position and power.[74]

7

This racial unity in political affairs could not, however, overcome deeper divisions within the race which often followed lines of color differentiation.   Those at the top of the socioeconomic scale continued to be predominantly of light complexion, while those at the bottom were generally much darker.   The ante-bellum free Negro population had been roughly split in this manner, and not unexpectedly, those who had succeeded in establishing positions of social prestige and leadership sought diligently to maintain them once the situation was complicated by universal Negro freedom.

These divisions along color lines were most evident in urban areas in the decades following Reconstruction, for it was there that social patterns were most fully developed.   Rural Afro-Americans generally tended to be poor, so that social stratification was for the most part lacking, and color differences consequently were relatively unimportant because other criteria of division were not present.   In urban areas, on the other hand, color combined with a variety of other factors (including wealth, religious denomination, occupation, family history, moral behavior, etc.) in creating sharp class divisions within the overall Afro-American community.

Constance McLaughlin Green has described such stratification in Washington, D.C. As early as 1863, leading native Washington Negroes organized the Lotus Club as a rallying point in differentiating themselves from the masses of black freedmen who were flooding into the city. In succeeding decades, "the well-educated aristocrats of predominately white blood" consciously drew away from the darker-skinned middle class, while the gulf between these two groups and the inarticulate black lower class widened even further. By the end of the century, Washington's Negro class structure resembled a pyramid, according to Green. "From the strata below," she notes, "the Negroes who danced on the point of the needle appeared not to be angels, but scarcely more accessible than heavenly creatures." The city's Negro aristocracy was made up of those who combined light-colored skin with the qualifications of antiquity of family, money, education, and a suitable occupation (chiefly in the professions, banking, real estate brokerage, a respectable business, or politics). Dubbed the Negro "Four Hundred" by the *Bee*, a leading Afro-American newspaper, the aristocracy probably did not number more than ninety to one hundred families.

Green contends that the city's middle class was also derived mainly from among the mixed-blood population. "Only less fully than the Four Hundred with their very light skins and generally non-Negroid features," she explains, "were the [middle-class] mulattoes conscious of gradations of color." The middle class was flexible, however, in that it could accept blacks who demonstrated ability and ambition.[75] The result was considerable tension and enmity among Washington Negroes. Lower-class blacks envied the status of upper-class mulattoes and were offended by their exclusiveness, while the latter resented the often uncouth behavior of the lower class, blaming it in part for generating white prejudice against the entire race.

In Savannah, color gradations divided the Negro community in a manner similar to that in Washington, D.C. The upper class was chiefly drawn from the free mulatto class of the pre-war period and their descendants. These mixed-bloods consciously strove to maintain white patterns of family life and conventional sex mores, while expressing contempt for what they viewed as the immorality and bad manners of the lower class. The upper class generally belonged to the Episcopal, Congregational, Presbyterian, and Catholic churches, while blacks were more often Baptists or Methodists. Savannah's mulatto elite did recognize the needs of the city's entire Negro population, however, and was active in political affairs and in founding the Savannah *Tribune*, the leading Afro-American newspaper in the city.[76]

Charleston and New Orleans also evidenced social stratification intensified by color differences. In post-war New Orleans, John

Blassingame reports, mulattoes had an overwhelming majority of the wealth and education in the Negro community. For the most part, this resulted from their elevated status during the ante-bellum period, including the patronage and aid of white fathers. Mulattoes also dominated a variety of skilled trades, so that occupationally they tended to be better off than their black brothers. Finally, cultural distinctions paralleled color gradations in many instances. Those who were most refined and who were most closely aligned with the French cultural patterns of the city's white elite were generally of mixed blood. The combination of all of these factors left mulattoes predominant among the elite Negroes of New Orleans, with little in common with the lower classes.[77] Similar divisions characterized the Afro-American community in Charleston, although again color was a contributive factor in determining an individual's social standing. Other aspects of importance included education, occupation, and a history of family freedom.[78]

The color stratification seen in the late nineteenth century was not limited to the Deep South. A student of religious life in Nashville, Tennessee, reported the existence of considerable color prejudice among Negroes in that city. Certain churches, for example, were regarded as "blue-vein" congregations, referring to the light skin color (with consequent visibility of blood vessels) of the membership. In general, the most progressive churches were those attended by upper-class mulattoes.[79] W. E. B. Du Bois' study of Negro life in Philadelphia also found color differences correlated to social class, although color itself was but one of a number of factors involved in social stratification.[80] The Negro upper class in Boston was likewise distinguished by the light complexion of its members, most of whom were professionals or literary people of Northern birth or long Northern residence.[81]

Little concrete, analytic research has yet been done on class structure within the Afro-American community in the late ninetenth and early twentieth centuries. At this point, however, it seems clear that the small upper class was characterized by light skin color, and that mulattoes were also heavily represented in the middle class which began to develop during this period. In most instances, color was not a determinative factor in an individual's socioeconomic status, but it was often associated with a number of other factors which influenced his position within at least the local Negro community. Without qualities of education, wealth, proper family background, acceptable behavior patterns, etc., color itself counted for little.[82]

This fact is made evident by a look at the census figures involving mulattoes that were reported in 1890 and 1910. By 1890, the nation's mulatto population had almost doubled from the 1860 figures (588,363) to 1,132,060. This represented 15.2 percent of the total Negro population. When the number of mulattoes was assessed again two decades later, it had increased another 81 percent to 2,050,686, or 20.9 percent of the overall Negro population.[83] Of this number, obviously few werre included in either the upper or middle classes. Most shared the lifestyle of poverty and deprivation which characterized the race as a whole.

Nevertheless, certain statistical peculiarities did tend to distinguish the mulatto population from the black population. First, the mulatto population was growing much faster then the black population. The 81 percent increase in the number of mulattoes between 1890 and 1910 dwarfed the 22.7 percent increase in blacks. This would seem to indicate that white blood was becoming continually more and more diffused throughout the Negro population, most often through intermarriage of blacks and mulattoes. This idea was underscored by the fact that the percentage of mulattoes in 1910 was greatest in the lower age categories.[84] The 1910 census figures also revealed that the mulatto population tended to be more urban than the black population. Mulattoes composed 27.2 percent of the urban Negro population (versus 20.9 percent overall), with the percentage being approximately the same in all sections of the country and in all different sizes of urban communities.[85]

Perhaps the most striking statistical differentiation between mulattoes and blacks was in the area of sexual distribution. There was a marked sexual imbalance within the mulatto population, with the number of females greatly exceeding the number of males. In 1910, the sex ratio, expressed in terms of the number of males per 1000 females,was 886 among mulattoes, compared with 1,018 among blacks and 1,066 among whites. There were also variations in the mulatto sex ratio among the three major sections of the United States. In the South, the sex ratio was lowest, at 877 (compared with 1,103 among blacks). In the North, it stood at 937 (versus 1,050 for blacks), while in the West there was an actual surplus of mulatto males. There the mulatto sex ratio was 1,041 (compared with a black sex ratio of 1,296). It might be hypothesized that the imbalance in the mulatto sex ratio reflected the dynamics of racial passing in America. It seems likely that among those mixed-bloods who were of the lightest complexions, men would have been more likely to leave the Negro race in favor of becoming white. Not only would men have been more mobile in terms of occupation, residence, and associates, but they would also have married outside the race somewhat more easily, thereby insuring their identification as white.

The geographical differences in the mulatto sex ratio also hint at this possibility. Mulatto males were proportionately most abundant in the West, where white prejudice and discriminatory practices might have been least wide-spread and galling (because relatively few Negroes lived there). In such a situation, light-skinned mulattoes might well have chosen to retain their original racial allegiance. Where prejudice and discrimination were more severe, however, this might not have been the case. The sex ratio was more unbalanced in the North than in the West, and most unbalanced in the South. Where life as a Negro was most oppressive, it is possible that a larger proportion of light mulattoes chose to slip quietly into the white race rather than bear the burden of being a Negro. Similar evidence is found in the unbalanced mulatto sex ratio characteristic of urban areas (810 mulatto men for every 1000 mulatto women in 1910), since cities were the places where passing might be most easily accomplished.[86]

8

Whatever distinctions and divisions characterized the Negro population by the first decades of the twentieth century, white Americans were more inclined than ever to view the entire group as a single, dark, anonymous mass. After 1920, the Census Bureau ceased to distinguish mulattoes from blacks, as if it were saying in reality there was no difference.[87] Throughout the South (and much of the West as well), states continued generally to define as Negro anyone with one-eighth or more of black blood, but this definition was itself simply a legal curiosity, important primarily in cases of racial intermarriage.[88] In everyday practice, as one student of the Negro's legal status concluded in 1910,

> one is a Negro or is classsed with that race if he has the least visible trace of Negro blood in his veins, or even if it is known that there was Negro blood in any one of his progenitors.[89]

"One drop" of black blood was enough to make an individual a Negro, as long as some white person knew about it. It was an enigmatic situation, though, for if no one knew, a "Negro" could become a "white" person, if he were light enough. For those of a slightly darker tinge, however, white racism and its inherent guilt and insecurity demanded banishment to the Negro race.

NOTES

[1] Melville J. Herskovits, *The American Negro: A Study in Race Crossing* (New York: Alfred A. Knopf, Inc., 1928), p.3. See also Edward Byron Reuter, *Race Mixture: Studies In Intermarriage and Miscegenation* (New York: Whittlesey House of McGraw-Hill Book Company, Inc., 1931), p. 3.

[2] *A Century of Population Growth: From the First Census of the United States to the Twelfth, 1790-1900* (Washington, D.C.: Government Printing Office, 1909), p. 185.

[3] Edward Byron Reuter, *The Mulatto in the United States, Including a Study of the Role of Mixed-Blood Races Throughout the World* (Boston: Richard G. Badger, 1918), p. 112.

[4] This was especially true of the 1890 returns, with their overly elaborate divisions. Even the Census Bureau itself admitted this fact. "The figures are of little value," it explained. "Indeed, as an indication of the extent to which the races have mingled, they are misleading." U.S., Department of Interior, Office of the Census, *Eleventh Census of the United States, 1890: Population*, Part I, p. xciii. The 1870 census was also notoriously inaccurate in its survey of Negro population in the South. See *Negro Population in the United States, 1790-1915* (Washington, D.C.: Government Printing Office, 1918), p. 26.

[5] *Negro Population*, pp. 220-221. For the 1850 white population, see J. D. B. DeBow, *Statistical View of the United States. . .Being a Compendium of the Seventh Census* (Washington, D.C.: A. O. P. Nicholson, Public Printer, 1854), p. 45. It is likely, it should be noted, that all census counts of mulattoes undercounted the number of mulattoes.

[6] *Negro Population*, pp. 220-221. It should be noted that here and elsewhere in this chapter I have included Missouri in the South, as opposed to the Census Bureau's classification of Missouri as being in the "West North Central" United States. The "South," then, includes the "South Atlantic" states of Delaware, Maryland, Virginia, West Virginia (from the 1870 census on), North Carolina, South Carolina, Georgia, and Florida: the "East South Central" states of Kentucky, Tennessee, Alabama, and Mississippi; the "West South Central" states of Arkansas, Louisiana, Oklahoma (from the 1910 census on), and Texas; and Missouri.

[7] For evidence of such stratification in Philadelphia, for instance, see [Joseph W. Wilson], *Sketches of the Higher Classes of Colored Society in Philadelphia* (Philadelphia: 1841).

[8] Leon F. Litwack, *North of Slavery: The Negro in the Free States, 1790-1860* (Chicago: University of Chicago Press, 1961), p. 182.

[9] *Ibid.* Among militant mulatto leaders of the ante-bellum Northern Negro population, one could list Frederick Douglass, James Forten, Robert Purvis, Charles L. Redmond, James McCune Smith, William Still, John Mercer Langston, William Wells Brown, and David Walker. Not all of these men had been born in the North, of course.

[10] This practice was evident among Negroes well into the twentieth century. One might, for instance, note the incidence of advertisements for skin bleaches or hair straighteners

in such popular post-1900 Afro-American periodicals as *Alexander's Magazine* or the *Colored American Magazine.* Ironically, such practices helped to promote important Negro business enterprises. For an ante-bellum Negro's protest against this attitude, see M. H. Freeman, "The Educational Wants of the Free Colored People," *Anglo-African Magazine,* I, 4 (April, 1859), 116-117.

[11]August Meier and Elliott M. Rudwick, *From Plantation to Ghetto: An Interpretive History of American Negroes* (New York: Hill and Wang, 1966), p. 91.

[12]Donald L. Horowitz, "Color Differentiation in the American System of Slavery," *Journal of Interdisciplinary History,* III, 3 (Winter, 1973), 527.

[13]*Ibid.,* pp. 528-530. The quotation is from p. 530. However, as will be shown below, where marked general exceptions to the rule of mulatto impoverishment did exist in the United States, i.e., in New Orleans and Charleston, there was some tendency to recognize free mulattoes as a separate and distinct group.

[14]Herbert S. Klein, "The Colored Freedmen in Brazilian Slave Society," *Journal of Social History,* III,, 1 (Fall, 1969), 47-49; Marvin Harris, *Patterns of Race in the Americas* (New York: Walker and Company, 1964), pp. 86-89. A similar situation developed in the Dutch colony of Surinam. See Harry Hoetink, "Race Relations in Curaçao and Surinam," in Laura Foner and Eugene D. Genovese, eds., *Slavery in the New World: A Reader in Comparative History* (Englewood Cliffs, N.J.: Prentice-Hall, Inc., 1969), pp. 178-188.

[15]This point is made by Harris, *Patterns of Race,* p. 87, and Harry Hoetink, *The Two Variants in Caribbean Race Relations: A Contribution to the Sociology of Segmented Societies,* trans. .by Eva M. Hooykaas (London and New York: Published for the Institute of Race Relations by Oxford University Press, 1967), p. 163.

[16]Horowitz, "Color Differentiation," pp. 528-529; Winthrop D. Jordon, "American Chiaroscuro: The Status and Definition of Mulattoes in the British Colonies," *William and Mary Quarterly,* 3rd. ser., XIX, 2 (April, 1962), 194-195.

[17]See the comments of one observer in A.C. Carmichael, *Domestic Manners and Social Condition of the White, Coloured, and Negro Population of the West Indies* (2 vols.; London: Whittaker, Treacher, and Co., 1833), I, 93-94.

[18]Carl N. Degler, *Neither Black Nor White: Slavery and Race Relations in Brazil and the United States* (New York: Macmillan Company, 1971), pp. 226-235.

[19]Klein, "Freedmen Brazilian Slave Society," p. 40.

[20]Gary B. Nash, *Red, White, and Black: The Peoples of Early America* (Englewood Cliffs, N.J.: Prentice-Hall, Inc., 1974), p. 286.

[21]Degler, *Neither Black Nor White,* pp. 235-239.

[22]Robert S. Cope, *Carry Me Back: Slavery and Servitude in Seventeenth Century Virginia* (Pikevile, KY.: Pikeville College Press of the Appalachian Studies Center, 1973), p. 114. The actual cases, one in 1630 and one in 1640, involved white men names Hugh Davis and Robert Sweat. See Helen Tunnicliff Catteral, ed., *Judicial Cases Concerning American Slavery and the Negro* (3 vols.; Washington, D.C.: Carnegie Institute of Washington, 1926-1937), I, 78.

[23]William Waller Hening, comp., *The Statutes at Large; Being A Collection of All the Laws of Virginia, from the First Session of the Legislature, in the Year 1619* (13 vols.: Richmond, New York, Philadelphia: 1819-1823), II, 170.

[24]*Ibid.*, III, 66-68. Maryland had passed a similar law in 1664 but rescinded it in 1681. See Jeffrey R. Brackett, *The Negro in Maryland: A Study of the Institution of Slavery*, Johns Hopkins University Studies in History and Political Science, Extra Volume VI (Baltimore: N. Murray, Publication Agent, John Hopkins University, 1889), pp. 32-34.

[25]Hening, *Statutes at Large*, III, 86-88; Cope, *Carry Me Back*, p. 115.

[26]Winthrop D. Jordan, *White Over Black: American Attitudes Toward the Negro, 1550-1812* (Chapel Hill: University of North Carolina Press, 1968), p. 139.

[27]Massachusetts did so in 1705, Maryland and North Carolina in 1715, South Carolina in 1717, Pennsylvania in 1726, and Georgia in 1750 (when Negroes were first admitted to the colony). See *The Acts and Resolves, Public and Private, of the Province of the Massachusetts Bay* (21 vols.; Boston: Wright & Potter, 1869-1922), I, 578-579; *Archives of Maryland* (69 vols.; Baltimore: Maryland Historical Society, 1883-), I, 533-534, VII, 204-205, XIII, 546-549, XXII, 259-260, XXX, 289-290, XXXIII, 112, XXXVI, 275-276; Walter Clark, ed., *The State Records of North Carolina* (26 vols.: Goldsboro, N.C.: Nash Brothers, Printers, 1886-1907), XXIII, 65, 106, 160, 195; Thomas Cooper and David J. McCord, eds., *Statutes at Large of South Carolina* (10 vols.: Columbia, S.C.: 1836-1841), III, 20; James T. Mitchell, *et al.*, *The Statutes at Large of Pennsylvania from 1682 to 1809* (18 vols.; Harrisburg, Pa.: C.M. Bush, 1896-1915), IV, 62-63; Allen D. Candler, comp., *The Colonial Records of the State of Georgia* (26 vols.; Atlanta: C. P. Byrd, 1904-1916), I, 59-60.

[28]Nash, *Red, White, and Black*, p. 290.

[29]Jordan, "American Chiaroscuro," pp. 199-200. This view was expressed in a much earlier and more caustic assessment of colonial white attitudes towards miscegenation and its mulatto product in Carter G. Woodson, "The Beginnings of Miscegenation of Whites and Blacks," *Journal of Negro History*, III, 4 (October, 1918), 349-351. For a superb overall explanation of the genesis and meaning of white American attitudes about miscegenation, see Jordan, *White Over Black*, pp. 136-178.

[30]In this regard, see Irene Diggs, "Color in Colonial Spanish America," *Journal of Negro History*, XXXVIII, 4 (October, 1953), 403-427; Jordan, *White Over Black*, pp. 174-175.

[31]Ira Berlin, *Slaves Without Masters: The Free Negro in the Antebellum South*, Vintage Books (New York: Random House, Inc., 1974). pp. 97-98.

[32]See *ibid.*, pp. 98-99, 161-162, n. 39.

[33]Charles S. Mangum Jr., *The Legal Status of the Negro* (Chapel Hill: University of North Carolina Press, 1940), pp. 3-4.

[34]James Hugo Johnston, *Race Relations in Virginia and Miscegenation in the South* (Amherst: University of Massachusetts Press, 1970), pp. 193-194, 215.

[35]Jordan, "American Chiaroscuro," p. 189.

[36]John D. Duncan, "Slave Emancipation in Colonial South Carolina," *American Chronicle, A Magazine of History*, I, 1 (January, 1972), 66.

[37]Peter H. Wood, *Black Majority: Negroes in Colonial South Carolina From 1670 through the Stono Rebellion* (New York: Alfred A. Knopf, Inc., 1974), pp. 233-236.

[38]Berlin, *Slaves Without Masters*, pp. 197-199.

[39]This does not mean that intermarriage was common. As one student of South Carolina's free Negro population has noted, social sanctions against intermarriage were strong during the ante-bellum period, so that most interracial sexual contact was extramarital. See Marina Wikramanayake, *A World in Shadow: The Free Black in Ante-bellum South Carolina* (Columbia: University of South Carolina Press, 1973), pp. 13, 76.

[40]Catterall, *Judicial Cases Concerning Slavery*, II, 269. See also Berlin, *Slaves Without Masters*, pp. 163-165.

[41]E. Horace Fitchett, "The Origin and Growth of the Free Negro Population of Charleston, South Carolina," *Journal of Negro History*, XXVI, 4 (October, 1941), 423.

[42]On the Brown Fellowship Society, see James B. Browning, "The Beginnings of Insurance Enterprise among Negroes," *Journal of Negro History*, XXII, 4 (October, 1937), 422-423, 426-427; E. Horace Fitchett, "The Traditions of the Free Negro in Charleston, South Carolina," *Journal of Negro History*, XXV, 2 (April, 1940), 145, 150; Wikramanayake, *World in Shadow*, p. 87.

[43]Fitchett, "Traditions of Free Negro in Charleston," pp. 144-151; Wikramanayake, *World in Shadow*, pp. 83-85, 88-89, 91.

[44]O. Vernon Burton, "The Slave Community in Edgefield, South Carolina, 1850-1880" (unpublished Ph.D. dissertation, Princeton University, 1975).

[45]For a description of some of these wealthy mulatto planters, see H. E. Sterkx, *The Free Negro in Ante-Bellum Louisiana* (Rutherford, N.J.: Fairleigh Dickinson University Press, 1972), pp. 202-213.

[46]John W. Blassingame, *Black New Orleans, 1860-1880* (Chicago: University of Chicago Press, 1973), p. 17.

[47]Frederick Law Olmsted described the institution of the *placage* in his *A Journey in the Seaboard States, with Remarks on Their Economy* (New York: Dix & Edwards, 1856), pp. 244-245. See also Sterkx, *Free Negro in Louisiana*, pp. 250-251; Blassingame, *Black New Orleans*, pp. 17-18.

[48]Laura Foner, "The Free People of Color in Louisiana and St. Domingue: A Comparative Portrait of Two Three-Caste Slave Societies," *Journal of Social History*, III, 4 (Summer, 1970), 414, 423, 427; Sterkx, *Free Negro in Louisiana*, pp. 240-284, *passim*.

[49]Sterkx, *Free Negro in Louisiana*, pp. 223-234; Foner, "Free People of Color," pp. 424-425; Berlin, *Slaves Without Masters*, pp. 112-114, 129.

[50]Charles S. Sydnor, "The Free Negro in Mississippi Before The Civil War," *American Historical Review*, XXXII, 4 (July, 1927), 781-783; D. Clayton James, *Antebellum*

Natchez (Baton Rouge: Louisiana State University Press, 1968), pp. 177-178. For insights into the lives of mulatto elites in Natchez, see two works based on the diaries of William Johnson, a light-skinned Natchez barber who stood at the top of the city's free Negro community and often even mixed with neighboring white aristocrats in the 1830s and 1840s: William Ransom Hogan and Edwin Adams Davis, *The Barber of Natchez* (Baton Rouge: Louisiana State University Press, 1954) and William Ransom Hogan and Edwin Adams Davis, eds., *William Johnson's Natchez: The Antebellum Diary of a Free Negro* (Baton Rouge: Louisiana State University Press, 1957).

[51]James Benson Sellers, *Slavery in Alabama* (University: University of Alabama Press, 1950), pp. 384-389; Morris Raymond Boucher, "The Free Negro in Alabama Prior to 1860" (unpublished Ph.D. dissertation, State University of Iowa, 1950), pp. 18-19 and *passim.*

[52]Russell Garvin, "The Free Negro in Florida Before the Civil War," *Florida Historical Quarterly*, XLVI, 1 (July, 1967), 11-12; David Y. Thomas, "The Free Negro in Florida Before 1865," *South Atlantic Quarterly*, X, 4 (October, 1911), 336, 338, 345.

[53]Berlin, *Slaves Without Masters*, p. 198.

[54]Catterall, *Judicial Cases Concerning Slavery*, III, 649.

[55]See Berlin, *Slaves Without Masters*, pp. 275-283.

[56][Edwin Clifford Holland], *A South Carolinian, A Refutation of the Calumnies Circulated against the Southern and Western States, Respecting the Existence of Slavery among Them, to Which is Added a Minute and Particular Account of the Actual Condition of Their Negro Population* (Charleston: A. E. Miller, 1822), pp. 84-85.

[57]Wikramanayake, *World in Shadow*, pp. 169-170.

[58]Ruth B. Barr and Modeste Hargis, "The Voluntary Exile of Free Negroes of Pensacola," *Florida Historical Quarterly*, XVII, 1 (July, 1938), 1-14.

[59]Monroe *Register*, April 12, 1860, quoted in Sterkx, *Free Negro in Louisiana*, p. 309. For a description of the rising tide of white opposition to the presence of free Negroes, including mulattoes, in Louisiana, see *ibid.*, pp. 285-315.

[60]Henry Hughes, *Treatise on Sociology, Theoretical and Practical* (Philadelphia: Lippincott, Grambo & Co., 1854), p. 31.

[61]See Luther Porter Jackson, *Free Negro Labor and Property Holding in Virginia, 1830-1860* (New York: D. Appleton-Century Co., Inc., 1942), pp. 125-127; Constance McLaughlin Green, *The Secret City: A History of Race Relations in the Nation's Capital* (Princeton, N.J.: Princeton University Press, 1967), pp. 42-44; Cyprian Clamorgan, *The Colored Aristocracy of St. Louis* (St. Louis: 1858).

[62]Berlin, *Slaves Without Masters*, pp. 28-29, 86, and 183-216, *passim.*

[63]See *Ibid.*, pp. 343-380, *passim.*

[64]Catterall, *Judicial Cases Concerning Slavery*, II, 359.

[65]For mulattoes being employed as domestic servants and the resulting stratification among the slave population, see Olmsted, *Seaboard States*, pp. 421, 427; Frances Ann

Kemble, *Journal of a Residence on a Georgia Plantation in 1838-1839* (New York: Harper and Brothers, 1863), pp. 193-194; E. Franklin Frazier, *The Negro in the United States* (Rev. ed.; New York: Macmillan Company, 1957), pp. 53-56; Kenneth M. Stampp, *The Peculiar Institution: Slavery in the Ante-Bellum South,* Vintage Books (New York: Random House, 1956), p. 196. The extent of this practice is questioned by Winthrop D. Jordan. See Jordan, "American Chiaroscuro," p. 186 and Jordan, *White Over Black,* pp. 169, 178. It should be noted, however, that Jordan's argument derives from a reading of colonial and not ante-bellum documents. Eugene D. Genovese seems to accept Jordan's position, although admitting differences in New Orleans and Charleston. See Genovese, *Roll, Jordan, Roll: The World the Slaves Made* (New York: Pantheon Books, 1974), pp. 327-328. Considerable impressionistic evidence nevertheless seems to indicate that there was widespread color differentiation between house servants and field hands, although many mulatto slaves clearly fell in the latter category as well. It is possible, though, that some white families tended to perceive their domestics as lighter in color than the anonymous field slaves, even if that were not actually the case. Perhaps to the degree that familiarity bred affection between white masters and house slaves, it also led the former to see the latter as more white-like.

[66]Berlin, *Slaves Without Masters,* pp. 386-387; Sellers, *Slavery in Alabama,* pp. 387-389, 397-398; Mary F. Berry, "Negro Troops in Blue and Gray: The Louisiana Native Guard, 1861-1863," *Louisiana History,* VIII, 2 (Spring, 1967), 165-190.

[67]Joel Williamson. *After Slavery: The Negro in South Carolina During Reconstruction, 1861-1877* (Chapel Hill: University of North Carolinan Press, 1965), pp. 316-317; George B. Tindall, *South Carolina Negroes, 1877-1900* (Columbia: University of South Carolina Press, 1952), pp. 195-197. Peter Kolchin notes a similar response among the mulatto Creoles of Mobile, Alabama. See Kolchin, *First Freedom: The Response of Alabama's Blacks to Emancipation and Reconstruction* (Westport, Conn.: Greenwood Press, 1972), pp. 142-143.

[68]*The Nation,* I, 11 (September 14, 1865), 332.

[69]Kolchin, *First Freedom,* pp. 163-167.

[70]Roger A. Fischer, *The Segregation Struggle in Louisiana, 1862-1877* (Urbana: University of Illinois Press, 1974), p. 48; E. Franklin Frazier, *The Negro Family in the United States* (Chicago: University of Chicago Press, 1939), p. 263.

[71]Luther Porter Jackson, *Negro Office-Holders in Virginia, 1865-1895* (Norfolk, Va.: Guide Quality Press, 1945 [c. 1946].

[72]Samuel Denny Smith, *The Negro in Congress, 1879-1901* (Chapel Hill: University of North Carolina Press, 1940), p. 7 and *passim.*

[73]Ada Piper, "Activities of Negroes in the Territorial Government of the District of Columbia, 1871-1874" (unpublished M.A. thesis, Howard University, 1943), esp. p. 61; Green, *Secret City,* pp. 97-99.

[74]In late 1864, a New Orleans newspaper summed up the situation well in noting the bond between the state's free mulattoes and the black freedmen:

> "These two populations, equally rejected and deprived of their rights, cannot be well estranged from one another. The emancipated will

find in the old free men, friends ready to guide them, to spread upon them the light of knowledge, and teach them their duties as well as their rights. But, at the same time, the free men will find in the recently liberated slaves a mass to uphold them; and with this mass behind them they will command the respect always bestowed to number[s] and strength."

New Orleans *Tribune*, December 29, 1864, quoted in Blassingame, *Black New Orleans*, p. 154.

[75]Green, *Secret City*, pp. 65, 121, 138-142. The quotations are from pp. 121 and 141. See also Frazier, *Negro in United States*, pp. 286-289.

[76]Robert E. Perdue, *The Negro in Savannah, 1865-1900* (Jerico, N.Y.: Exposition Press, 1973), pp. 90-93.

[77]Blassingame, *Black New Orleans*, pp. 153-156; Frazier, *Negro Family in United States*, pp. 263-265.

[78]Williamson, *After Slavery*, pp. 313-317.

[79]Louis Clausiel Perry, "Studies in the Religious Life of the Negroes of Nashville, Tennessee," *Vanderbilt University Quarterly*, IV, 2 (April, 1904), 90-91.

[80]W. E. B. DuBois, *The Philadelphia Negro: A Social Study*, Publications of the University of Pennsylvania in Economy and Public Law No. 14 (Philadelphia: University of Pennsylvania Press, 1899), pp. 310-311.

[81]John Daniels, *In Freedom's Birthplace* (Boston: Houghton, Mifflin Co., 1914), pp. 174-183.

[82]For a suggestive essay on the relationship between class structure and ideology in the Negro community of the turn-of-the-century decades, see August Meier, "Negro Class Structure and Ideology in the Age of Booker T. Washington," *Phylon*, XXIII, 3 (Fall, 1962), 258-266. Meier gives little attention to the interplay of color in this situation, however. For the role of mulattoes in the Negro middle class, see Frazier, *Negro Family in United States*, pp. 423-429; Reuter, *Mulatto in United States*, pp. 358ff.

[83]*Negro Population*, p. 208.

[84]*Ibid.*, pp. 212-213.

[85]*Ibid.*, pp. 213-214.

[86]*Ibid.*, pp. 211-212, 214. For an interesting discussion of this general topic, see "Sex Distribution in the Mulatto Population" in Reuter, *Race Mixture*, pp. 59-71.

[87]In point of fact, the Census Bureau even reported a massive decline in the mulatto population in 1920. That year, it claimed, there were only 1,660,554 mulattoes in the United States, down 19 percent from the figure reported ten years earlier. It would seem that mulattoes were simply becoming less visible to white Americans.

[88]On the legal aspects of racial intermarriage, see Gilbert Thomas Stephenson, *Race Distinctions in American Law* (New York: D. Appleton and Company, 1910), pp. 78-101; Albert Ernest Jenks, "The Legal Status of Negro-White Amalgamation in the

United States," *American Journal of Sociology,* XXI, 5 (March, 1916), 666-678. On the legal definition of a Negro, see Stephenson, *Race Distinctions,* pp. 12-20.

[89]Stephenson, *Race Distinctions,* p. 19. Thirty years later, another student of legal aspects of race relations was led to make the same conclusions. See Mangum, *Legal Status of Negro,* p. 248.

CHAPTER II

SCIENCE, AMALGAMATION, AND THE "ONE DROP RULE"

The decline in the status of the mulatto during the half-century after emancipation resulted, to a considerable degree, from a growing passion within the white community for racial purity. This attitude spread somewhat simultaneously through the popular mind and various scientific circles with the gradual development of a distinct set of ideas about race and racial differences. Indeed, for many years popular attitudes and scientific theories interacted with and reinforced each other. Ultimately, these ideas involved the nearly universal acceptance of what might be termed the "one drop rule," the belief that regardless of how distant a mulatto's black ancestry might be, regardless of how white he might appear to be physically, he nevertheless remained a Negro. Booker T. Washington explained the situation quite graphically in 1900:

> It is a fact that, if a person is known to have one per cent of African blood in his veins, he ceases to be a white man.. The ninety-nine per cent of Caucasian blood does not weigh by the side of one per cent of African blood. The white blood counts for nothing. The person is a Negro every time.[1]

"One drop of black blood makes a Negro" was the common axiom, and it was this notion which eventually colored all discussions on the subject of racial amalgamation and the mulatto's place in America's clearly biracial society.

Whites, of course, had long been conscious of a myriad of characteristics which apparently served to distinguish different races. With regard to the black man, as Winthrop Jordan has noted, the white man's perception of these racial differences served as an important factor in rationalizing the decision to enslave Africans. In many ways these ideas were rather nebulous and sometimes even contradictory, but their overall effect was to establish in the white mind a strong connection between black skin on the one hand, and savagery and inferiority on the other.[2] However, it was not until the nineteenth century that scientists began intensely to study and catalog these differences with a goal of better understanding the relationships between races and the degree to which certain races were superior or inferior to others.

Nineteenth-century anthropology relied upon a system for the classification of man developed in the previous century by two Europeans, Carl von Linnaeus and Johann Friedrich Blumenbach. Both men were primarily concerned with simply designating the races or varieties of man and based their considerations on such external factors as skin color, the texture and color of hair, and skull and facial characteristics. It was Blumenbach who originated the name "Caucasian," taking it from Mount Caucasus because its southern slope, he believed, had cradled what he felt to be the most beautiful race of man. The other two primary races, the Ethiopian and the Mongolian, were extreme degenerations from the Caucasian, while the other races of which he spoke, the American and the Malayan, he saw as transitional groups of only minor significance. Blumenbach, however, did not question the fundamental belief in the common origin of all races of mankind.[3]

Working from this basis of classification, considerable anthropological effort in the nineteenth century concentrated on anthropometry in an attempt to clarify and distinguish the characteristics peculiar to each racial grouping.[4] Perhaps the most important initial phase was phrenology and other forms of cranial measurement, which sought through studying head shapes and sizes and brain weights to determine variations in intelligence and mental processes. While the importance of such studies themselves was eventually discounted in favor of the new evolutionary psychology propounded by Herbert Spencer, the essential notions developed during this early stage of investigation had a lasting impact upon anthropological considerations of race and racial differences. This was especially true of the ideas of racial inferiority established in part by the phrenologists, which relegated the Mongolian, Malayan, American, and Ethiopian races to varying positions of inferiority below the Caucasian depending upon skull shapes and sizes.[5]

The mulatto posed a particular problem for those who sought to establish distinct racial classifications on the basis of highly tangible physical features, for he clearly combined the characteristics of both of the races from which he sprang. In America, the mulatto and the idea of racial amalgamation had long held an ambiguous position in the minds of whites. There was considerable confusion about the relations between mixed-bloods and the pure black. The mulatto was generally perceived to be more intelligent than the black, as well as physically more attractive because of the predominance of white rather than black physical characteristics. In these terms, the mulatto was clearly superior to blacks. At the same time, it was widely believed that the mulatto was constitutionally weak, prone to debilitating diseases, and like all hybrids, basically infertile--facts which indicated certain basic inferiorities to both of the parent races. Despite the relative frequency with which it was practiced in the ante-bellum period, then, racial amalgamation was not seen as a wise course. It produced a weak being, with little or no future, who obviously was not a desirable representative of the American people.

It was the American Civil War which marked a watershed in anthropometric studies of racial differences and the development of concrete theories about the unique status of the mulatto. Both the Provost Marshall-General's Bureau and the United States Sanitary Commission established procedures for the wide-scale measurement of soldiers during the war years. The conclusions drawn from these studies were not important so much because they were new, but because they helped to crystallize and give scientific substantiation to earlier, largely impressionistic attitudes and ideas about race. As a result, they had considerable impact on ensuing racial theory. As historian John S. Haller, Jr., has noted,

> nearly all subsequent late nineteenth-century institutionalized attitudes of racial inferiority focused upon war anthropometry as the basis for their beliefs. . . . The directions and conclusions of the Civil War anthropometric evidence buttressed the conservative ethos of American social order and stability and, at the same time, encouraged a new "scientific" attitude.[6]

Through a variety of measurements of body dimensions, head size, vision, teeth, strength, respiration, and pulmonary capacity, the researchers in both groups found, as might be expected, that Negroes were distinctly inferior to whites. More important for the present study, they established that, as earlier racialists had argued, the mulatto was physiologically inferior to both of the original stocks. It seemed a logical conclusion, then, that mixing of the races was no real remedy for the racial inferiority of the black man. The mulatto would not be able to stand the rigors of competitive life. Benjamin A. Gould, who headed most of the Sanitary Commission's studies, reported that the organization's efforts confirmed "the well known phenomenon" of the mulatto's "inferior vitality."[7] For example, the difference between mulattoes and full blacks in terms of chest size and respiration, important measures of physical vigor, was "very conspicuous . . . the blacks in their turn falling below the Indians, and these vastly below the whites, of whatever class."[8]

In 1875, Jedediah Hyde Baxter published the findings of the Provost Marshall-General's Bureau in two weighty tomes, corroborating on an even larger scale the findings of Gould. Through one aspect of his study, a questionnaire to Union doctors, Baxter also confirmed the popular belief in the mulatto's physical inferiority. The mulatto was clearly incapable of enduring hardship and was weaker than either the pure black or the white. Although, according to one responding physician, a larger proportion of Negroes successfully passed the physical examination than any other group, those rejected were invariably mulattoes. The capabilities of the mixed-blood, though imitative, were a good deal less than the full black, and the mulatto exhibited a markedly greater tendency to scrofulous and tubercular diseases.[9]

Perhaps the Civil War study most frequently cited in later decades was that of Sanford B. Hunt, a surgeon in the United States Volunteers. In 1869 he published an article entitled "The Negro as a Soldier" in the London *Anthropological Review*. Of particular concern to Hunt were physiological signs of intellectual differences between the races. Presuming that "the size and weight of the brain is the measure of its intellectuality," Hunt made studies of the autopsies performed at several different Army hospitals. From 405 autopsies, 381 of which were performed on Negroes, he concluded that the brain of the full-blooded Negro weighed five ounces less than that of the white, while slight admixture of white blood in the Negro served to "diminish the negro brain from its normal standard." Where the admixture of white blood was greater, however, "it determines a positive increase in the negro brain, which in the quadroon is only three ounces below the white standard." It was clear, therefore, that the addition of the blood of the superior white man increased the intellectual capabilities of the Negro, but never to the point of making the mixed-blood the equal of the white man. Further, because other evidence demonstrated the proclivity of mulattoes to tuberculosis and lower fecundity, it was evident that overall the amalgamation of the races had a deleterious effect, since its mixed-blooded product was not the equal of the white man himself.[10]

The anthropometric studies of the mid-nineteenth century served to confirm most earlier beliefs about mixed-bloods. Inevitably, they were carried over into the last quarter of the century and shaped, to a remarkable degree, the theories and attitudes about mulattoes and racial mixing which were developed in a variety of increasingly sophisticated social and biological sciences. It was not until after the turn of the century that many of these earlier concepts were reevaluated and discarded, although they lingered on in the works of popularizers of scientific theories and therefore continued to have considerable impact on popular racial thought. In particular, the contributions of Franz Boas to anthropology and social thought in general--most significantly the idea of cultural relativism and the recognition of culture as a phenomenon distinct from race--remained largely unknown to the American public. As a result, while the academic world was gradually revising its understanding of the meaning of race, the vast majority of Americans clung to older ideas which served to explain their everyday perceptions.

The questions to be developed in this and the next chapter revolve around just how biological and social scientists, and the popular writers who followed in their wake, understood the process of racial amalgamation and perceived its product, the mulatto. How did they see the forces of heredity at operation in the mixing of the races? What, in fact, did those forces involve? Why was the great majority of these men led to conclude that miscegenation was a grave error? Why did "one drop of black blood" make a Negro? Why was such an outlook necessary? Finally, how were these ideas conveyed to the general public, and what effect did they have on popular attitudes about the mulatto and race mixing? It is in this latter realm, of course, that theories were converted into practice and basic patterns of race relations developed and enforced.

2

In the late nineteenth century, three distinct strains of thought combined to shape white America's attitudes about race and racial differences, including evolving notions about racial intermixture and the nature of the mulatto. The most obvious was Darwinism. Its effects were felt not only in the realm of biology, but in a wide variety of social, economic, and political theorizings as well.[11] In the area of racial theory, however, Darwinism was most important because of the way it interacted with other concepts, both competing and complementary, in molding both popular and scientific attitudes and perceptions. Many people, including a sizable segment of the scientific community, rejected the idea of Darwinian hereditarian determinism, while others accepted it only to a limited degree. Certainly of equal importance were the revived and reinvigorated notions of environmentalism, whose most important theoretical precursor was the French naturalist, Jean Baptiste Pierre Antoinne Lamarck (1744-1829). Further, both Darwinism and Lamarckianism interacted with polygenist concepts surviving from earlier debates about the origin of different races.

The argument between polygenists, or those who believed that the races of man were distinct species with separate origins, and the monogenists, who insisted on the unity of mankind and a single creation, had played an important part in the intellectual wranglings over slavery during the ante-bellum period. Yet the debate did not die with the Civil War and the coming of emancipation. As George W. Stocking has noted, the difference in the two positions ultimately involved much more than the essentially academic question of whether or not mankind had descended from a single monogenetic type. "From a broader point of view," he explains,

> polygenism and monogenism can be regarded as specific expressions of enduring alternative attitudes toward the variety of mankind. Confronted by antipodal man, one could marvel at his fundamental

likeness to oneself, or one could grasp at his immediately striking differences.[12]

Perhaps it is this wider context which serves to explain the persistence of the polygenist/monogenist issue. Certainly the external forces of the era were doing little to undermine the ideas upon which the polygenist position was founded. If anything, those ideas might have been intensified, as imperialistic white men increased their contacts with people of other races in the latter half of the nineteenth century. Not only were the differences between the civilized white man and the dark-skinned savage even more visible than before, but now there was a greater need to justify the former's imperial domination of the latter.

Monogenism was the traditional belief, derived for the most part from a strict reading of the Biblical account of creation. It held that all races had sprung from a single family. Basic differences in color, bodily form, and intelligence were the result of environmental changes affecting migrating groups as they adapted themselves over many generations. From this perspective, there were no true "pure" races, only the relative permanence of marked varieties which were suited to different geographical and climatic regions. These varieties were gradually produced by the inheritance of acquired variations which represented the influence of external, environmental conditions, and were fixed (although not necessarily permanently) through long periods of close breeding.

It should not be assumed, however, that monogenists were necessarily egalitarians (although some indeed were), despite their belief in humanity's single origin. During centuries of formation, races had acquired certain characteristics which, upon overall comparison, established an obvious inequality among them. Clearly the Negro, as such, had never been the white man's equal. Indeed, one historian has argued that the theory of monogenism grew out of an a priori belief in degradation from the original prototype, and most whites were convinced that this degeneration had proceeded farthest in the case of the black man. The monogenists' environmentalism led them to classify races in terms of changes in the genus *Homo*, so that inherent feelings of superiority often resulted in an adamant classification of the Negro as inferior.[13]

Polygenism, on the other hand, struck many as being a heretical doctrine, inasmuch as it represented something of a denial of the Biblical story of man's origins. Yet for many people the theory of multiple origins, as it was developed in the first half of the nineteenth century, was an entirely logical explanation of easily perceived differences among men. Much of the impetus for the polygenist position derived from the mania for classification and categorization which swept both academic and amateur natural scientists in America in the early decades of the

1800s. In particular, the study of cranial shapes and other physical features of various racial types led a number of the nation's most eminent scientific figures, including Samual George Morton and Louis Agassiz, to adopt a polygenist outlook. Some even tried to reconcile their ideas with the Bible, arguing that other peoples had existed along with the Adamite family, or in extreme cases, that non-whites were actually sub-human and had been created before Adam.

The essential point of the polygenist view was that man had originated in several places by several special acts of creation, and that from that time forward the various types had remained distinct. Consequently, there was considerable inclination among polygenists to speak of different "species" of men to emphasize the distinct separation of different races. Again, classification systems resulting from such a point of view usually involved a hierarchical perception of the races, reflecting notions inherent in the traditional concept of the Great Chain of Being.[14] Altogether, polygenism represented a distinctly pre-Darwinian outlook, and was ostensibly discarded as the hereditarian doctrine reshaped Western thought in the second half of the nineteenth century. Nevertheless, powerful remnants of polygenist thought, especially those concerning racial inferiority, survived the earlier debate over the origin of man and influenced both the thought and vocabulary of post-Darwinian anthropological studies.[15]

The survival of polygenist ideas was of particular significance in shaping notions about the mulatto and race mixture. Racial amalgamation had been an issue of acute importance in the earlier debate between the monogenists and the polygenists. The very use of the term "species" by the polygenists indicates how unnatural they felt racial mixing to be--different species would interbeed only under artificial conditions. Further, if the races of man were in fact distinct species and had been created as such for some deliberate reason (though perhaps unknown to man), then it followed that maintaining racial purity was a task of extreme importance. Josiah Clark Nott, an Alabama physician and pre-Darwinian polygenist, expressed this view quite firmly. If the races were separated by differences which were essential rather than accidental, he wrote in 1854, "it is evident . . . that the superior races ought to be kept free from all adulterations, otherwise the world will retrograde, instead of advancing, in civilization."[16] It was a notion that would be echoed by a multitude of writers for the next sixty years.

Of equal importance for later thought was the polygenist belief that because the union of distinct species was "unnatural," the offspring of such unions were sterile or tended toward sterility. As a result, there could be no stable mixed or mulatto race. Although prolific when backcrossed with either of the original races, mulattoes were not fully fertile among themselves. Without continued mixture with whites or blacks, the mulatto group, already believed to be physically weak and short-lived, would either die out or "revert" to the characteristics of the lower of its two progenitors. In a similar vein, polygenists tended to be convinced that mixed-bloods were generally mentally, morally, and physically inferior to either parent group.[17]

It might be noted, perhaps parenthetically, that monogenists generally took a different view of the mulatto. While at times granting that not all racial mixings produced equally viable offspring, they tended to explain the apparent or presumed ill effects of amalgamation as resulting from social or environmental factors, especially the absence of a normal family life which often characterized interracial unions. A number of monogenists even defended racial mixing as a positive social good. This view was particularly evident among the more radical element of abolitionists at the time of the Civil War. This group saw in racial amalgamation the key to the eradication of racial prejudice and ultimately believed that intermixture would serve to combine the best characteristics of each race into a single superior type.[18] All monogenists, however, contended that new and stable mixed races could be formed by the intermarriage of disparate racial groups.

This more positive view of mulattoes and race mixture, like that of the polygenists, survived into the late nineteenth and early twentieth centuries, although it was accepted by only a minority of racial thinkers and certainly not by the public itself. Residual polygenist notions, on the other hand, had a considerably greater effect. Indeed, polygenist ideas of mulatto inferiority and sterility, the unnaturalness of racial mixing, and the need to maintain racial purity subsequently did much to determine how white America in the late nineteenth and early twentieth centuries perceived mixed-bloods and reacted to the idea of racial amalgamation.

The point to be made is that although Darwinism revolutionized patterns of thought in the Western world in the latter decades of the 1800s, and although the biological and social sciences themselves underwent considerable change during this period towards greater sophistication both in terms of analytical approach and reliance upon systematic measurement, older polygenist notions, often built upon little more than impressionistic and anecdotal argument, continued to have considerable impact upon racial thought. Physical anthropology, for instance, was an increasingly important scientific discipline in generating many of the notions which eventually made their way into popular thoughts on race and racial differences. It was one discipline clearly affected by polygenist survivals. Major areas of concern to physical anthropologists--the idea that cultural differences among men were the direct product of differences in their racial physical structure; the assumption that these distinguishing physical differences were virtually primordial in nature; the idea that the most important of these differences involved the human skull and brain; and the notion that out of the heterogeneity of modern populations one could reconstruct "types" which were representative of the "pure races" from whose mixture these modern populations derived--all indicate the impact of polygenist elements.[19]   While a separate discipline, cultural anthropology (then called "ethnology") borrowed heavily from the principles of physical anthropology. This reflects the manner in which certain polygenist ideas spread easily from one field of research to another, eventually becoming important facets of white America's general ideas about race.

3

The significance of these polygenist survivals in shaping popular and scientific ideas about race and racial differences can best be appreciated when they are seen in conjunction with the widespread contemporary belief in a Lamarckian theory of inheritance.   In its most elemental form, the polygenist notion of race was built upon the idea of racial essence, conceived at this time in what were ultimately almost Platonic terms. It was assumed, explains one historian, that there existed

> some hereditary essence expressing itself in a number of visible peculiarities that mark every member of a "pure" race and distinguish it from other races, the clarity of the distinction depending on the purity of the essence--since the only process which could significantly modify a race was racial mixture.[20]

Related to this was the long-standing organismic strain in social and political thought.   Races were often thought of as supraindividual entities which had a common "genius" or "soul" which distinguished them from other races. Further, they followed the individual life cycle of birth, growth, maturity and perhaps death. Such thought was a part of the Romantic philosophy growing out of the late eighteenth century work of Johann Gottfried von Herder, who emphasized the unique characteristics of different cultural or national groups.[21] Given the basic predisposition of white Americans towards a strong cultural chauvinism, it was not difficult to transmute Herder's optimistic view of cultural differences into notions of racial superiority.   The process merely involved comparative value judgments about the "genius" of the white race, generally as perceived in its social, political, and economic achievements, in contrast to the achievements of the darker races of the world.   In late nineteenth-century racial thought, there was a strong inclination to feel that this racial "genius" was the key to understanding both the past and the future of individual racial groups.[22] How it was developed, maintained, and transmitted is where the belief in a Lamarckian scheme of inheritance came into play.

Lamarckianism essentially held that an organism's environmentally generated needs brought about an "inclination" towards actions appropriate to meet those needs. Such actions, becoming habitual, occasioned the development of organs to execute them. Further, such structural modifications which were acquired in the lifetime of an individual organism might be preserved by reproduction and thereby passed on to the next generation. This notion was commonly referred to as the doctrine of the inheritance of acquired characteristics, for it involved the belief that an organism specifically developed the physical means of dealing with its environment and then was able to pass such characteristics on to its offspring. Although obviously sharply at odds with the notion of hereditary variation which is now seen as the basis of Darwinian evolution, at the time Lamarckianism was an appealing and widely accepted explanation of biological adjustment to environmental changes. Indeed, Darwin himself leaned towards a Lamarckian explanation of the origin of varietal characteristics, and in the latter part of the nineteenth century a significant portion of the American scientific community subscribed to what was termed a "Neo-Lamarckian" school for just that reason--the inability of basic Darwinian concepts of the survival of the fittest to explain the *origin* of the fittest in the first place.

Of greater importance here, however, is the fact that Lamarckianism, with roots deep within the tradition of nineteenth-century social thought, was a valuable tool for explaining the origins of racial differences. Consequently, it was diffused throughout the racial speculations of the period, both among those who leaned towards a Darwinian, largely biological explanation of evolution, as well as among those who might better be classed as environmentalists.[23] As George W. Stocking has commented, the idea of the inheritance of acquired characteristics

> explained certain biological (or sociobiological) givens which underlay the social behavior of contemporary man: the racial differences which limited or qualified the generalizations of sociologists as to the behavior of man in society, and the evolution of the mental characteristics which were the foundation of human society in general. But beyond what might be called these manifest functions, it also had certain latent functions and consequences. It had much to do with determining the character of the prevailing racialism. Furthermore, in the context of "Social Darwinism" it helped to legitimitize in *biological* terms the causal efficacy of *social* processes.[24]

The significance of Lamarckian concepts in shaping racial thought is explained by the fact that at this time there was considerable confusion as to the boundaries of biological and social phenomena. The two realms overlapped in the minds of most Americans, including trained scientists. Perhaps this is most evident in the way Darwinian principles of biological evolution were easily adopted to explain what was characterized as social evolution,[25] but this is only one indication of the very blurred distinction between biological and social processes. Such confusion was particularly true in the area of racial thought, for race itself (and this is surely the essential point) was viewed as much as a cultural or social phenomenon as it was a biological one, both in terms of formation and subsequent development or evolution.

The central idea in the Lamarckian view of race formation was "adaptation"--changes in organic behavior or physical structure caused by specific environmental influences were then transmitted by heredity from parent to child. Over an adequately long period of close breeding, such characteristics became common to the group as a whole and served to distinguish it from other racial groups. A similar process was felt to be at work in mental evolution, a concept of central concern to anthropologists and other scientists in the late 1800s and early 1900s who sought to understand the cultural differences (including the apparent inferiority of certain cultures) characterizing mankind.[26] Lamarckianism offered a seemingly logical explanation of the evolution of instincts, the factors which were viewed as the foundation of cultural practices. From the Lamarckian point of view, instincts were somehow the gradually internalized product of habitual behavior, both in an individual and a social sense. A group's habitual responses to its environment were eventually absorbed into its collective psyche, and this could clearly account not only for basic differences in cultural practices but more importantly for what were generally perceived to be the crucial differences in racial "geniuses." In this pattern of thought, one can see the interaction of social and biological concepts, as essentially social practices were absorbed and then transmitted by the biological mechanism of Lamarckian heredity. Such a view of race formation as a social process operating through biological means of transmission or inheritance explains the widespread casual but erroneous designation of various national and cultural groups as "races." More important, however, was the compelling explanation it offered for the highly visible cultural distinctions between races.

As long as race continued to be thought of in both biological and cultural terms, this notion of a Lamarckian transmission of social characteristics allowed many racial theorists to explain differential evolutionary patterns among races. Quite simply, a race's cultural characteristics, generated in response to its peculiar geoclimatic environment, determined both the nature of its development and its tendencies at the present time. With these social characteristics being transmitted in a biological sense from generation to generation, it was not hard to see the future of a racial group as following patterns thoroughly established in the past. For the white man, with his heritage of impressive political and economic achievements, this of course offered an optimistic outlook. For less civilized people like the black man, whose African heritage evidenced only savagery and sensual excess, the future was clearly much bleaker.

To a degree, such pessimistic notions about non-white peoples violated a basic Lamarckian tenet, i.e., racial plasticity resulting from exposure to new environments. Such thinking underlay much of the reform activity of the late nineteenth century, and is itself a partial explanation for the resurgence of Lamarckian thought at that time. Many environmentalists were responding, consciously or not, to the negative implications of hereditarianism in their emphasis upon the power of new environments to alter racial characteristics for the better.[27] In general, however, an individual's own racial outlook or attitude seemed to determine just how far he would apply his belief in Lamarckian environmentalism. To some, the process of racial cultural change was a continuing one, but for others, particularly those who had the most negative feelings about blacks and other "inferior" races, Lamarkianism only operated in past tense. Racial characteristics had been set and now, being "in the blood," shaped subsequent patterns of race development. From such a perspective, there was little hope for significant improvement and/or change among blacks. Racial characteristics in the blood limited black potential for cultural advancement. Blacks could clearly never become the equal of the white man.

Overall, the power of this Lamarckian view of race derived its strength from the manner in which it fit in and interacted with ideas of Darwinian evolutionism and residual polygenist notions. It was the three perspectives working together which served to shape racial thought in the years from Reconstruction to the First World War. Polygenism contributed ideas about racial differences and inferiority, especially through its emphasis upon notions of racial "genius" and of race as something of a supraindividual entity. Lamarckianism offered an explanation for the evolution of races and the development of the instincts which represented racial genius. It then explained how this racial essence, once in the blood, was passed on to succeeding generations. Finally, hereditarianism, while reinforcing feelings of racial superiority and inferiority, in its concentration upon evolutionary change underscored the need for care in terms of which characteristics should be perpetuated and which eliminated. These three strains of thought, operating together and separately upon the notion of race as an organic, biosocial phenomenon, provided the basis for both scientific and popular ideas and attitudes among whites about race and racial differences.

The patterns of race relations which developed in the half-century after emancipation were a direct reflection of these beliefs. Segregation and disfranchisement were the concrete manifestations of these attitudes, but their effects actually went much deeper. Ultimately these notions determined how whites perceived blacks as people and as competitors in a world-wide struggle for survival and domination. In this vein, scientific and social scientific theories served to explain and reinforce everyday observations about black people and interracial relations, and vice versa. A society coming to worship the very concept of science found in the latter's developing theories on race convenient justifications for its relegation of blacks to the status of inferiors, and then ready explanations for why blacks appeared to *be* inferior. Science and society were interacting in a vicious cycle of which the black man was the inevitable victim.[28] Until the concept of culture was divorced from the biological phenomenon of race, there was little chance that white America would perceive the Negro in anything but negative terms.[29]

How did this evolving racial outlook affect white attitudes about the mulatto? As has been noted, the mulatto was already burdened by impressionistic evidence which held him to be physically weak, intellectually inferior at least to the white man, and probably morally inferior to both races. Important anthropometric studies in the mid-nineteenth century largely confirmed these beliefs, and in doing so set the tone for subsequent scientific and social scientific investigations and theorizings about the mulatto and the consequences of racial amalgamation. These theories naturally reflected the ripening racial perspective of the period. Indeed, as with general attitudes about blacks, the development of the white racial position and ideas about mulattoes and race mixture went hand in hand, each reinforcing the other. Theories generated by the scientific community often reflected popularly held assumptions about mixed-bloods, while scientific notions were passed on to the public through a variety of popular writers. However, the fact that a growing number of scientists and social scientists gradually began to deviate from traditional racial positions, particularly after the turn of the century, seemed to have little significant effect on the material which reached the popular audience. Notions long discarded by much of the scientific community continued to reach the lay reader and presumably thereby to shape or confirm his beliefs about the mulatto and the Negro in general until well into the twentieth century. Certainly it is questionable whether even today all of the late nineteenth century suppositions and superstitions about race, racial differences, and the effects of race mixture have disappeared from the mind of white America.[30]

In sum, how did white Americans--scientists, social scientists, and the general public--view the mulatto and the idea of racial mixture in the fifty years after emancipation? How did the assumptions of these different groups intersect and interact? What were their sources? What were their effects upon public policy towards mixed-bloods and race mixing itself?

4

It has already been noted that polygenists of the pre-Civil War era were acutely conscious of the seemingly detrimental effects of racial mixing, and that this position was a direct outgrowth of their belief that the races of man actually represented distinct "species." This inclination to emphasize the distinctness of races became a cornerstone of the so-called "American School" of anthropology in the late nineteenth century and serves to explain much of the direction which ideas about the mulatto and race mixing took during that period.

Dr. Josiah Clark Nott, generally regarded by his contemporaries as one of the founders of the "American School" and co-author of the widely read anthropological treatise *Types of Mankind* (1854),[31] was a major figure in establishing the initial scientific position vis-à-vis the mulatto and race mixture. Indeed, Nott himself was first drawn to the study of anthropology by the problem of the mulatto and miscegenation. As early as 1843, in an article entitled "The Mulatto a Hybrid--Probable Extermination of Two Races If the Whites and Blacks are Allowed to Intermarry," he expounded on his own observations made during fifteen years of medical practice among the mixed races of the South. Mulattoes, he felt, were clearly less intelligent than whites, but more intelligent than blacks. Mulattoes were also less hardy and shorter-lived than either of the two original races, with mulatto women being "particularly delicate" and "subject to many chronic diseases." Further, mixed-bloods were less prolific among themselves than when mated with either white or black. Clearly, the mulatto was a hybrid, the offspring of "two distinct species--as the mule from the horse and the ass."[32]

Nott reiterated these notions ten years later in *Types of Mankind*,[33] and then again in 1866 in an article in the *Anthropological Review*. The latter essay, an open letter to Major General Otis O. Howard, superintendent of the Freedman's Bureau, was designed to reveal to Howard and reform-minded Northerners in general the true nature of the Negro. What intellectual capabilities the race had shown, Nott explained, were invariably evidenced by mixed-bloods, although mulattoes still fell far short of the white man in intelligence. The history of the Haitian republic offered clear evidence of the true nature of the mulatto's ability. Haiti's mulatto rulers "swept every remnant of civilization from the country, which soon relapsed into savageism." Mixing of the white and black races, Nott insisted, produced a variety that was both physically and intellectually intermediate between the two original stocks. "They are more intelligent than the blacks," he said of mulattoes, "and less so than the whites." It was questionable, though, whether the added intellectual power of mixed-bloods was enough to improve them "to any useful degree." On the other hand, Nott declared, "it is certain that the white race is deteriorated by every drop of black blood infiltrated into it--just as surely as the blood of the greyhound or pointer is polluted by that of a cur."[34]

Although Josiah Nott was converted rather quickly to an essentially Darwinian belief in evolutionary development and the antiquity of man,[35] his notions about mulattoes and racial mixture clearly reflected basic polygenist beliefs. Because of his reputation as a scientist, however, these ideas were readily picked up by other learned men of his day and influenced not only their work but that of scholars in later decades as well. Many of Nott's ideas were not original, and he was obviously inclined personally to accept the impressionistic sort of evidence which played an important role in the anthropological speculations of that time. Yet his own eminence certainly led to wider adoption of such ideas among scientists and laymen of the period. Indeed, such theories about mulattoes and racial mixing were an integral part of the "American School" of anthropology, and they clearly formed the interpretive basis of the Civil War anthropometrists' conclusions about mulattoes. Further, Nott and the ideas he espoused were still being cited at the end of the century as the "scientific" position with regard to mulattoes and the consequences of race mixing.

The work of Frederick L. Hoffman (1865-1946) provides evidence of how such theories were perpetuated. Hoffman, a statistician who worked for the Prudential Insurance Company of America, published a study of the *Race Traits and Tendencies of the American Negro* in 1896 through the American Economic Association. In essence, the work reflected "a summation of the century's medical and anthropological accumulations concerning race relations in America,"[36] with the usual confusion of social and biological processes tied together in a basically polygenist framework. After sifting through an immense amount of statistical and anthropological data, Hoffman came to the conclusion that despite census figures showing the Negro race to have an increasing birth rate and to be growing in numbers, its movement from the plantation to urban surroundings, together with the change from slavery to freedom, had undermined both its health and its race future. The high incidence of tuberculosis, syphilis, gonorrhea, scrofula, and other diseases among Negroes (often in themselves indicative of the immorality he saw as a "race trait") clearly pointed, he insisted, to the eventual extinction of the race.[37] The same fate faced the mulatto even sooner. In a chapter concerned with anthropometric details, Hoffman repeatedly cited the findings of Sanford B. Hunt, Benjamin A. Gould and other researchers of the Civil War period to demonstrate the physical inferiority of the mulatto.[38] He then expanded on this position in a chapter dealing specifically with the subject of racial amalgamation.

Although noting that there was "no agreement amongst high authorities" as to whether race mixing led to the improvement or deterioration of races, Hoffman's statistics led him to the quick conclusion that the mulatto was "possessed of the least vital force" of all races, a view largely derived from the work of Josiah Nott a half-century before. Looking at the findings of Civil War anthropometrists, particularly the smaller lung capacity of mulattoes, Hoffman ruled that

> the mixed race is physically the inferior of the white and pure black, and as a result of this inferior degree of vital power we meet with a lesser degree of resistance to disease and death among the mixed population, in contrast with the more favorable condition prevailing among the whites and pure blacks. Morally, the mulatto cannot be said to be superior to the pure black . . . . most of the illicit intercourse between whites and coloreds is with mulatto women and seldom with those of the pure type.[39]

Intellectually, however, "the mulatto is undoubtedly the superior of the pure black," Hoffman maintained, basing his view on studies which showed the brain weight of mulattoes to be greater than that of pure blacks. Yet this fact in itself held little hope for the mixed-blood, given the overwhelming evidence of his physical debility.[40]

With these facts in mind, it was clear to Hoffman that racial amalgamation was detrimental to the true progress of both races and resulted in an "inferior social efficiency and diminishing power as a force in American national life."[41]

> Hence the conclusion is unavoidable [he announced] that the amalgamation of the two races through the channels of prostitution or concubinage, as well as through the intermarrying of the lower types of both races [the only level at which he felt legitimate mixing actually took place], is contrary to the interest of the colored race, a positive hindrance to its social, mental and moral development. But aside from these considerations, important as they are, the physiological consequences alone demand race purity and a stern reprobation of any infusion of white blood. Whatever the race may have gained in an intellectual way, which is a matter of speculation, it has been losing its greatest resources in the struggle

for life, a sound physical organism and power of rapid reproduction.[42]

Hoffman's conclusions with regard to mulattoes, hybridity, and miscegenation were manifestly conditioned by traditional polygenist ideas about these subjects. Not only were his opinions clearly within this vein, but the sources for much of his data were themselves consciously or unconsciously working within a polygenist framework. To this, Hoffman linked a Darwinian emphasis on racial competition, with the result that there appeared to be little future, in his view, for the black man or the mulatto in America. In this manner, older notions became tied to newer racialist beliefs, and together they composed a scientific, ostensibly impartial statement on race relations which less sophisticated white Americans were subsequently inclined to accept unquestioningly.[43] In point of fact, Hoffman's study was itself cited for the next two decades by a variety of scientific and popular writers to bolster what were essentially racist attitudes towards blacks, mulattoes and the subject of race mixing. His recognized standing in the scientific world only served to enhance the significance of his findings in the eyes of white America.[44]

The true import of Hoffman's findings, however, does not lie in the mere fact of his personal impact upon later writers on race relations. Rather, these ideas were significant because they were held by a wide variety of thinkers throughout the years between the Civil War and World War I. Indeed, a sampling of literature on race and race mixing throughout this period indicates how pervasive were the ideas expressed in Hoffman's study. Men with a variety of backgrounds--educational, geographic, occupational, etc.--all held to a cluster of ideas about race, race mixing, and the nature of the mulatto which reflected the interaction of the Darwinian, Lamarckian, and polygenist outlooks described above. Further, just as Hoffman relied upon the work of earlier writers like Nott, Hunt, Gould, and Baxter and was himself subsequently cited by other writers of the era, there is a strong sense in which all of the works of this period served to reinforce each other. The result was that new ideas, particularly those which might have challenged traditional notions with regard to blacks, mulattoes, and miscegenation, were often stifled by the force of existing "scientific" evidence. Even after biologists, anthropologists, and sociologists began to turn away from earlier doctrines which necessarily held the Negro to be inferior and race mixture therefore a mistake, most popular writers continued to cite "scientific" authorities like Hoffman or even Nott to substantiate claims about black or mulatto inferiority. Of course, it was the work of these writers which was most often consumed by lay readers, thereby shaping popular racial attitudes, although many respected scientists from various disciplines also at times wrote for a wider audience in different popular publications like the *Arena, Atlantic Monthly, Open Court* and *Popular Science Monthly.* The fact that leading scientists and social scientists were propounding theories of a racist slant only served to strengthen already powerful popular beliefs about the inferiority of non-white peoples and the evils of racial amalgamation.

5

Among the many scientific and social scientific figures of the late nineteenth century who held attitudes about mulattoes and race mixture similar to Frederick Hoffman's, a number was active in disciplines which bore directly or indirectly on questions involving race and race distinctions. Others, however, were attracted to racial questions largely by personal biases. In the eyes of the general public, though, such an individual's standing as a scientist was often sufficient to imply that his findings or opinions on racial matters bore the stamp of scientific objectivity. Numerous physicians, for instance, wrote on a variety of racial matters, frequently from the vantage point of "personal observation." As doctors, they had no formal training in matters dealing with race, but their status as physicians could make such a fact less than distinct for the average reader, who might view medical credentials as evidence of scientific authority. In this manner, highly unscientific notions were able to seep into general racial attitudes under the guise of "scientific" findings.

In the late nineteenth and early twentieth centuries, however, there were many true academicians, both scientists and social scientists, actively involved in shaping the direction of racial thought. One such figure was Nathaniel Southgate Shaler (1841-1906), a leading geologist and paleontologist and dean of the Lawrence Scientific School at Harvard University. With such credentials, Shaler's opinons on racial matters carried considerable weight both within the scientific community of the time as well as with the general public. Shaler's own thoughts, however, typify how scientific and impressionistic evidence often combined in determining racial attitudes. One historian has noted Shaler's role in this regard:

> Mixing anecdote with science, reminscence with experimentation, he carried forward a systematic study of American science and social science that had implications for the era's most controversial social and political issues. His views about mankind, half scientific, half opinion and recollection, gave him a position of immense authority in the ripening of America's attitudes on race.[45]

Shaler's background was that of a Kentucky slaveholding aristocrat, and his views on race reflected that fact. He was also an ardent evolutionist, but viewed evolution from an admittedly Lamarckian point of view. Consequently, he was inclined to stress the interaction of organic and social processes. It was environment which had had the greatest effect in shaping mankind's characteristics. "The creature of to-day," he wrote, "though it endures for but a moment in time, is the heir of all the ages and embodies in its life the experiences of the past." The environmental forces peculiar to each land mass had had a particular influence on the development of each division of mankind. It was in each cradle-land that the races had developed their more permanent qualities. Such permanent race characteristics, the "assemblage of physical and mental motives," reflected the geographic circumstances of each race's prehistoric existence. These race characteristics became fixed, according to Shaler, and were then carried by each race during its subsequent wanderings. Aryan, Moor, African, and Hun were "still to a great extent what their primitive nature made them." Their race quality reflected this early development of essential characteristics and determined, to a considerable extent, their future race course as well as the "vigor with which they do their appointed work."[46]

Somewhat paradoxically, perhaps, Shaler held that the forces of environment no longer had great power to shape the races of man. Clearly this was to be seen in the case of the Negro, since he remained unchanged after centuries of exposure to new conditions of life in America. Citing the earlier medical and anthropometric studies of the race's inferior brain size and structure, Shaler concluded that physiological traits conferred on a race during its earliest stages of development posed restrictive barriers upon subsequent race development.[47] "The varieties of men," Shaler explained,

> following a common original law, hold fast to the ways of their forefathers, and the moral as well as the physical characteristics of a race are to a greater or less degree indelible, whether the given kind belong to the human or to lower creatures.[48]

It was essential to realize, he declared, that the Negro was not "a black white man," but rather a distinct type marked by characteristics which had been shaped in an environment far different from that which molded the white race. Were the black race left to itself, the civilized veneer developed through long contact with the white man would soon be dissolved, and the old savage ways so much a part of the Negro's primitive, barbaric African background would forcefully reassert themselves. This savage heritage was in the blood of the black man, and it made him not only inferior to the white race, but an alien, unassimilable element in American society.[49]

Given this basic understanding of race and racial differences, it is not surprising that Shaler adamantly opposed racial amalgamation between whites and blacks. Shaler was essentially a polygenist, and consequently held the basic notions about the results of miscegenation which were fundamental to a polygenist outlook. The hybridization of distinct racial groups was "almost always disadvantageous," he declared, for the mulatto product of such unions was generally sterile and lacking in the vitality characteristic of the parent races. As early as 1870, in commenting on the large proportion of mulattoes he found while visiting Charleston, South Carolina, Shaler emphasized their obvious physical and reproductive inferiority. Although admittedly quick-witted, mulattoes were "generally more unfitted and indisposed to hard labor than the pure blacks," the result of the blending of two disparate bloods.[50] The idea that mulattoes were physically weak and short-lived was central to Shaler's opposition to amalgamation, but his position reflected the sort of impressionistic stance characteristic of the previous generation's beliefs about mulattoes. He cited, for instance, the experience of his father, a physician and "critical observer" who had spent more than fifty years in Cuba and the slaveholding South and who staunchly maintained that he "had never seen mulattos [sic] . . . who had attained the age of sixty years, and that they were often sterile."[51] Similarly, Shaler noted, "all the medical men I have questioned" were in agreement that mulattoes were "usually of much weaker body than the average people of pure blood of either race." Further, it was questionable whether mulattoes exhibited the moral character otherwise found in the original races, although it did appear that the mulatto was intellectually superior to the pure black.[52] The latter point was evidenced by the fact that "almost all the Negroes of this country who have shown marked capacity of any kind have had an evident admixture of white blood."[53]

Not only was miscegenation unwise because it produced a physically inferior being, it as also inadvisable since it resulted in a "third something" which led not to greater racial harmony and unification but to increased racial discord. The people of mixed blood tended to set themselves apart from the mass of blacks, Shaler noted, only further complicating the racial picture.[54] The mulatto was "peculiarly inflammable material," the victim of an incompatible heritage which left him out of joint with basic racial patterns. Shaler could sympathize with the mulatto's plight, citing the prejudices from which the mixed-blood suffered and the limitations upon his field of association,[55] yet the inevitable conclusion remained that racial mixing was a dire mistake, one for which both races, but particularly the whites, would eventually pay dearly. "It is not possible," he insisted, to unite their blood with that of our race. The results of centuries of experiment show beyond all question that this union cannot be effected without the loss of the qualities which give our Aryan race its singular value. The conditions demand that the blood of the races be kept entirely apart.[56]

Such a statement reveals a strain of thinking fundamental to most arguments during this period about racial differences and the detrimental effects of racial amalgamation, for Shaler here reflects the intersection of polygenist and Lamarckian ideas in explaining why miscegenation is bad. Because basic racial characteristics were carried in the blood, any mixing of the bloods of two races would jumble those characteristics. Since the traits of the Negro were so obviously inferior to those of the white man, the latter would surely suffer by any such mixture--his superior characteristics would be weakened or perhaps even overwhelmed by the savage traits which the Negro had developed during ages of African barbarism. It was this type of thinking which underlay much of the white opposition to amalgamation, both among academicians like Shaler and among the public at large. However, the fact that men like Shaler lent their support to such ideas only served to reinforce their hold on the public mind.

Shaler was not alone among late nineteenth-century scientists. Edward Drinker Cope (1840-1897) was a respected zoologist and paleontologist who for many years was professor of geology at the University of Pennsylvania. He was also editor of the *American Naturalist* and contributed considerable work to the United States Geological Survey. A leading figure in the school of thought contemporarily designated as "Neo-Lamarckianism," Cope evidenced a remarkably wide range of interests in social as well as scientific questions of the day. Perhaps because of their apparent relation to evolutionary processes, race and racial distinctions were subjects of particular concern to him.[57]

"We all admit," Cope wrote in 1870, "the existence of higher and lower races, the latter being those which we now find to present greater or less approximation to the apes." Citing the anthropometric studies of the U.S. Sanitary Commission, he held that there was conclusive evidence of the Negro's close structural approximation to the anthropoid in a variety of physical traits.[58] It was not until the 1890s, however, that he took a strong public stand against the Negro. In a series of articles in *Open Court*, a magazine devoted to the "religion of science," Cope summed up many of his earlier findings about racial characteristics and the relative positions of the black and white races on the evolutionary scale, ultimately advocating both disfranchisement and the forced migration of American blacks. The Negro, particularly due to his mental faculties, was simply unfit for American citizenship. He lacked sufficient rational and moral capacity, yet equally important, his development had seemingly reached its end so that he was no longer susceptible to the evolutionary influence of the environment.

Convinced as he was of the Negro's inherent inferiority, Cope saw no future for him in America. Moreover, the Negro's continued presence represented a menace to whites, given what Cope felt was the inevitability of race mixture. Cope was truly alarmed at the danger this entailed, especially since he was sure of the inferiority of the mulatto. "With few exceptions," he declared, "the hybrid is not as good a race as the white, and in some respects it often falls below the black especially in the sturdy qualities that accompany vigorous physique."[59] Whites could not afford to compromise the superior qualities which had taken their race thousands of years of toil and hardship to develop. Miscegenation, therefore, would be "a shameful sacrifice," "an unpardonable sale of a noble birthright for a mess of pottage."

> We cannot cloud or extinguish the fine nervous susceptibility, and the mental force, which cultivation develops in the constitution of the Indo-European, by the fleshly instincts, and the dark mind of the African. Not only is the mind stagnated, and the life of mere living introduced in its stead, but the possibility of resurrection is rendered doubtful or impossible. The greatest danger which flows from the presence of the negro in this country, is the certainty of the contamination of the race.[60]

So detrimental were the inferior characteristics carried in the blood of the black man, miscegenation represented "a crime of gigantic proportions," for it would necessarily destroy the superior qualities of the white man.[61] Yet since "hybridization is the rule and not the exception," Cope urged the drastic step of deporting the nation's black population, lest the white man fall to temptation and carelessly lose his hard-won heritage.

Similar fears about the detrimental effects of miscegenation were expressed by another leading geologist, Joseph LeConte (1823-1901). Reared on a large plantation in Liberty County, Georgia, LeConte held positions at several Southern universities prior to the Civil War. After the war, he accepted a position at the new University of California where he remained for three decades, nationally acclaimed for his scientific contributions and philosophical speculations on the principles of evolution. LeConte was somewhat more optimistic about the future of the Negro, seeing him as "plastic, docile, impressionable, sympathetic, imitative, and therefore in a high degree improvable by contact with a superior race and under suitable conditions."[62] Yet like Nathaniel Shaler, LeConte held to a basically polygenist definition of race and generally spoke of the primary races in specific terms. While favorable results might be produced by the mixing of two relatively close varieties, the crossing of the primary races themselves caused bad effects. The product of such a crossing was a hybrid, by nature weaker than either of the two parent races. LeConte did contend that mulattoes were intellectually superior to pure blacks, but citing the work of Josiah C. Nott and Sanford B. Hunt, he maintained that the mulatto was physically weaker than either of the original races and was therefore destined to die out in a laissez-faire environment characterized by race struggle.[63] The obvious mental and physiological differences separating the white man and the Negro were barriers which made primary crossing a mistake.[64]

Numerous other late nineteenth- and early twentieth-century scientists, some well known, some not, offered like arguments as to the inferiority of the mulatto and the dangers involved in miscegenation. In 1893, W. A. Dixon, a physician in Ripley, Ohio (a town on the Ohio River), wrote of the prosperity, refinement, and physical vigor which had characterized the mulatto population of his town during the ante-bellum period. Three or four generations later, however, these families had virtually disappeared, victims of declining fertility and a proclivity for a variety of debilitating diseases. Despite favorable conditions, these mulattoes proved unable to preserve their type. Questioning other physicians in the area, Dixon was confirmed in his belief that mulattoes were particularly prone to tuberculosis, and they were "inferior in vitality, intelligence, and consequently morality," with increasing tendencies towards complete sterility.[65] Dixon's findings merely reaffirmed the earlier contentions of Baxter, Gould, and others who insisted on the mulatto's inferiority.

In the next decade, Robert Bennett Bean, an anatomist then at the John Hopkins Hospital in Baltimore, published a widely cited study of "the Negro Brain" which painted another negative picture of the mulatto. "The Caucasian and the negro are fundamentally opposite extremes of evolution," Bean declared, differing in brain structure, mental functioning, and basic emotional activity and inclinations.[66] When the two types are crossed, improvement in the size and capabilities of the Negro brain did result, but other effects were less desirable. Three classes of mulattoes resulted from interracial mixing. One was physically powerful and Negroid in all characteristics save color, while a second was physically and mentally weak and of mottled color. These two types represented the gravest menaces to society, for they inherited, as tradition had it, "all the bad of both black and white."

> They have all the sensuality of the aboriginal African, and all the savage nature of the primitives from the wilds of Europe, without the self-control of the Caucasian or the amiability of the negro.[67]

The third class closely resembled the Caucasian, both in physical features and in basic mental abilities, but was a type to be pitied.

> They have the inclinations and often the abilities of more favored individuals in the white race, yet an inexorable law has decreed that they shall marry in their own race or die out. They are almost invariably of a delicate mold, and die young.[68]

While there was little hope for the Negro in competition with the white man, given the great differences in mental development of the two races, it was clear to Bean that the solution did not lie in amalgamation, for its beneficial results did not outweigh its overall negative effects.

The baneful consequences of race mixing were of particular concern to Eugene S. Talbot, author of a respected study of degeneracy and physical deformities. Given the "decided differences in the state of evolution of the two races," amalgamation tended to weaken the qualities of the superior white race, rendering it "more liable to the action of the factors producing degeneracy."[69] The problem lay in the different manner in which members of each race developed. As whites matured, the greatest developmental energy went toward the growth of the brain, while in blacks the reproductive organs took precedence. The mulatto, unfortunately, followed the latter course, for his energies were channeled into sexual rather than cerebral development. The fact, Talbot wrote,

> that the conflict for existence between brain growth and reproductive organ growth at puberty, results, in the mulatto, as in the negro and anthropoids, in the triumph of the reproductive, indicates that the mulatto has factors of degeneracy which would be fatal to the establishment of an intermediate type on the environment of the white.[70]

Talbot was willing to admit that in some instances the mulatto was "better adapted to the white environment than the pure black," but overall, the degenerative effect of amalgamation was too great to ignore. Not only was mental development stultified, but other Negro traits, always present in the blood of the mulatto, were liable to reassert themselves. Witness, for instance, "the relapse into voodooism and cannibalism of the Hayti and Louisiana French hybrids and the Anglo-Saxon hybrids of Liberia."[71]

In Talbot's argument against racial mixing there was an overt statement of the sort of thinking which ultimately underlay all white objectives to amalgamation and which explained the nature of white perceptions of the mulatto. Given the belief in the existence of fundamental racial traits which were carried in the blood and transmitted from one geneation to the next, miscegenation necessarily became an evil. It mixed these racial traits and led to the weakening or destruction of the superior qualities of the white man by the savage traits the Negro had developed through centuries of sensual, barbaric life in Africa. Images of Africa (and to a lesser extent of Haiti) as a land of wild, sexual excesses, superstitious religious practices, and widespread cannibalism greatly influenced how white Americans saw and understood the black people around them.[72] Not only physical but cultural differences as well were explained in terms of this African heritage and seen as basic racial characteristics being transmitted in a hereditary fashion. Such traits posed a grave threat to the civilized characteristics in the blood of the Caucasian, and therefore could not justifiably be intermixed with those superior white qualities.

These notions also explain at least one reason for white perceptions of mulattoes as Negroes. Even those mixed-bloods who were ostensibly white in appearance still carried in their blood the savage traits of their African ancestors. Those ancestors might be many generations removed, but the basic characteristics remained, lurking beneath the surface of white skin and straight hair and ultimately guiding many of the actions, attitudes, and sensibilities of the mulatto. Furthermore, these black traits might one day reappear unexpectedly in an atavistic child, one whose parents were white but who itself evidenced strong Negro characteristics. It was this sort of thinking, based upon notions of racial essences and the interworkings of socio-cultural and biological processes, which was at the heart of the "one drop rule." One drop of black blood, carrying as it did these myriad undesirable characteristics, was enough to brand its possessor as a child of Africa, with all of the connotations of savagery and sensuality which such a designation inherently involved in the white mind. There seemed little inclination to question the power of these African traits to overwhelm the civilized white traits which flowed in the blood of the lightest mulatto. The ideas fit together in a powerful argument against racial amalgamation as well as any political policy which smacked of the "social equality" which necessarily implied intermarriage in the minds of whites.[73]

Perhaps because of the nature of their own disciplines, the scientists whose attitudes were discussed above were particularly concerned with the physical manifestations of racial differences. Ideas about inferior brain sizes, the physical weakness and reproductive deficiencies of mulattoes, the degenerative results of racial mixing, etc., appealed to men whose studies involved physical evidence of evolutionary development and race traits.[74] Yet race was viewed at this time as as much a cultural as a physical phenomenon. Overall, considerably more attention was given to race by social scientists than by those working in biology, geology, and allied natural science disciplines. Ideas from the latter realm did overlap with the theories of social scientists, however, so that often the two groups were not really too distinct.   Nevertheless, social scientists were most conscious of social manifestations of racial differences, although they did tend to explain the transmission of social characteristics in essentially biological terms.   This reflects once again the strength and pervasiveness of Lamarckian ideas about heredity and evolution.   Popular writers on racial matters in turn derived their ideas from both groups, generally selecting those theories which suited their own personal outlooks about race and racial differences.   Many social scientists and popular writers also tended to hang on to these older notions of the biological transmission of cultural characteristics and the Lamarckian outlook of which they were a part after biologists and related scientists had discarded such beliefs around the turn of the century.   Certainly part of the explanation for this fact must lie in the ease with which these out-dated ideas served to, explain racial differences in which white Americans *wanted* to believe.

6

The generation between 1890 and 1915 was probably the most important period in the development and institutionalization of patterns of race relations between Reconstruction and the civil rights movement of the 1960s. This was also the period during which the social sciences became established as distinct academic disciplines and the major professional journals and organizations were founded. As a part of this development, the era witnessed the beginnings of what would become a widespread reaction to certain aspects of evolutionary thought, especially the "organic analogy" of Herbert Spencer's sociology.   Some anthropologists, most notably Franz Boas, even began to challenge the theory of social evolution itself. But aside from this small group of anthropologists who were to fashion the modern position on race and culture and the distinctions between them, the great majority of social scientists continued to think in evolutionary terms which clearly followed the Spencerian tradition, with all of the Lamarckian mechanisms which that often entailed. Darwinian evolution, Lamarckian evolutionary ethnology, and polygenism continued to interact in the minds of most social scientists to support the idea of a racio-cultural hierarchy which placed the civilized white man at the top and the dark-skinned savage at the bottom.[75]

The work of Herbert Spencer and his American disciple, John Fiske, served as the most important bridge between biology and the social sciences. In this regard, of course, it really only reinforced older notions which saw race as both a cultural and biological phenomenon. By drawing strong parallels between social and physiological evolution, Spencer also reaffirmed hierarchical perceptions of racial development.

Like so many other racial theories of the day, Spencer's sociology was built upon a foundation of travelers' accounts, impressionistic evidence, and speculative assumptions, but the result was a sweeping portrait of race character which greatly influenced the thinking of most other social scientists of the period. The overriding conclusion generally drawn from Spencer's works was the superiority of the white man and the inferiority of other races.[76]

The solution to racial inferiority, Spencer insisted, did not lie in mixing the diverse races. Although the mixture of slightly divergent varieties of the same stock might prove beneficial, union of widely divergent varieties was "physically injurious" to the offspring. It produced a "worthless type of mind--a mind fitted neither for the kind of life led by the higher of the two races, nor for that led by the lower--a mind out of adjustment to all conditions of life."[77] Spencer expanded on this point in his *Principles of Sociology*, once again denouncing the mixture of races who were "widely unlike":

> The conflicting tendencies towards different social types, instead of existing in separate individuals, now [after interracial mixing] exist in the same individual. The half-caste, inheriting from one line of ancestry proclivities adapted to one set of institutions, and from the other line of ancestry proclivities adapted to another set of institutions, is not fitted for either. He is a unit whose nature has not been moulded by any social type, and therefore cannot, with others like himself, evolve any social type. Modern Mexico and the South American Republics, with their perpetual revolutions, show us the result.[78]

From Spencer's point of view, since cultural characteristics were as much a part of the inheritance of an individual (or a race) as were physical traits, amalgamation was unwise since it mixed those characteristics into an incompatible combination unsuited to life with either parent's social order.

Similar thinking underlay the racial speculations of numerous other social scientists of the period. Among anthropologists, Daniel Garrison Brinton (1837-1899) typified this view. A specialist in the study of American Indians, Brinton was professor of American linguistics and archeology at the University of Pennsylvania and a leading figure in the early years of academic anthropology.[79] Like most of his fellow white Americans, Brinton was convinced of the basic inequality of the races of mankind, with "the European or white race standing at the head of the list, the African or negro at its foot."[80] Given this basic pattern of racial superiority and inferiority, Brinton was convinced that miscegenation was unwise, for it brought an "indelible degradation" on the descendants of the white partner in a mixed union.[81] It was the white man's blood which suffered through an intermixture with that of the Negro. "It is essential to remember," Brinton explained,

> that it is the inferior race only which reaps the psychical advantage [from amalgamation]. Compared to the parent of the higher race, the children are a deteriorated product. Only when contrasted with the average of the lower race can they be expected to take some precedence. The mixture, if general and continued through generations, will infallibly entail a lower grade of power in the descendent. The net balance of the two accounts will show a loss when compared with the result of unions among the higher race alone.[82]

Brinton was not concerned simply with physical deterioration through race mixing, although he was "tolerably certain" of the physical weakness of the mulatto.[83] His Lamarckian perspective, like Spencer's, led him to fear dangers of mixing cultural traits through amalgamation. As with the individual, Brinton wrote, "the future of a people is already written in its past history." Because "psychical traits" were passed on from generation to generation in the same manner as physical characteristics, there was the peril that the superior qualities of the white man would be polluted by the inferior traits of the Negro.[84] The key to the preservation of white racial purity, he was convinced, lay in the moral sense of the white American woman. Her proper Victorian sensibilities placed her above the sexual temptations which might lead to interracial mixing. As he explained in 1890,

> It is to the women alone of the highest race that we must look to preserve the purity of the type, and with it the claims of the race to be the highest. They have no holier duty, no more sacred mission, than that of transmitting in its integrity the heritage of ethnic endowment gained by the race through thousands of generations of struggle. That philanthropy is false, that religion is rotten, which would sanction a white woman enduring the embrace of a colored man.[85]

Anthropologist W J McGee (1853-1912), head of the Bureau of American Ethnology, evidenced a similar Lamarckian outlook about race traits and the negataive consequences of amalgamation in addition to a polygenist belief in multiple origins and differential rates of racial evolution. McGee (who insisted on being known by his two unpunctuated initials) was convinced that intertribal and international blending would one day produce a superior human type. Yet he drew back at the thought of interracial mixing, arguing that it was "often apparently injurious, generally of doubtful effect, and only rarely of unquestionable benefit." While admitting that the outstanding figures of the Negro race were in fact mulattoes, he was inclined to see them as atypical. For the most part, mulattoes resulted from illicit matings "between the lower specimens of one or both lines of blood, so that the evil of miscegenation may well have been intensified." The general tendency, then, was to produce clearly inferior types, especially since they were burdened by the negative physical and cultural traits of the black man.[86]

Like the statistical compendium of Frederick L. Hoffman, Joseph Alexander Tillinghast's study of *The Negro in Africa and Ameria* (1902) stands as a summation of the nineteenth century's ethnological findings about the American Negro's African heritage. Drawing on a variety of impressive sources, Tillinghast painted a picture which confirmed popular notions about life in sub-Saharan Africa.[87] Africans lived a primitive, savage life shaped by religious fetishism, social and political disorganization, and unbridled licentiousness. Slavery, polygamy, and cannibalism were widespread, while the intense heat and humidity and the abundance of nature stifled industriousness and initiative. "From time immemorial," concluded Tillinghast, the people of Africa "have been weak in self-command, they have been dominated by impulse, and inclined to an indolent semi-nomadic existence, and they have possessed an extremely primitive code of morality."[88] These were the characteristics which blacks brought with them as slaves to America, and although mitigated somewhat by contact with the white man during the ante-bellum years, they remained the "hereditary instincts" which left the Negro so much at odds with the basic patterns of American social organization.

The fact that the Negro possessed such obviously inferior physical, mental and moral traits convinced Tillinghast that amalgamation between the white man and the Negro was a mistake. In discussing the mulatto and the question of racial mixture, Tillinghast relied heavily on the findings of Frederick L. Hoffman and Paul Broca (1824-1880), a renowned French anthropologist whose essay on "The Phenomenon of Hybridity in the Genus Homo" (1864) summarized the polygenist position on racial mixing and was itself largely drawn from the work of Josiah C. Nott. Tillinghast repeated the common assumption that mulattoes were "more or less degenerate in physical vigor and fertility," while insisting that immorality prevailed even more along mixed-bloods than among pure blacks. Similarly, he reiterated the theory that "the mulatto tends to approximate the Caucasian in cerebral structure," in that the mixed-blood exhibited "more intellectual capacity and nervious energy" than the pure Negro, and was "more alert and deft in movement." The result was that the mulatto exhibited "more of the Caucasian temperament," which led Tillinghast to speculate that among the more prominent and successful American Negroes of that time, "mulattoes constitute a much larger proportion than they bear to the colored population as a whole." Yet it was the "Caucasian heredity" in the blood of the mulatto which explained his relative capacity for acquiring civilization. He remained held back by the hereditary traits of his black African ancestors, so that the obvious conclusion for Tillinghast was that, overall, miscegenation led to a degeneration of white blood and therefore represented a serious social error.[89]

Such was the general pattern of anthropological thought on race and the consequences of racial amalgamation through the early years of the twentieth century. However, by this time there were stirrings of new lines of thought and investigation among anthropologists, especially in the research and writing of Franz Boas (1858-1942). Boas' work between 1890 and 1910 clearly reveals the conflicting trends of thought which were revolving around the concepts of race, heredity, and environment, and his own mind seems to have struggled through different empirical and theoretical positions as he gradually evolved the concept of culture as distinct from race. This was the necessary first step in the development of the modern outlook with regard to race, race formation, and racial differences.

Boas most visibly began moving in this direction in an 1894 essay entitled "Human Faculty as Determined by Race," with the process essentially being capped with the 1911 publication *The Mind of Primitive Man*.[90] By emphasizing that culture was a phenomenon which was not a direct function of race as a biological entity, Boas succeeded in breaking the conceptual bonds of nineteenth-century anthropology and turning that discipline in a significantly new direction. In terms of racial theory, this meant new ideas about the basic equality of all men and all races, especially in terms of mental ability. Cultural achievement, Boas explained, did not specifically reflect mental ability, but rather was the product of the general course of history experienced by different racial groups. Accident and environment played as important roles in shaping the development of culture as did the inner resources of the racial group itself, if not more so. The only point of certainty, he insisted, was that the "differences between the average types of the white and the Negro, that have a bearing upon vitality and mental ability, are much less than the individual variations in each race."[91] In this sense, men were more alike than different, and all were essentially plastic and adaptable to a variety of social and cultural situations.

If this was the direction that anthropological thought was moving by the turn of the century, other social scientific disciplines were noticeably slower in adopting such a shift in orientation. This is not to say, however, that changes were not occuring among sociologists, psychologists, and other social scientists with regard to attitudes about race and racial differences. Indeed, in *The Mind of Primitive Man*, Boas himself made note of the contributions of a number of psychologists and sociologists, as well as several physicians, who offered critiques of older physical anthropological ideas.[92]   Nevertheless, many social scientists continued to hold to older notions which served to buttress essentially racist arguments among those who were less objective in their racial outlooks.

Many sociologists, for instance, continued to think in terms of distinct racial differences and characteristics through the second decade of the century, and such a perspective was reflected in their notions about mulattoes and race mixing. As might be anticipated, their concern over the issue of miscegenation was especially intense with regard to the social effects of mixing. Edward A. Ross, for example, was a leading liberal Progressive of the age and not particularly interested in "the Negro question," as it was then phrased. Yet speaking before the American Academy of Political and Social Science in 1901, Ross demonstrated the type of thinking common to many of his fellow sociologists. Although warning against too dogmatic an insistence on "the race factor" and the hereditary and fixed differences between peoples, Ross nevertheless provided an extensive list of characteristics by which races differed. His inevitable conclusion was that the American white man was clearly superior to all other peoples, "in capacity and efficiency" and only now reaching his prime. The Negro, on the other hand, was "an inferior race." Considering these basic racial differences, it was absolutely essential that racial purity be maintained at all costs. "The superiority of a race cannot be preserved," Ross adamantly declared, "without *pride of blood* and an uncompromising attitude toward the lower races." Only with a "strong sense of its superiority" could the "higher culture" of white America survive, for pollution of the blood through race crossing meant cultural degradation. One had only to look at the superiority of British America, where racial purity was emphasized, in comparison with the rest of the hemisphere, which for centuries more would continue to "drag the ball and chain of hybridism" and remain subordinate.[93]

Ross' position typified the thinking of many sociologists at the turn of the century, especially in the belief that races differed in their degree of cultural evolution, with the Negro's cultural level being at the bottom of the scale. The capacity for cultural achievement, of course, was an hereditary trait carried "in the blood." Sociologists and psychologists tended to speak of such traits as racial "instincts," and their understanding of the operation of these instincts (generally in a Lamarckian sense) was central to their feelings about race mixture.

Charles A. Ellwood, a sociologist at the University of Missouri who was later to become president of the American Sociological Society, reflected this sort of attitude about racial differences in an article published in 1901. Instincts, he insisted, were dominant factors in shaping the development of races and individuals. "The important thing to recognize," explained Ellwood,

> is that race heredity has fixed in us . . . through a process of evolution by natural selection, certain coordinations of nerve cells and muscle fibers which tend to discharge in one way rather than another, and which make personal and social development tend to take one direction rather than another.

Although he spoke of the forces of natural selection, Ellwood still conceived of "race instincts" or "race habits" as basically Lamarckian "innate tendencies." This explained why children developed the general "mental and moral characteristics" of their particular race regardless of the cultural environment in which they were raised. As Ellwood described the process:

> The negro child, even when reared in a white family under the most favorable conditions, fails to take on the mental and moral characteristics of the Caucasian race. His mental attitudes toward persons and things, toward organized society, toward life, and toward religion never become quite the same as those of the white. His natural instincts, it is true, may be modified by training, and perhaps indefinitely in the course of generations; but the race habit of a thousand generations or more is not lightly set aside by the voluntary or enforced imitation of visible models, and there is always a strong tendency to reversion. The reappearance of voodooism and fetishism among the negroes of the South, though surrounded by Christian influences, is indeed to be regarded as due not so much to the preservation of some primitive copy of such religious practices brought over from Africa as to the innate tendency of the Negro mind to take such attitudes toward nature and the universe as tend to develop such religions.[94]

From a sociological perspective, the racial traits of the Negro were an obvious explanation of his inferior status in America. Surveying "The Evolution of Negro Labor" in 1903, Carl Kelsey, a sociologist at the University of Pennsylvania, denied the common Northern belief that it was the Southern white man who held the black man back. Rather, Kelsey explained, it was the Negro's "inheritance from thousands of years in Africa." The Negro's racial heritage was inimical to his economic progress.[95] Howard Odum made the point even more explicitly in 1910. His *Social and Mental Traits of the Negro*, while supposedly an objective cataloging of black racial traits and characteristics, in fact repeated the myriad stereotyped impressions whites had long held of blacks and their way of life, a way of life which was believed to reflect inherent racial characteristics.[96] All of these qualities were traceable to the life of indolence, licentiousness, and savagery which was the American Negro's African heritage. "The tendencies of the present-day Negro," wrote Odum,

> his restlessness, his vagrancy and loafing, his love of excitement and sensuality, his bumptiousness, the child and savage elements in his nature, still reflect forcibly the prevalent traits of the Negro in Africa. It is thus expedient to take into consideration the fact that the Negro inherits these chief traits and inherent tendencies through many generations.[97]

Other social scientists were equally convinced of the existence and importance of these biocultural racial instincts. The psychologist G. Stanley Hall, president of Clark University, was much impressed with the persistence of African traits among American blacks, traits which served to separate the black man from the white in decisive ways. "No two races in history, taken as a whole," Hall argued in 1905,

> differ so much in their traits, both physical and psychical, as the Caucasian and the African. The color of the skin and the crookedness of the hair are only the outward signs of many far deeper differences, including cranial and thoracic capacity, proportions of body, nervous system, disposition, character, longevity, instincts, customs, emotional traits, and diseases. All these differences, as they are coming to be better understood, are seen to be so great as to qualify if not imperil every inference from one race to another, whether theoretical or practical, so that what is true and good for one is often false and bad for the other.[98]

In essence, Hall was saying, it was what was inside that counted-- biologically and culturally. Racial traits in the blood determined the entire pattern of an individual's life.

This sharp sense of racial differences based upon essential racial traits was also emphasized by James Bardin, a psychologist at the University of Virginia, and by John R. Commons, the widely renowned liberal economist. In discussing racial characteristics and differences, Commons reflected the impact upon anthropological theories of Franz Boas. He believed it necessary to distinguish between the basic capacities of racial groups and the level of culture or civilization which a particular group might have developed. There was not always a direct correlation between the two, Commons maintained, since a superior race might be only in the process of evolving a superior culture, while at present appearing backward in the eyes of more advanced peoples. This argument did not extend as far as the black man, however. The division between inherently superior and inferior races mirrored the division between the temperate and tropic zones of the earth. Races evolving in the latter region, because of the geo-climatic factors involved, developed traits involving "ignorance, superstition, physical prowess, and sexual passion" which made them basically unassimilable into the superior races who were characterized by "intelligence, foresight, thrift, and self-control."[99]

Bardin likewise stressed the unassimilable nature of the black man. Negroes had, according to Bardin,

> physically and mentally, definite and easily recognized characteristics, indicative of a common origin different from our own, and expressed in a similarity of Negro cultures throughout the world.[100]

Blacks possessed a distinctive racial "mind-set" which reflected the course of their evolutionary development in both a physical and mental context. This racial mentality meant that the Negro retained a peculiar black outlook and understanding of the world around him, regardless of how much the white man might try to educate him in the ways of Caucasian civilization.[101]

Such an understanding of the role of racial instincts militated against the idea of racial mixing in the minds of most social scientists. Because the Negro was not a white man with black skin but an inherently different being driven by a distinct set of instincts and traits, a union of black and white would produce a discordant individual, an impossible individual, at war within himself and ultimately self-destructive. Many social scientists believed that these instincts also involved, fortunately, a sense of aversion to unlike peoples and therefore made the chances of extensive racial amalgamation unlikely. In essence, this meant that race prejudice was an instinctive psychological reaction, ultimately for self-preservation. William I. Thomas, a sociologist at the University of Chicago, exemplified this view when he spoke of conditions "in the course of the biological development of a species which . . . lead to a predilection for those of one's own kind and a prejudice against organically different groups." Such a response was universal throughout the animal world, beginning perhaps as a subconscious reaction to physical features which differentiated racial groups and developing into a conscious dislike for those features. Race prejudice, Thomas concluded,

> is an instinct originating in the tribal stage of society, when solidarity in feeling and action were essential to the preservation of the group. It, or some analogue of it, will probably never disappear completely.[102]

Thomas was clearly operating here from a basically Lamarckian perspective. Race prejudice, like all racial instincts, developed in response to felt needs and was then transmitted in a biosocial manner. Of course, this was the ultimate explanation for the operation and continuation of any racial instinct or trait. Racial instincts and characteristics represented the heritage of the race, and in the case of the white man, at least, that heritage had to be staunchly guarded against the encroachment of unacceptable racial types, most specifically through amalgamation. Racial prejudice thus was an essential factor in preserving white civilization. "Behind physical aversion to alien types," declared Ulysses G. Weatherly, a University of Indiana sociologist who later became president of the American Sociological Society, "there lurks an instinctive recognition of racial standards as a social capital that must not be dissipated by surrendering race purity."[103] Weatherly was willing to admit that at times a race might face "the danger of physical exhaustion through overdevelopment of the intellect" and therefore require the infusion of blood from "more sturdy stocks." However, he warned, "if physical amelioration be purchased at the expense of any fundamental elements of civilization the balance of the advantage will be destroyed."[104] Mixing could not be allowed with clearly inferior races, for it would jeopardize the white man's fundamental superiority.[105]

7

Despite this general opposition to race mixing, by the end of the first decade of the twentieth century social scientists began taking a new, less prejudiced look at the mulatto and his status with regard to the two races. Some did reiterate older notions about the mulatto's physical and possible moral weaknesses, but many proved more objective in their assessments of the mixed-blood's position.

It was as though the traditional pattern of ideas was beginning to decay and to fertilize new conceptions even as it was just reaching maturity. Social scientific thought, prodded by the theorizings of Franz Boas, was moving into a more egalitarian stance. As the modern outlook toward culture and race evolved among anthropologists, its effects gradually began to be felt among a variety of other academic disciplines. Yet older notions gave way only with great reluctance, or quite often were subsumed into newer theoretical orientations. In sum, while many social scientists were gradually breaking with traditional ideas and perceptions about race, at the same time they were often merely rephrasing or recasting them in new, more sophisticated forms.

One question of particular concern to many social scientists was why mulattoes seemed to dominate the most influential and prestigious positions in the Negro race, both at the local and national levels. A number was quick to suggest the intellectual superiority of the mulatto in comparison with pure blacks as the most likely explanation. John R. Commons remarked that mixed-bloods "on the average differ but little if at all from those of the white race in their capacity for advancement."[106] Sociologist Charles A. Ellwood, noting that recent findings dismissed the idea of amalgamation having detrimental physiological effects, also emphasized the intellectual superiority of mulattoes to pure blacks. He accounted for this fact, however, in terms of the superior contribution made by the mulattoes' white ancestors.[107]   Likewise, G. Stanley Hall stressed the mulatto's inheritance "more or less of the best Anglo-Saxon cavalier blood, brain, and temper."[108]

Hall was writing in 1905, Ellwood a year later. By the next decade, the impact of Boas and other more egalitarian thinkers was beginning to be felt throughout the social sciences. In 1910, even before the publication of Boas' *The Mind of Primitive Man*, Robert S. Woodworth, a psychologist at Columbia University, was backing off from his own earlier beliefs in differences in mental capacities among races. In an important article which set the tone for much revisionist work in the forthcoming decade, Woodworth declared that "sensory and motor processes, and the elementary brain activities, though differing in degree from one individual to another, are about the same from one race to another."   In addition, Woodworth was challenging the traditional techniques for measuring such differences, for his own earlier studies had emphasized cranial measurements and brain weights. In their place, he offered cultural explanations for what appeared to be major racial differences.[109]

Other social scientists soon picked up on this more egalitarian train of thought. In 1912, for example, William I. Thomas, who in 1904 had spoken of the inexorability of race prejudice against different, inferior groups, was noting that "individual variation is of more importance than racial difference." Racial differences were no longer so much biological as social in origin, so that there did not exist a truly racial quality of mind.[110] George W. Ellis likewise stressed the impact of new ethnological perspectives on sociological and psychological investigations of race, while Wilson D. Wallis of the University of Pennsylvania reflected the Boasian notion of cultural relativism in discussing what sociologists were increasingly recognizing as culturally imposed racial prejudice.[111]

One hallmark of this new attitude and outlook among social scientists after about 1910 was the rapid demise of the adherence to Lamarckianism. The shift had been underway for a decade or more, but it was a difficult struggle. In 1907, however, William I. Thomas argued that "the characters of body and mind acquired by the parent after birth are probably not inherited by the child."[112] A year later, Charles A. Ellwood criticized sociologist Jerome P. Dowd's book on *The Negro Races* for coming "dangerously close to indorsing the exploded use-theory of racial development,"[113] while Carl Kelsey, who in 1903 had spoken of the Negro's "inheritance from thousands of years in Africa, commented, "We know pretty definitely today that acquired characteristics are not passed on from generation to generation."[114]

Social scientists' gradual abandonment of Lamarckianism, spurred by the theory's earlier rejection by biologists in favor of new genetic viewpoints, redounded upon polygenist notions of racial traits and temperaments. The evolution of a concept of culture meant that the biological phenomenon of race could be, and gradually was, divorced from the idea of race as a socio-cultural phenomenon. The process by which such thinking changed was gradual, although following a rather logical course. As George Stocking has commented, in many cases it essentially involved merely the substitution of one word or another:

> For "race" read "culture" or "civilization," for "racial heredity" read "cultural heritage," and the change had taken place. From explicitly Lamarckian "racial instincts" to an ambiguous "centuries of racial experience" to a purely cultural "centuries of tradition" was a fairly easy transition--especially when the notion of "racial instincts" had in fact been largely based on centuries of experience and tradition.[115]

The decline of these older modes of thought, however, did not necessarily mean that social scientists abandoned their basic notions about racial hierarchies, with their implications of white superiority and Negro inferiority. Indeed, after 1910 the advent of various psychological tests for measuring intelligence often served to strengthen earlier prejudicial attitudes. The work of George Oscar Ferguson, a reputable psychologist at the University of Virginia, was especially important in setting the tone of this scientific racism by using intelligence tests to demonstrate the inequality of races. In his most important volume, *The Psychology of the Negro*, Ferguson announced that the average IQ of whites was one hundred, while the average IQ among blacks was only seventy-five. He did admit that there was considerable overlapping, however, since many Negroes scored above the white average. Ferguson's explanation of this fact involved chance and/or the admixture of white blood. Indeed, he was so struck by the significance of the latter factor that he sought to determine scientifically the effect of race mixture on intelligence. He consequently divided his subjects according to the amount of racial intermixture, judging this fact by the color of their skin. The results confirmed his expectations: "The percentage of success for Negroes compared to whites on the test were 69.27% for pure Negroes; 73.2% for 3/4 Negroes; 81.2% for mulattoes (half whites); 98.7% for quadroons."[116] Perhaps not surprisingly, Ferguson's findings mirrored the conclusions of nineteenth-century studies which measured cranial capacity and equated intelligence with brain weight. Nevertheless, they provided something of an explanation of why color stratification reflected other patterns of social stratification within the Negro community.

The fact that mulattoes composed a disproportionately large segment of the Negro middle and upper classes had long been recognized by whites. Nathaniel Southgate Shaler had mentioned this fact when writing about his observations in Charleston, South Carolina in 1870.[117] By the turn of the century, though, it was a point of considerable comment and speculation among social scientists. In a sense, such notions were but a newer statement of older ideas about the inherent superiority of the mulatto over the pure black, but explanations now reflected more sophisticated lines of social scientific thought. Carl Kelsey, for instance, observed in 1903 that a traveler in the South could not miss the fact that "the leaders in industry and education are not pure negroes," and insisted that it was unwise to measure the achievements and potential of the race by the accomplishments of mixed-bloods.[118] The psychologist G. Stanley Hall similarly remarked that, "while there are some pure Africans born with gifts far above the average of their race, most of its leaders are those to have by heredity, association, or both, derived most from the whites."[119] H. S. Dickerson likewise wrote,

> There are full-blooded negroes of ability, but a very large proportion of those one sees in places of responsibility and honor among negroes are of mixed race. It is so with teachers, ministers, and physicians. In many of the most celebrated schools a large part of the pupils are very light, and in the cities one finds congregations in some of the more aristocratic churches in which nearly all are mulattoes.[120]

Charles A. Ellwood also noted that "the leaders of the negro race, its van and its hope today, are almost without exception of mixed blood."[121]

Beyond the mere observation of the mulatto's elevated status in the Afro-American community, there are some division of thought as to both the cause and the desirability of this fact. As noted above, most social scientists, particularly before about 1910, would have agreed with Ellwood in explaining the mulatto's superiority in terms of the beneficial hereditary contribution of his white ancestors. Indeed, Ellwood himself was optimistic that the gradual diffusion of white blood throughout the Negro race would lead to a general improvement of the race as a whole.[122] The political scientist Paul S. Reinsch was also impressed by the results of amalgamation, commenting that mulatto women in particular developed "gentle and attractive qualities."[123] He noted the role of the mulatto in pacifying black/white relations in the Caribbean region, a point reiterated by H. E. Jordan of the University of Virginia. Citing Sir Sidney Olivier's favorable assessment of the mixed-blood's position in Jamaica, Jordan asserted that the mulatto "forms the most intelligent and potentially useful element of our colored population."[124] Jordan flatly rejected traditional notions that race mixing necessarily resulted from degeneracy.   Arguing instead from a Mendelian perspective, he contended that the product of any union was only as good as its parents, so that the mixing of favorably endowed whites and blacks could produce desirable combinations.   Jordan, it seems, would have hybridized the entire Negro race in hopes that this would elevate it to a higher level.   In this process, the mulatto was the key, already being the intermediate between black and white.   Through him, white blood could eventually be spread through the whole race.

> The mulatto is the leaven with which to lift the negro race.   He serves as our best lever for negro elevation.   The mulatto does not feel the instinctual mental nausea to negro mating.   He might even be made to feel a sacred mission in this respect. The negro aspires to be mulatto, the mulatto to be white.   These aspirations are worthy, and should be encouraged.   Possibility of marriage with a mulatto would be a very real incentive to serious efforts for development on the part of the negro. The logical conclusion may follow in the course of the ages.   At any rate from present indications our hope lies in the mulatto.   A wise statesmanship and rational patriotism will make every effort to conserve him, and imbue him with his mission in the interests of the brotherhood of a better man.   The problem seems possible of solution only as the mulatto will undertake it, with the earnest help of the white.[125]

Jordan was writing from an essentially eugenist viewpoint, for he believed that through rational planning and careful selection in mating the human species could be improved (at least the Negro part of the species). Because he saw the mulatto as a distinct improvement over the pure black, he ultimately favored hybridizing the entire race.

Sociologist Frances Hoggan similarly noted the beneficial aspects of amalgamation, given favorable social conditions under which the mixing might take place.[126] John R. Commons also held that ultimately, amalgamation was the only true means for the Negro to be assimilated into American society, considering the basic temperamental and hereditary characteristics which separated him from the white man. Until such time as that might occur (and Commons was not overly optimistic in that regard), Commons felt that the mulatto had to fulfill an important role as "the natural leader, instructor, and spokesman of the black." "A new era for the blacks is beginning," he declared, "when the mulatto sees his future with theirs."[127] Personally, Commons was sympathetic to the plight of the mixed-blood, "in whose veins run the blood of white aristocracy." He believed that most mulattoes had roughly the same potentials and sensibilities as white men, so that it was "the tragedy of race antagonism that they with their longings should suffer the fate of the more contented and thoughtless blacks." "It is a curious psychology of the Anglo-Saxon," Commons wrote, "that assigns to the inferior race those equally entitled to a place among the superior."[128]

Other social scientists, regardless of their professional attitudes about the mulatto, also seemed to sense the injustice of banishing him to the Negro race. "The position of the half-caste," declared Ulysses G. Weatherly,

> is usually an unfortunate one. The consciousness of his superiority to the more primitive stock raises a barrier against sympathetic co-operation on that side, while on the side of the dominant race he finds an unwillingness to grant social equality.[129]

Some observers, however, were wary of the pressures and discontent which this rejection generated among mixed-bloods. Weatherly, for example, feared the mulatto as a disruptive force in black/white relations in America.[130] G. Stanley Hall also cited the discontent stirring within the mulatto as a result of his unusual racial position:

> It is their aspirations, discontent, struggles, ending often in discouragement, which makes them either sink to vice or grow revengeful and desperate, that constitute the pathos of the present condition, and make it hardest for the men to preserve their hope and just ambition, and for the women to keep their virtue in the presence of whites.[131]

Many of the lightest mulattoes, Frances Hoggan claimed, were passing over into the white race surreptitiously, unable to bear the burdens of life as a black person. Yet these were the cowards of the race, she maintained, "vulgar representatives of commercialism, self-interest, and duplicity," who deserted the race that needed their talents. For this element of the mulatto population Hoggan had no sympathy, although she understood their dilemma. She had only praise, however, for those who remained a part of the Negro race:

> A black skin is a very serious handicap in the United States, and those who, from race love and devotion, elect to remain with the dark race, though fair enough to escape into the white one, are cast in heroic mold, and deserve in fullest measure the admiration and respect of both races.[132]

Among social scientists, then, attitudes about the mulatto and racial mixture remained ambiguous and sometimes contradictory. At a time when various disciplines were refining their methods of research and analysis as well as their basic theoretical foundations, many social scientists continued to hold on to older, often impressionistic ideas about race. Most important of these was the fundamental belief in the inferiority of the Negro race. Neither the decline of Lamarckianism and polygenist ideas nor the development of the culture concept essentially affected basic, deeply ingrained ideas about race and the existence of a racial hierarchy. Although the feeling that socioeconomic factors might be at least partially responsible for shaping racial differences was spreading among social scientists,[133] it could not overcome fundamental attitudes about racial inequality between whites and blacks. The initiation of intelligence testing after 1910 only provided further evidence of black inferiority, now under the guise of new scientific "proof."[134]

Given the notion that blacks were inferior, white social scientists looked at the Negro community, saw that mulattoes stood out in middle- and upper-class positions, and then made the logical inference that the mulattoes' superior status resulted, at least in part, from their admixture of superior white qualities. Many made the "common observation," as Ulysses G. Weatherly put it, that Negroes in the United States placed a premium on light color as a factor in social prestige and as an element of attraction in marriage.[135] Surely this was proof that even Negroes recognized the superiority of the white race. Such perceptions and beliefs underlay much of the social scientific speculation about mulattoes and race mixture during the first decades of the twentieth century. Meanwhile, this train of thought continued to interact with other changing theoretical positions about the nature of man, race, and society during this same period.

8

By about 1910, most serious social scientists had discarded notions about physical degeneration resulting from race mixture.[136] Nevertheless, they continued to see the mulatto was something different-- clearly not a white man, but perhaps not wholly a black man either. Sometimes they sought to differentiate the mulatto from the mass of blacks, but in the end they had only the categories of black and white with which to work. Some writers might advocate a separate classification for mulattoes, as was generally the case in Latin America and the West Indies, but America's racial heritage left no room for such a third group.

Limited by the confines of America's biracial system, social scientists were forced to deal with the mulatto on those terms. Clearly he was not a white man, for he carried some degree of black blood in his veins. As long as race connoted differences, the possession of that black blood forever made the mulatto non-white. Further, since the racial traits of blacks were distinct from those of whites (whether those traits be polygenist racial instincts, Lamarckian biocultural factors, or simple genetic traits which shaped the Negro's physical appearance and mental capacities), there was no logical choice but to see the mulatto as black. The traits of the Negro were such powerful entities in the minds of whites, such distinctive characteristics, that their possession could undermine or override whatever white traits a mixed-blood might also possess.   Mulattoes might be different from blacks--in physical appearance, in mental capabilities, in aspirations and sensitivities--but those black traits were there somewhere--hidden, perhaps, but still potent. Ultimately, even in the minds of trained scientific thinkers, this necessarily meant that the mulatto was a Negro.

Edward Byron Reuter's study of *The Mulatto in the United States* (1918) was the capstone of pre-World War I efforts to understand the role of the mixed-blood in America and the true consequences of racial amalgamation. As such, it typified the manner in which traditional ideas about racial inferiority and racial differences molded otherwise essentially objective social science investigations of the subject. The book was the published version of Reuter's doctoral dissertation in sociology, completed at the University of Chicago. He received his degree itself in 1919. At that time, Chicago's Sociology Department was among the most prestigious and progressive in the country, and was on the brink of becoming the leading center for the sociological study of American race relations.   Indeed, when the full effect of Franz Boas' revolutionary impact on social science finally made itself felt at Chicago in the 1920s, the Department, especially through the work of Robert Ezra Park, became a major force in reshaping academic attitudes about the question of race.[137]   Reuter himself would make important contributions to the study of race and race relations in the coming decades (particularly involving the subject of race mixture), but in the mid-1910s his ideas and attitudes reflected the clash of earlier modes of thought with new social scientific perspectives.

Reuter's book was the first full-scale, academic treatment of the mulatto in America.   It involved a depth and sophistication of research and analysis not found in earlier studies of the subject.   Reuter used census materials to develop a picture of the growth of the mulatto population.   Drawing on a wide variety of historical studies of the colonial and ante-bellum South, he described the factors promoting miscegenation while attacking the notion that most mulattoes derived their white blood from aristocratic planters.   Instead, he emphasized mixing between lower-class whites (especially servants during the colonial period) and blacks and mulattoes.   Reuter felt that amalgamation had declined somewhat during the ante-bellum period because of the growing antipathy of poor whites for Negroes, but argued that in the post-bellum era it was proceeding at a much faster pace.   For the most part, this involved casual liaisons of white men and black or mulatto women, especially in urban areas.   In general, Reuter felt, intermixture had always gone on to the extent of the white man's wishes. The Negro woman partner, he contended,

> never has objected to, and has generally courted, the relationship. It was never at any time a matter of compulsion; on the contrary, it was a matter of being honored by a man of a superior race. Speaking generally, the amount of intermixture is limited only by the self-respect of the white man and the compelling strength of the community sentiment.[138]

These lines reveal something of the attitude Reuter seemed to have about Negroes. While only "vicious" or "dissolute" white men were the primary participants in interracial unions, Reuter implied that almost any Negro woman would gladly accept such a role. He seemed convinced of the greater sensuality and lower moral state of Negroes, and saw this as an obvious explanation of their eager participation in such mixing.[139]   Reuter seemed to be caught amid conflicting personal attitudes about Negroes, and the confusion affected his subsequent interpretation of the nature of the mulatto.   On the one hand, his training as a sociologist led him to discount most traditional theories about Negro inferiority. In "The Superiority of the Mulatto," an article published in 1917, Reuter reflected the Boasian outlook about differences in cultural levels among races. He noted that culture was a social product and not a biological fact, and that it was unwise to judge the potential of any racial group simply from its actual cultural attainments. Similarly, he challenged theories claiming great mental differences between whites and blacks, although admitting that early intelligence testing did indicate that Negro capacity in this realm might not be quite equal to that of whites. Yet on the other hand, Reuter was struck by the overwhelming evidence that mulattoes *were* somehow different and superior to pure blacks. As many white writers had noted, there were distinct parallels between color and class stratification within the Afro-American commuity, a fact which to Reuter emphasized the inherent superiority of the mixed-blood over pure blacks. As he explained in 1917,

> In all times in the history of the American Negro and in all fields of human effort in which the Negroes have entered, the successful individuals, with very few exceptions have been mulattoes.   The black Negroes, either past or present, who have made any marked degree of success are decidedly rare exceptions.[140]

To date, this notion had been largely built upon loose, impressionistic evidence.   Reuter set out to establish the truth in the matter. From a wide variety of sources--publications like *The Negro Year Book*, numerous histories of the Negro race and its accomplishments, and several compilations of essays by prominent men of the race, as well as an extensive network of correspondence with both whites and Negroes--Reuter composed a list of 4,267 Negroes which included "every member of the race who has made any marked success in life." By various means he attempted to determine the racial background of each individual, eventually coming to the conclusion that 3,820, or nearly 90 percent, were of mixed blood. Since the ratio of pure blacks to mulattoes in the Negro population as a whole was approximately four to one, mulattoes held a highly disproportionate share of the race's prestigious positions. Further, when Reuter raised the standards of achievement, the proportion of mulattoes grew considerably higher. To Reuter, this was convincing argument for the superiority of the mulatto.[141]

In explaining this phenomenon, Reuter rejected the simple assumption that mulattoes benefited from a superior heritage because of their white ancestry. His reading of Boas, as well as the influence upon him of Robert E. Park and William I. Thomas at Chicago, led him to doubt both inherent mental differences between blacks and whites and the importance of cultural differences in determining the ability of mulattoes. Nor was the assumption of superior cultural advantages for mixed-bloods enough to explain "the great gulf that exists between the yellow and the black." Reuter's speculations led him to settle upon the factor of biological selection, acting through Mendelian principles of genetics, as the essential clue to the mulatto's apparent abilities. Further, the key to this process of selection was in the Negroes involved in racial mixing, not with the whites. Since most mixing did not involve whites of the higher social classes, Reuter held that "from the Caucasian side the mulattoes' ancestry has been, if not an inferior one, at last not above the average." From the Negro side, however, mulattoes were descended "from the best of the race." In this point, Reuter came back to the notion that amalgamation involved willing and even eager participation on the Negro woman's part. As he explained it,

> There is no question as to the opportunity of white men to intermix with women of the lower race. It was not a question of opportunity on the part of the white male so much as it was a question of desire. Such association was to the Negro woman an honor sought and not a relation avoided. The choicest females of the black group became the mothers of a race of half-breeds. The female offspring of these mixed unions became chosen in turn to serve the pleasure of the superior group. By this process of repeated selection of the choicer girls of the black and mulatto groups to become the mothers of a new generation of mixed-blood individuals there has been a

constant force making for the production of a choicer type of female. So far as a correlation maintains between physical perfection and mental superiority and in so far as such superiority is a heritable thing, the mulattoes, from one side of their ancestry, at least, have tended to produce a superior type.[142]

Further, since much of the mixing went on with black house servants, traditionally the more intelligent members of the slave population, mulattoes had the extra advantage of a superior intellectual heredity.

The operation of these basic principles was coupled with a social factor to ensure the mulatto's superior status, i.e., the attitudes of whites about mixed-bloods and pure blacks. Because whites believed themselves inherently superior to blacks, they were naturally inclined to see mulattoes as also somewhat superior to blacks because of their white blood. At the same time their black blood equally marked mulattoes as inferior to pure-blooded whites. Therefore, mulattoes from an early point took on the status of an intermediate group in the minds of whites, even if not in actual social relations. Since blacks did not question their own inferiority to the white man, Reuter argued, mulattoes were inclined to accept the prevailing way of thinking. They saw the white man as superior and the black as their inferior, and because both groups generally treated mullatoes in this manner, caste feelings developed over time which separated mulattoes from the mass of blacks and served to perpetuate their unique and often privileged position.

Given this social prestige, the mixed-blooded group was able to attract to itself all of the superior men who did appear among the pure blacks. The desire of such men to be included among the elite group resulted in their almost inevitable decision to marry a mulatto wife. Reuter cited various statistics to demonstrate the fact that the leading black men of the day actually were married to women lighter than themselves. The overall result, he believed, was that

> whatever talent there is among the mulattoes remains among the mulattoes; whatever talent there is among the black group marries into the mulatto caste. In either event the talent of the whole race finds its way into the mulatto group.[143]

To Reuter, this long-standing fact of biological selection, both in interracial mixing and in marriage within the Negro race itself, provided a means of accounting for the "demonstrated superiority of the mulatto group" without relying on questionable assumptions about the inherent inferiority of the black race and without exaggerating the cultural opportunities mixed-bloods might have possessed.

Due to their superiority, Reuter saw mulattoes as both "the key to the race problem" and "the real and natural leaders" of the Negro race. Like other sociologists, he sensed a tension among mulattoes arising from their frequent inability to fit into America's two-caste racial system. This was not as true in the South, Reuter contended, where most mulattoes willingly identified with the Negro race and its problems and took leadership roles in guiding the race to a new day. Southern blacks acquiesced to the superiority of the mulatto, Reuter claimed, and mulattoes adjusted relatively easily to their status:

> The superior education of the mulattoes qualifies them for leadership; their superior ambition and greater self-confidence pushes them to the front. The mulatto, even though only slightly superior, is assured of success once he has cast his lot with the Negro people. His role on the Southern situation is the role of leadership.[144]

In the North, however, mulattoes and pure blacks were more estranged. There even more of the successful men were of mixed blood, but they tended to be "proud of their European blood, their smoother features, their 'better' hair and their higher economic status; they are not always careful to conceal the fact."[145] While maintaining an attitude of "kindly toleration and mild contempt" toward the black masses, Northern mulattoes nevertheless assumed the role of spokesmen for the race. In that position, they often became bitter agitators, a role which Reuter, a proponent of Booker T. Washington's conservative approach to race relations, found distasteful. In Reuter's view,

> The agitations voice the bitterness of the superior mulattoes, of the deracialized men of education, culture, and refinement who resent and rebel against the intolerant social edict that excludes them from white society and classes them with the despised race.[146]

Reuter was convinced that "the desire of the mixed-blood man is always and everywhere to be a white man; to be classed with and become a member of the superior race." Were it possible, mulattoes would break with their dark brothers and seek assimilation into the white race.[147] Their agitations for equal rights ultimately meant the right to escape from the Negro race.[148] Fortunately, in Reuter's opinion, this agitation only solidified white opposition to Negro rights and thereby forced the mulatto back into the Negro race where he was most needed. As the vanguard of the race, however, mulattoes represented a vital point in the eventual adjustment of race relations in America.

Reuter, then, offered a curious combination of old and new ideas about mulattoes and race mixture. In this sense, he represented a transitional phase in academic thought about the meaning of race and racial differences. He could speak of Negroes as "the lower race" while challenging traditional theories of racial inferiority. While viewing amalgamation as good for the Negro race, he did not support it as a positive policy for whites to follow because it still created something that was not a white man. He could support goals of mulatto leaders of the race as long as they held to conservative approaches for furthering the needs of Afro-Americans, but would not tolerate malcontented mulattoes who demanded equal rights with the white man. He could cite the statistics of Frederick L. Hoffman or the opinions of Philip Alexander Bruce, an apologist for the Old South and traditional race relations, while at the same time reflecting the newer teachings of Franz Boas, Robert E. Park, and William I. Thomas. Most importantly, he was able to take long-established notions about the superiority of mixed-bloods and give them a new, scientific explanation. Ultimately, while he might question ideas about racial inferiority, Reuter could still divide groups into "superior" and "inferior," and it was the black man who inevitably ended up on the bottom. In that sense, Reuter had not passed far beyond the thinking of less sophisticated men who flatly denied the essential equality of all peoples.

What Reuter basically sought to impress upon his readers, however, was the need to consider all elements of the racial situation in the search for a solution to America's race problems. He recognized that Negroes could not be dealt with as a monolithic block any more than the white population could. Such assessments, he insisted, would necessarily be "either worthless or vicious."[149]   Perhaps this in itself was an important early step towards the realization that ultimately justice demands that all men be treated as individuals rather than as members of a racial grouping.

9

From today's perspective, it would be quite easy to label virtually all of the individuals discussed here as clear-cut racists. Despite their extensive training in a variety of natural and social sciences, they obviously continued to subscribe to traditional beliefs about Negro inferiority and the grand significance of ostensible racial differences. Yet this should be taken more as testimony to the pervasiveness of the era's racial attitudes rather than as an indictment of these particular people. Certainly to their credit is the fact that by the early years of the twentieth century, many were moving to question traditional ideas about race and the meaning of racial differences.

In the decades after the Civil War and Reconstruction, the racial thought of even these trained observers was largely stifled by a variety of residual, older points of view. Polygenist ideas, spawned by the ready perception of the myriad apparent physiological and cultural differences between races, led most racial thinkers to emphasize differences rather than similarities among races and peoples. Ultimately, it was believed, these differences sprang from inherently unique racial "geniuses," a conglomeration of instincts and traits which had developed in response to each race's initial geo-climatic environment. In this vein, polygenism merged with a powerful Lamarckian strain of thought pervading much of the scientific outlook of the period. Lamarckianism emphasized the development and then perpetuation of specific traits in response to an individual's and a race's physical and cultural environment. Polygenism and Lamarckianism were further cemented by the nearly universal acceptance of Darwinian principles in explaining the operation of social as well as biological phenomema. Indeed, in the latter decades of the nineteenth century, social thought was almost entirely dominated by biological concepts and points of view. Nowhere was this truer than in the realm of racial thinking, for race was itself seen as a biocultural phenomenon.

As Edward Byron Reuter later explained, the dominance of this biological perspective was not conducive to serious and objective racial study:

> It directed attention along lines that prevented the emergence of significant questions and productive procedures. Classification emphasized differences; this led to the definition and measurement of physical and mental traits. But these racial traits had no meaning, or at least the meaning was not clear without interpretation. Interpretation involved the dubious procedure of explaining social reality in biological terms.[150]

It was not really until after the turn of the century that social scientists began to realize that the social significance of race could not be discovered and understood by the enumeration and definition of physical characteristics and mental differences or through an examination of biological processes. With the gradual development of a concept of culture divorced from biological classifications of race, racial study eventually moved into a new frame of references. Eventually, this meant the relevant data for studying racial questions became social interrelationships rather than physical traits and biological processes.

It is within this overall picture of the racial thought and basic intellectual trends of the period that we must seek to understand the racial attitudes of these academic figures. They were as much men of their own age as we are of ours, and their perspectives were inevitably molded by the intellectual currents of their time. This fact is particularly evident in their attitudes about mulattoes and the question of race mixture, for ultimately these two related ideas stood at the core of the era's understanding of just what race itself meant.

Whites had long conceived of mulattoes as somehow different from both of the two parent races. Mulattoes were physically weak, notably infertile, and prone to debilitating diseases. At the same time, they were clearly intellectually superior to pure blacks, although certainly not the equal of the white man. There was also a question as to their moral character, especially since they often sprang from illegitimate interracial unions. These were the traditional ideas about mulattoes in circulation at the end of the nineteenth century, and by their very nature are indicative of the racial thought of the period. Mulattoes were superior to blacks because of their admixture of white blood. Nevertheless, they were not and never could be white, because black racial instincts and traits, understood in an essentially Lamarckian framework, continued to affect mixed-bloods' physical appearance and, more important, their psychic make-up. The mulatto might be both black and white, but because he possessed even the remotest black traits and instincts somewhere in his blood, he was not a white man. The dynamics of America's two-caste racial system therefore demanded that he be relegated to the status of a Negro.

After 1900, the rediscovery of Mendel's law of inheritance and the development of a new science of genetics gradually undermined many of the older, generally impressionistic notions white Americans held about mulattoes. This changing perspective was particularly evident among social scientists, where more objective attempts were made to understand the nature and role of the mulatto. Yet deeply ingrained beliefs about racial inferiority continued, often unconsciously, to affect academic assessments of the mulatto and the effects of race mixture. It was difficult to put aside the idea that mulattoes derived their abilities from the superior qualities of their white progenitors. It was even harder to discard ideas about racial differences and distinctiveness in favor of a positive (or at least neutral) attitude toward racial amalgamation. Even among those who did not condemn miscegenation, its benefits were universally seen as accruing not to whites but to the Negro, who would receive the superior qualities of the white man but who had little to offer in return. Further, since no one would claim that the mulatto was overall the equal of the white man, there seemed little reason for the white man to demean himself and his blood by mixing it with that of the Negro. Ultimately, though, race mixing was bad because it produced someone who was not white, and by the definition imposed by the period's racial persepective, being non-white necessarily implied inferior. It was this position which very few scientists were able to move beyond in the years prior to World War I.

10

In assessing the significance of the pronouncements of these scientists and social scientists, it is important to recognize that most were in no way outspoken racists. Indeed, their views on race and racial inferiority were generally not the primary subjects of their academic concerns, but rather were merely elements within their larger spheres of intellectualization. Their reputations were built upon achievements in areas other than simply racial theory. Their ideas about race are most important instead for what they reveal about the general tenor of racial thought in this period of a half-century.

As Idus A. Newby has commented, the link between science and racism was not so much the result of deliberate endorsement of racist ideas by the learned men of the day, but rather due to "the errors of judgment and scientific shortcomings of scientists themselves, which led them to endorse the 'obvious' fact of racial inequality without adequate empirical proof."[151] It was often the limitations of their own disciplines, many of which were still in the formative stages, which caused respected scientists and social scientists to support ideas about the racial inferiority of the Negro and other non-white peoples. Nevertheless, science did provide both a vocabulary and a set of concepts which rationalized and eventually helped to justify the value system upon which ideas of racial inferiority rested in American thought. John S. Haller has argued that,

> For many educated Americans who shunned the stigma of racial prejudice, science became an instrument which "verified" the presumptive inferiority of the Negro and rationalized the politics of disfranchisement and segregation into a social-scientific terminology that satisfied the troubled conscience of the middle class.[152]

Perhaps one might question just how troubled the majority of the middle class was about racial inequities, but it is clear that the work of many men who saw themselves as objective and impartial in racial matters did lend considerable support to doctrines of a more viciously racist slant. Many of the individuals discussed above themselves often wrote for a popular audience. Most were intent on acquainting America with the facts and the meaning of the evolutionary outlook to which they universally subscribed. Whether optimistic environmentalists or more dispassionate Darwinians, their ideas about race nevertheless frequently served to reinforce existent notions about Negro inferiority in the minds of white Americans. Moreover, many of their ideas were seized upon by popularizers and disseminated to the public in less sophisticated and often more overtly racist forms.

Perhaps this, then, is the second importance of the writings of these academic figures--their works provided scientific support for racial propagandists intent upon convincing white America of the magnitude of the race problem and especially the evils entailed in policies which threatened to bring "social equality." When the learned men of the day spoke out against the detrimental effects of race mixture, their words provided a strong argument against any policy which might conceivably undermine white racial purity. That the result was often the denial of basic rights to the Negro was a consequence that most academicians generally failed to foresee.

NOTES

[1]Booker T. Washington, *The Future of the American Negro* (Boston: Small, Maynard & Company, 1900), p. 158.

[2]Winthrop D. Jordan, *White Over Black: American Attitudes Toward the Negro, 1550-1812* (Chapel Hill: University of North Carolina Press, 1968).

[3]Johann Friedrich Blumenbach, *The Anthropological Treaties of Johann Friedrich Blumenbach*, ed. by Thomas Bendyshe (London: Published for the Anthropological Society by Longman, Green, Longman, Roberts, & Green, 1865), p. 269.

[4]As one historian has noted, "The hallmark of anthropolgy in the nineteenth century was anthropometry." John S. Haller, Jr., *Outcasts From Evolution: Scientific Attitudes of Racial Inferiority, 1859-1900* (Urbana: University of Illinois Press, 1971), p. 7.

[5]The early stages of anthropometric studies and the popularity of various types of cranial measurements are described in *ibid.*, pp. 6-19. For the effect on the basic pattern of thought regarding racial inferiority, see John S. Haller, Jr., "Race and the Concept of Progress in Nineteenth Century American Ethnology," *American Anthropologist,* LXXIII, 3 (June, 1971), 710-724.

[6]Haller, *Outcasts From Evolution*, pp. 19-20. See also John S. Haller, Jr., "Civil War Anthropometry: The Making of a Racial Ideology," *Civil War History*, XVI, 4 (December, 1970), 309-324.

[7]Benjamin Apthorp Gould, *Investigations in the Military and Anthropological Statistics of American Soldiers* (New York: Published for the United States Sanitary Commission by Hurd and Houghton, 1869), p. 319.

[8]Benjamin Apthorp Gould, "The Negroes and Indians of the United States," *Anthropological Review*, IV, 1 (January, 1866), 40-42.

[9]J[edediah] H[yde] Baxter, *Statistics, Medical and Anthropological, of the Provost-Marshal-General's Bureau, derived from Records of the Examination for Military Service in the Armies of the United States During the Late War of the Rebellion, of Over A Million Recruits, Drafted Men, Substitutes, and Enrolled Men* (2 vols.; Washington, D.C.: Government Printing Office, 1875), pp. 394, 403, 285.

[10]Sanford B. Hunt, "The Negro as a Soldier," *Anthropological Review*, VII, 1 (January, 1869), 40-54. The quotations are from p. 52.

[11]For a discussion of the impact of Darwinism on Western thought, see Paul F. Boller, Jr., *American Thought in Transition: The Impact of Evolutionary Naturalism, 1865-1900* (Chicago: Rand McNally, 1969); John C. Greene, *The Death of Adam: Evolution and Its Impact on Western Thought* (Ames: Iowa State University Press, 1959); and Richard M. Hofstadter, *Social Darwinism in American Thought* (Rev. ed.; Boston: Beacon Press, 1955).

[12]George W. Stocking, *Race, Culture, and Evolution: Essays in the History of Anthropology* (New York: The Free Press, 1968), p. 45.

[13]See Haller, *Outcasts From Evolution*, pp. 70-74.

[14]*Ibid.*, pp. 75-76. The concept of the Great Chain of Being and its role in Western thought is treated in Arthur O. Lovejoy. *The Great Chain of Being: A Study of the History of an Idea* (Cambridge: Harvard University Press. 1936).

[15]Haller, *Outcasts From Evolution*, pp. 88-94. The origins of the polygenist view and the debate which ensued in nineteenth-century American scientific circles is the subject of William Stanton, *The Leopoard's Spots: Scientific Attitudes Toward Race in America, 1815-1859* (Chicago: University of Chicago Press, 1960). Stanton's overall opinion that polygenism found little support in ante-bellum American, particularly in the South, seems to be questionable. For polygenism's effects on intellectual patterns in one Southern state, see William Henry Longton, "Some Aspects of Intellectural Activity in Ante-Bellum South Carolina, 1830-1860: An Introductory Study" (unpublished Ph.D. dissertation, University of North Carolina at Chapel Hill, 1969), pp. 100ff. On polygenism's acceptance in America, see George M. Frederickson, *The Black Image in the White Mind: The Debate on Afro-American Character and Destiny, 1817-1914* (New York: Harper & Row, Publishers, 1971), pp. 84-96. For a good summary of the polygenist/monogenist debate and its effects on overall racial thought, see John S. Haller, Jr., "The Species Problem: Nineteenth-Century Concepts of Racial Inferiority in the Origin of Man Controversy," *American Anthropologist*, LXXII, 6 (December, 1970), 1319-1329.

[16]Josiah C. Nott and George R. Glidden, *Tyes of Mankind: or, Ethnological Researches, Based upon the Ancient Monuments, Paintings, Sculptures, and Crania of Races, and upon their Natural, Geographical, Philological, and Biblical History* (London: Truber & Co., 1854), p. 405.

[17]Stocking, *Race, Culture, and Evolution*, pp. 48-49. Among the most important contemporary statements of this position was Paul Broca, *On the Phenomena of Hybridity in the Genus Homo*, trans. and ed. by C. C. Blake (London: Published for the Anthropological Society by Longman, Green & Roberts, 1864), esp. pp. 16ff., 27-29, 38-40.

[18]This group, which included such figures as Wendell Phillips, Bishop Gilbert Haven, and Theodore Tilton, is included among those who had a "romantic" view of race, according to George M. Frederickson. See his *Black Image in the White Mind*, pp. 97-129.

[19]Stocking, *Race, Culture, and Evolution*, pp. 55-56.

[20]*Ibid.*, p. 57.

[21]Herder actually espoused what might be termed a cultural relativism, since he was able to see good qualities in a variety of different cultures. His basic stance is to be found in his *Reflections on the Philosophy of the History of Mankind*, Abridged, and with an introd., by Frank E. Manuel (Chicago: University of Chicago Press, 1968).

[22]See Stocking, *Race, Culture, and Evolution*. pp. 65-66; Frederickson, *Black Image in White Mind*, pp. 97ff.

[23]Stocking, *Race, Culture, and Evolution*, pp. 238-243. My debt in this line of thought to Stocking's essay, "Lamarckianism in American Social Science, 1890-1915" is

considerable, as well as to the entire book in which it is found, *Race, Culture, and Evolution*.

[24] *Ibid.,* pp. 242-243.

[25] Quite simply, little or no distinction was made between social and organic development. Cultural organization became strictly analagous with physiological organization, and facts pertaining to one were readily applied to the other. See Haller, *Outcasts From Evolution*, pp. 121-122 and ff. For the manner in which evolutionary principles were applied to many social processes, see Hofstadter, *Social Darwinism*.

[26] Stocking, *Race, Culture, and Evolution*, p. 245.

[27] For the pessimistic impact of Darwinism on American racial thought see Frederickson, *Black Image in White Mind*, pp. 228-255; Hofstadter, *Social Darwinism*, pp. 170-200; Haller, *Outcasts from Evolution*, pp. 207-210; and Thomas F. Gossett, *Race: The History of an Idea in America* (New York: Schocken Books, 1965), pp. 144-175. For Lamarckianism's more optimistic view, see Gossett, *Race*, pp. 163-164; Stocking, *Race, Culture, and Evolution*, pp. 247, 253; and Haller, *Outcasts From Evolution*, pp. x-xi, 154ff.

[28] Haller, *Outcasts From Evolution*, pp. 208-210.

[29] The development of the culture concept gradually took place in the years after 1900, the milestone in this process being the publication of Franz Boas' book *The Mind of Primitive Man* in 1911. Boas' book revolutionized much scientific thought about race and culture. For the growth of this idea, see Stocking, *Race, Culture, and Evolution*, pp. 133-233.

[30] This would seem particularly true given the rise in the last twenty years of new scientific ideas emphasizing the Negro's apparent inferiority to whites. For a summary of such recent views, see Idus A. Newby, *Challenge to the Court: Social Scientists and the Defense of Segregation, 1954-1966* (Rev. ed.; Baton Rouge: Louisiana State University Press, 1969).

[31] *Types of Mankind* might be viewed as the capstone of pre-Civil War polygenist thought. It eventually appeared in at least nine editions before the end of the century. For the genesis and significance of the book, see Stanton, *Leopard's Spots*, pp. 161-173.

[32] Josiah C. Nott, "The Mulatto a Hybrid--Probable Extermination of the Two Races If the Whites and Blacks Are Allowed to Intermarrry," *American Journal of the Medical Sciences*, VI (1843), 252-256.

[33] Josiah C. Nott, "Hybridity in Animals, Viewed in Connection with the Natural History of Mankind," in Nott and Gliddon, *Types of Mankind*, pp. 372-410.

[34] Josiah C. Nott, "The Negro Race," *Anthropological Review*, IV, 3 (July, 1866), 103-116. The quotations are from p. 111.

[35] Stanton, *Leopard's Spots*, pp. 185-187.

[36] Haller, *Outcasts From Evolution*, p. 60.

[37] Hoffman's mortality statistics became the basis upon which both the Metropolitan and the Prudential Life Insurance Companies refused to write life insurance policies on

blacks. See John S. Haller, Jr., "Race, Mortality, and Life Insurance: Negro Vital Statistics in the Late Nineteenth Century," *Journal of the History of Medicine and Allied Sciences*, XXV, 3 (July, 1970), 247-261.

[38]Frederick L. Hoffman, *Race Traits and Tendencies of the American Negro* (New York: Published for the American Economic Association by the Macmillan Company, 1896), pp. 149-176.

[39]*Ibid.*, p. 184.

[40]*Ibid.*, pp. 185-187.

[41]*Ibid.*, p. 188.

[42]*Ibid.*, pp. 206-207.

[43]Hoffman was himself especially proud of his objectivity. Since he had been born in Germany and therefore was not native American, he said, he could write without "a personal bias which might have made an impartial treatment of the subject difficult." *Ibid.*, pp. 327-328.

[44]Hoffman was a member of the American Academy of Medicine, the American Statistics Association, and the Royal Statistics Society of London.

[45]Haller, *Outcasts From Evolution*, p. 187. For an indication of Shaler's contemporary standing, see Frank W. Noxen, "College Professors Who Are Men of Letters," *The Critic*, XLII, 2 (February, 1903), 127.

[46]Nathaniel S. Shaler, "The African Element in America," *Arena*, II (November, 1890), 661; Nathaniel S. Shaler, *The Individual: A Study of Life and Death* (New York: D. Appleton and Company, 1900), pp. 252-254, 313-314.

[47]Nathaniel S. Shaler, *The Citizen: A Study of the Individual and the Government* (New York: Barnes & Co., 1904), pp. 327-328; Shaler, "African Element in America," p. 671.

[48]Nathaniel S. Shaler, "The Nature of the Negro," *Arena*, III (December, 1890), 24.

[49]Nathaniel S. Shaler, "Science and the African Problem," *Atlantic Monthly*, LXVI (July, 1890), 42; Shaler, "African Element in America," p. 672.

[50]Nathaniel S. Shaler, "An Ex-Southerner in South Carolina," *Atlantic Monthly*, XXVI (July, 1870), 57.

[51]Nathaniel S. Shaler, *The Neighbor: The Natural History of Human Contacts* (Boston and New York: Houghton, Mifflin and Company, 1904), pp. 161-162. Elsewhere, Shaler claimed never personally to have seen a mulatto over fifty years of age. See Nathaniel S. Shaler, "The Negro Problem," *Atlantic Monthly*, LIV (November, 1884), 706.

[52]Shaler, "African Element in America," p. 672; Nathaniel S. Shaler, "The Negro Since the Civil War," *Popular Science Monthly*, LVII (May, 1900), 36.

[53]Shaler, *The Neighbor*, pp. 162-163.

[54]Shaler, "Science and African Problem," p. 37; Shaler, *The Neighbor*, pp. 163-164.

[55]Shaler, "Ex-Southerner in South Carolina," p. 57; Shaler, "Negro Since Civil War," pp. 36-37.

[56]Shaler, *The Neighbor*, p. 330.

[57]Cope's Neo-Lamarckian attitudes can best be seen in his *The Origin of the Fittest: Essays on Evolution* (New York: D. Appleton and Company, 1887) and *The Primary Factors of Organic Evolution* (Chicago: Open Court Publishing Company, 1896). For Cope's career, see Henry F. Osborn, *Cope: Master Naturalist* (Princeton, N.J.: Princeton University Press, 1931) and Marcus Benjamin, "Edward Drinker Cope," in David Starr Jordan, ed., *Leading American Men of Science* (New York: H. Holt and Company, 1910), pp. 313-340.

[58]Edward D. Cope, "On the Hypothesis of Evolution, Physical and Metaphysical," *Lippincott's Magazine*, VI (July, 1870), 40-41. See also Edward D. Cope, "Evolution and Its Consequences," *Penn Monthly*, III (May, 1872), 230-238, and Edward D. Cope, "The Developmental Significance of Human Physiognomy," *American Naturalist*, XVII, 6 (June, 1883), 618-627.

[59]Edward D. Cope, "Two Perils of the Indo-European," *Open Court*, III, 48 (January 23, 1890), 2054.

[60]*Ibid.*

[61]Edward D. Cope, "The African in America," *Open Court*, IV, 21 (July 17, 1890), 2400. Also, Edward D. Cope, "The Return of the Negroes to Africa, " *Open Court*, IV, 16 (June 12, 1890), 2331.

[62]Joseph LeConte, "The Race Problem in the South," in Brooklyn Ethical Society, *Man and the State: Studies in Applied Sociology* (New York: D. Appleton and Company, 1892), pp. 362, 367.

[63]*Ibid.*, p. 372; Joseph LeConte, "The Effect of Mixture of Races on Human Progress, " *Berkeley Quarterly*, I, 1 (April, 1880), 100-101. LeConte explained the biological processes involved in race mixing and evolutionary development in his "The Genesis of Sex," *Popular Science Monthly*, XVI, 2 (December, 1879), 169-179.

[64]LeConte did speak in favor of mixing "marginal varieties" of the Caucasian race with inferior races as a humanitarian solution to the otherwise inevitable decline of the Negro in the competitive evolutionary struggle. See LeConte, "Effect of Mixture of Races," p. 101 and "Race Problem in South," p. 374.

[65]W. A. Dixon, "The Morbid Proclivities and Retrogressive Tendencies in the Offspring of Mulattoes," *Journal of the American Medical Association*, XX, 1 (January 7, 1893), 1-2.

[66]Bean's differentiation of white and black characteristics closely resembled Herbert Spencer's conception of primitive and civilized mentalities:

> The Caucasian is subjective, the Negro objective. The Caucasian--
> more particularly the Anglo-Saxon, which was derived from the
> primitives of Europe, is dominant and domineering, and possessed
> primarily with determination, will power, self-control, self-government,

and all the attributes of the subjective self, with a high development
of the ethical and aesthetic faculties. The Negro is in direct contrast
by reason of a certain lack of these powers, and a great development
of the objective qualities. The Negro is primarily affectionate,
immensely emotional, then sensual and under stimulation passionate.
There is love of ostentation, of outward show, of approbation; there
is love of music, and capacity for melodious articulation; there is
undeveloped artistic power and taste--Negroes make good artisans,
handicraftsmen--and there is instability of character incident to lack
of self-control, especially in connection with the sexual relation; and
there is lack of *orientation*, or recognition of position and condition
of self and environment, evidenced by a peculiar bumptiousness.

Bean here was clearly seeing cultural race traits in Lamarckian terms. Robert Bennett
Bean, "Some Racial Peculiarities of the Negro Brain." *American Journal of Anatomy*,
V, 4 (September, 1906), 379.

[67]Robert Bennett Bean, "The Negro Brain," *Century Magazine*, LXXII, 5 (September,
1906), 780.

[68]*Ibid.*, pp. 780-781.

[69]Eugene S. Talbot, *Degeneracy: Its Causes, Signs, and Results* (New York: Charles
Scribner's Sons, 1904), p. 102. Talbot in fact cited the observations of W. A. Dixon
as evidence of the inferiority of the mulatto.

[70]*Ibid.*, pp. 102-103.

[71]*Ibid.*, p. 99.

[72]The exact nature of how whites perceived Africa at this time has not been given
adequate attention as yet by historians of American race relations, despite the fact
that much of the racial literature of the day contained numerous references to the
savage way of life that characterized black African peoples. The sources of such
images seem to have been varied, including travelers' accounts, missionary reports,
and inferential impressions drawn from descriptions of life in Haiti. Much criticism
of American blacks, however, was couched in terms of their retrogression to so-called
African patterns of life. Further, American blacks were frequently referred to as
"Africans," again demonstrating that white Americans had a very strong sense of the
Negro's origin and what that origin entailed. For a rather unsatisfactory treatment of
this general topic by an African scholar who was personally shocked by the
ethnocentrism of present-day white Americans, see Felix N. Okoye, *The American
Image of Africa: Myth and Reality* (Buffalo: Black Academy Press, Inc., 1971). For
a suggestive discussion of how ideas about primitive peoples affected anthropologists
in the pre-Boas era, see Stocking, "The Dark-Skinned Savage: The Image of Primitive
Man in Evolutionary Anthropology," in *Race, Culture, and Evolution*, pp. 110-132.

[73]See Claude H. Nolen, *The Negro's Image in the South: The Anatomy of White
Supremacy* (Lexington: University of Kentucky Press, 1967), pp. 29-39; Frederickson,
Black Image in White Mind, pp. 49, 132-133, 218-219, 248-249, 321.

[74]For an extended discussion of nineteenth-century studies of black/white physical differences, including ideas about black sexual peculiarities, see Haller, *Outcasts From Evolution,* pp. 40-68, esp. pp. 50-58.

[75]Stocking, *Race, Culture, and Evolution,* p. 122.

[76]Haller, *Outcasts From Evolution,* pp. 121-130.

[77]Herbert Spencer, "Comparative Psychology of Man," *Popular Science Monthly,* VIII, 3 (January, 1876), 262-263.

[78]Herbert Spencer, *The Principles of Sociology* (3 vols; New York: D. Appleton and Company, 1876-1897), I, 572.

[79]For a discussion of Brinton's career, see Regna Darnell, "Daniel Garrison Brinton: An Intellectual Biography" (unpublished M.A. thesis, University of Pennsylvania, 1967).

[80]Daniel G. Brinton, *Races and Peoples: Lectures on the Science of Ethnography* (New York: N. D. C. Hodges, Publisher, 1890), pp. 47-48.

[81]*Ibid.,* p. 287.

[82]Daniel G. Brinton, *The Basis of Social Relations: A Study in Ethnic Psychology,* ed. by Livington Farrand (New York and London: G. P. Putnam's Sons, 1902), p. 155.

[83]Brinton, *Races and Peoples,* pp. 283-284. See also Daniel G. Brinton, *Negroes* (Philadelphia: J. B. Lippincott Company, 1891).

[84]Brinton, *Social Relations,* pp. xiii, 6, 150.

[85]Brinton, *Races and Peoples,* p. 287.

[86]W J McGee, "The Trend of Human Progress," *American Anthropologist,* N.S., I, 3 (July, 1899), 419.

[87]Major sources for Tillinghast's depiction of the Negro in Africa included traveler's accounts like those of Mary Kingsley, David Livingstone, and Paul Du Chaillu, as well as the works of major anthropologists like A. B. Ellis, A. H. Keane, Daniel G. Brinton, and Paul Topinard.

[88]Joseph A. Tillinghast, *The Negro in Africa and America,* Publications of the American Economic Association, 3rd. ser., III, 2 (New York: Macmillan Company, 1902), p. 225.

[89]*Ibid.,* pp. 121-122.

[90]Franz Boas, "Human Faculty as Determined by Race," *Proceedings of the American Association for the Advancement of Science,* XLIII (1894), 301-327; Franz Boas, *The Mind of Primitive Man* (New York: Macmillan Company, 1911).

[91]Boas, *Mind of Primitive Man,* p. 269. The nature of Franz Boas' contribution to the reorientation of anthropological thought is essentially the subject of Stocking's *Race, Culture, and Evolution.* See esp. pp. 161-233.

[92]Boas, *Mind of Primitive Man,* pp. 24, 28, 29, 117-118. Among those cited were the psychologists William H. R. Rivers and Robert S. Woodworth (who had taken his

anthropological and statistical training under Boas), the neurologist Henry H. Donaldson, and Dr. Franklin Mall at the Johns Hopkins Hospital, who had challenged the findings of Robert Bennett Bean on the inferiority of the Negro brain.

[93]Edward A. Ross, "The Causes of Race Superiority," *Annals of the American Academy of Political and Social Science,* XVIII (July, 1901), 67-89. Ross' essay was included in a special volume devoted to *America's Race Problem.*

[94]Charles A. Ellwood, "The Theory of Imitation in Social Psychology," *American Journal of Sociology,* VI, 6 (May, 1901), 721-741. The long quotation is from pp. 735-736.

[95]Carl Kelsey, "The Evolution of Negro Labor," *Annals of the American Academy of Political and Social Science,* XXI, 1 (January, 1903), 73.

[96]Howard W. Odum, *Social and Mental Traits of the Negro: A Study of Race Traits, Tendencies, and Prospects,* Columbia University Studies in History, Economics and Public Law, Vol. XXXVII, No. 3 (New York: Columbia University Press, 1910). The Negro's many so-called traits are largely summarized on pp. 270-275.

[97]*Ibid.,* p. 186.

[98]G. Stanley Hall, "The Negro in Africa and America," *Pedagogical Seminary,* XII, 3 (September, 1905), 358.

[99]John R. Commons, *Races and Immigrants in America* (New York: Macmillan Company, 1907), pp. 209-213.

[100]James Bardin, "The Psychological Factor in Southern Race Problems," *Popular Science Monthly,* LXXXIII (October, 1913), 371.

[101]*Ibid.,* pp. 372-374.

[102]William I. Thomas, "The Psychology of Race Prejudice," *American Journal of Sociology,* IX, 5 (March, 1904), 593-611.

[103]Ulysses G. Weatherly, "Race and Marriage," *American Journal of Sociology,* XV, 4 (January, 1910), 450.

[104]*Ibid.,* pp. 448-449.

[105]Like Daniel G. Brinton, Weatherly placed his faith in white women as the preservators of racial purity: "It is to be expected that women, as the conservative sex, will be found more rigorous than men in resisting social change through cross-breeding. Women dominte the intimate social standards and fix the taboos which set off social classes from each other." *Ibid.,* p. 450.

[106]Commons, *Races and Immigrants,* p. 209.

[107]Charles A. Ellwood, "Review of *The Color Line: A Brief in Behalf of the Unborn,* by William Benjamin Smith," *American Journal of Sociology,* XI, 4 (January, 1906), 573. "If heredity counts for anything," Ellwood wrote, "this good white blood must greatly improve the negroid stock."

[108]Hall, "Negro in Africa and America," p. 360.

[109]Robert S. Woodworth, "Racial Differences in Mental Traits," *Science*, N.S., XXXI (February 4, 1910), 171-186.

[110]William I. Thomas, "Race Psychology: Standpoint and Questionnaire, with Particular Reference to the Immigrant and the Negro," *American Journal of Sociology*, XVII, 6 (May, 1912), 726, 728.

[111]George W. Ellis, "The Psychology of American Race Prejudice," *Journal of Race Development*, V, 3 (January, 1915), 297-315, esp. 312-313; Wilson D. Wallis, "Moral and Racial Prejudice," *Journal of Race Development*, V, 2 (October, 1914), 212-229.

[112]William I. Thomas, *Source Book for Social Origins* (Chicago: University of Chicago Press, 1909), p. 316.

[113]Charles A. Ellwood, "Review of *The Negro Races*, by Jerome P. Dowd," *American Journal of Sociology*, XIII, 6 (May, 1908), 857. See Jerome P. Dowd, *The Negro Races: A Social Study* (New York: Macmillan Company, 1907), for continuing, essentially Lamarckian ideas about race. Dowd was a sociologist at the University of Oklahoma who produced numerous works on race and the Negro in particular during his career.

[114]Carl Kelsey, "Discussion of an article by D. Collin Wells on 'Social Darwinism',"*American Journal of Sociology*, XII, 5 (March, 1907), 711. Kelsey specifically noted that it was the rejection of Lamarckianism in biology which was "reacting powerfully upon our social theories." Kelsey's earlier comment was in his "Evolution of Negro Labor," p. 73.

[115]Stocking, *Race, Culture, and Evolution*, p. 266.

[116]George Oscar Ferguson, *The Psychology of the Negro, An Experimental Study* (New York: Science Press, 1916); George Oscar Ferguson, "The Mental Status of the American Negro," *Scientific Monthly*, XII (June, 1921), 533-543.

[117]Shaler, "Ex-Southerner in South Carolina," p. 57.

[118]Kelsy, "Evolution of Negro Labor," pp. 55-56.

[119]Hall, "Negro in Africa and America," p. 361.

[120]Quoted in *ibid.*, p. 361.

[121]Ellwood, "Review of *The Color Line*," p. 573.

[122]*Ibid.*, pp. 573-574.

[123]Paul S. Reinsch, "The Negro Race and European Civilization," *American Journal of Sociology*, XI, 2 (September, 1905), 147.

[124]H. E. Jordan, "The Biological Status and Social Worth of the Mulatto," *Popular Science Monthly*, LXXXII (June, 1913), 576.

[125]*Ibid.*, 580-581. Jordan cited several "desirable negro traits" which the black man could contribute to a union with white blood: physical strength, resistance or relative immunity to certain infections, capacity for routine, cheerful temperament, vivid imagination, and rhythmic and melodic endowment. Presumably these would be

coupled with "white traits" like high intelligence, thrift, perseverance, self-control, and other characteristics ethnologists had traditionally ascribed to whites.

[126]Frances Hoggan, "The American Negro and Race Blending," *Sociological Review*, II, 4 (October, 1909), 349-360.

[127]Commons, *Races and Immigrants*, p. 210.

[128]*Ibid.*, pp. 209-210.

[129]Weatherly, "Race and Marriage," p. 444.

[130]Ulysses G. Weatherly, "A World-Wide Color Line," *Popular Science Monthly*, LXXIX (November, 1911), 480-481.

[131]Hall, "Negro in Africa and America," p. 361.

[132]Hoggan, "American Negro and Race Blending," pp. 354-355.

[133]See, for instance, Thomas, "Race Psychology," pp. 726, 745-746.

[134]For a summary of the literature generated by the first two decades of these tests, see Morris S. Vitales, "The Mental Status of the Negro," *Annals of the American Academy of Political and Social Science*, CXL (November, 1928), 166-177.

[135]Weatherly, "Race and Marriage," p. 441.

[136]Ellwood, "Review of *The Color Line*," pp. 572-574.

[137]For the development and importance of sociological study at the University of Chicago, see Robert E. L. Faris, *Chicago Sociology, 1920-1932* (San Francisco: Chandler Publishing Co., 1967); John Hylton Madge, *The Origins of Scientific Sociology* (New York: Free Press of Glencoe, 1962), pp. 88-126; and Roscoe C. Hinkle and Gisela J. Hinkle, *The Development of Modern Sociology, Its Nature and Growth in the United States* (New York: Random House, 1954), pp. 28-40.

[138]Edward Byron Reuter, *The Mulatto in the United States, Including a Study of the Role of Mixed-Blood Races Throughout the World* (Boston: Richard G. Badger, 1918), pp. 162-163.

[139]See, for instance, *ibid.*, pp. 137, n. 38; 145, n. 51.

[140]Edward Byron Reuter, "The Superiority of the Mulatto," *American Journal of Sociology*, XXIII, 1 (July, 1917), 85.

[141]Reuter, *Mulatto in United States*, pp. 183-314.

[142]Reuter, "Superiority of Mulatto," pp. 98-99.

[143]*Ibid.*, pp. 105.

[144]Reuter, *Mulatto in United States*, p. 364.

[145]*Ibid.*, p. 367.

[146]*Ibid.*, p. 370.

[147] *Ibid.*, pp. 315-316.

[148] *Ibid.*, pp. 369-371.

[149] *Ibid.*, p. 397.

[150] Edward Byron Reuter, "Racial Theory," *American Journal of Sociology,* L, 6 (May, 1945), 454-455.

[151] Idus A. Newby, *Jim Crow's Defense: Anti-Negro Thought in America, 1900-1930,* (Baton Rouge: Louisiana State Univrsity Press, 1965), p. 50.

[152] Haller, *Outcasts From Evolution,* p. x.

CHAPTER III

POPULAR RACIAL THEORY AND THE MULATTO

The racial and intellectual perspectives of American scientists and social scientists, particularly before 1900, were important because they absorbed, reflected, and even justified what could be called the popular racial thought of the day. Indeed, the work of these academic figures, to the degree that the public encountered it directly, more often reinforced than challenged prevailing racial attitudes. However, it was through the efforts of popularizers and propagandists that the works of scientists and social scientists had their greatest impact on white America's racial attitudes and outlook. Such writers drew freely upon theories and researches from a variety of disciplines--biology, genetics, psychology, sociology, anthropology, physiology, and others--in assembling a formidable array of authoritative evidence to support essentially racist doctrines. Moreover, their efforts were facilitated by the fact that most scientists and social scientists accepted the basic premise that races were unequal and that the Negro was inferior to the white man. In this manner, scientific findings became a part of the racial ideology of the period, greatly strengthening popular prejudice by clothing it in the mantle of academic and scientific authority.

In the mid-nineteenth century, the line between true scientists and what might be termed "popular writers" was often a rather fine one. Many times the distinction chiefly involved how an individual was regarded by others who were recognized as authorities in a particular field. Josiah C. Nott, for instance, had no formal training in anthropology, yet because his work was accepted as authoritative by anthropologists, he can be distinguished from less sophisticated writers of the period whose works had no academic standing. In terms of racial theory, this distinction was even fuzzier, since scientists and non-scientists alike were operating from essentially the same racial perspective in the mid-nineteenth century. This outlook, derived from the intersection of polygenism, Lamarckianism, and Darwinism described in the preceding chapter, pervaded the racial thought of virtually all Americans, regardless of their academic background or reputation. It is this fact which explains why science, even through the turn of the century, provided such ready support for the racist attitudes of the day. Further, until about the turn of the century, many reputable scientific figures themselves freely discussed racial issues in a wide variety of popular periodicals, since these were often the primary outlets for even rather sophisticated scientific articles. In this manner, the public was frequently exposed to authoritative pronouncements on race which actually differed little, if any, from the opinions of more overt racial propagandists.

After 1900, scientific attitudes about race and racial differences slowly began to change, gradually diverging from the mainstream of American racial thought. At the level of popular thought, however, such change left little or no real impression. Sociologist Edward Byron Reuter described the manner in which popular beliefs resist the scientific forces pushing for a reorientation of basic attitudes:

> Folk beliefs and sentiments, rooted in traditional and customary adjustments, are transmitted and flourish for decades and centuries after they are shown to be fallacious and inefficient; . . . folklore persists beside scientific understanding and often prevents the acceptance of the New. The genuine contributions to human understanding are sometimes slow to be recognized as such; they are likely to be less colorful and more difficult than the currently familiar doctrines; and they often demand a mental reorientation that meets great resistance.[1]

This fact is particularly true, Reuter argued, in the areas of race and race relations, because they involve an elaborate, emotionally deep-seated popular philosophy. Older ideas and doctrines compete with new scientific theories for acceptance, or frequently are even interwoven into ostensibly sophisticated theoretical outlooks.

When scientists and social scientists began to redefine their attitudes about race, then, most popularizers continued to hold to older views. For their purposes, virtually any scientific authority could serve as substantiation for notions of black inferiority. Not infrequently, this meant that popularizers gave little heed to how old these scientific statements might be, or to how an individuals's personal outlook might have changed in the meantime. In addition, the late nineteenth century also brought with it the professionalization of most major academic disciplines and the establishment of the leading professional journals. While this fact undoubtedly led to an acceleration of research among academicians and may have contributed to the gradual development of new ideas about race within such circles, it also meant that the scientific/academic community was becoming more isolated from the public. New ideas were now reported in publications like the *American Journal of Sociology*, the *American Anthropologist*, and the *Journal of Race Development*, or in books aimed at an essentially academic audience. The public had little contact with such publications and consequently was not significantly influenced by new modes of thought developing within scientific circles about race.

The overall result was that popular racial attitudes in 1917 differed little from those of a half-century before. This was especially true with regard to ideas about mulattoes and the consequences of racial mixing. By World War I, the impressionistic beliefs characteristic of the ante-bellum and Civil War eras had hardened into a virtual orthodoxy which saw the mulatto as degenerate and amalgamation as a grave threat to the supremacy of the white man. What factors were responsible for the solidification of these ideas? Why did white Americans become so frenzied over the threat of racial mixture? How was this concern linked to perceptions of the nature of the mulatto? Finally, what do these attitudes reveal about white America's basic understanding of the meaning and dynamics of race?

2

Just as Josiah C. Nott's *Types of Mankind* (1854) set the tone for much late nineteenth-century academic thought about race, mulattoes, and the effects of amalgamation, John H. Van Evrie's *White Supremacy and Negro Subordination* (1868) likewise exemplifies the patterns of thought which characterized popular writing about mulattoes and race mixture during that period. Van Evrie was an irascible New York physician, editor, and uncompromising Democratic foe of Republican war and Reconstruction policies. George M. Frederickson has labeled him "perhaps the first professional racist in American history."[2] An avowed polygenist, Van Evrie was staunchly convinced of the innate inferiority of the Negro and consequently saw no place for him in America outside the bonds of slavery. His late ante-bellum writings had had considerable influence in the South among pro-slavery theorists.[3] *White Supremacy and Negro Subordination* had orginally been printed in pamphlet form under a different title in 1853, then enlarged and printed in book form in 1861 and 1863.[4] The essence of each edition, though, was that the Negro's natural condition was slavery. As a writer on the fringe of the scientific racism of the period, Van Evrie employed various anthropological, ethnological, and physiological theories to substantiate his position that the races of man represented distinct species. From this perspective, Van Evrie necessarily concluded that miscegenation was a grave error.

Van Evrie's attitudes about mulattoes and race mixture gave expression to virtually all of the themes which constituted the popular train of thought in that realm in the late 1800s. The mulatto, he argued, was remarkable for "its fragility and incapacity to endure hardships," and was inevitably given to absolute sterility. This was clear evidence that mulattoism represented an "abnormal or diseased condition," although Van Evrie did admit that "as a general principle the mongrel has intellectual ability in proportion as he approximates to the superior race." Nevertheless, he was convinced that the moral qualities of the mixed-blood were weakened. "Everyone's observations, as well as history and statistics," he held, testified to "the greater viciousness of the mulatto when compared with either of the original types or typical races." Ninety precent of the crime committed by Negroes, charged Van Evrie, was in fact the work of mulattoes, "the females almost all being as lewd and lascivious as the men are idle, sensual, and dishonest."[5]

Given this perception of the nature of the mulatto, Van Evrie lashed out at those who would (or did) mix white blood with black:

> Mulattoism is to the South what prostitution is to the North--that is, those depraved persons who give themselves up to a wicked perversion of the sexual instincts, resort to the mongrel or "colored women" instead of houses of ill-fame, as in the former case. Such a thing as love, or natural affection, never has nor can attract persons of different races, and therefore all the co-habitations of white men and negro women are abnormal--a perversion of the instincts of reproduction.[6]

Extensive amalgamation, Van Evrie contended, would inevitably lead to the degeneration of the entire nation, both morally and physically. So weakened would America be that it would doubtless fall to a purer strain of the master race and once again become the province of a European power. All history testified to the punishment which God inflicted upon those nations which committed such sinful crimes. The example of the Latin American republics with their continual turmoil and poverty evidenced the consequences of widescale mixing of two disparate peoples. As a result, Van Evrie insisted, no policies should be condoned which might ultimately lead to "social equality" and the race mixing which that necessarily implied. "All the links in the chain are continuous," he declared,

> --all the series of events dependent on each other--all the steps of the process naturally united; the emancipation, the legal equality, the social level, the admixture of blood, and the ultimate extinction, are part and parcel of the same awful crime against nature and against God, against the laws of organization and against the decrees of the Eternal.[7]

In Van Evrie's eyes, because the races were distinct species, mixing represented a monstrous sin. This same polygenist outlook found expression in other works of race theory at that time and in subsequent decades. Buckner H. Payne, a Nashville publisher writing under the pseudonym of "Ariel," likewise expounded a polygenist interpretation in an 1867 pamphlet entitled *The Negro: What Is His Ethnological Status?*. To Payne, as to a number of earlier pro-slavery commentators, the Negro's status was that of a pre-Adamite--he had been "created before

Adam and Eve" as "a *separate* and *distinct* species of *the genus homo.*"
It was because Adam's sons had intermarried with this inferior, ape-like
species that God had sent the flood as a punishment for human
wrongdoing.   Payne therefore decried the present tendencies of
Reconstruction policy, for like most radical racists he was convinced that
Negro equality would inevitably lead to amalgamation. The resultant
debasement of the white race would bring about catastrophic intervention
by an angry God:

> The states and people that favor this equality and amalgamation of
> the white and black races, *God will exterminate.* . . A man cannot
> commit so great an offense against his race, against his country,
> against his God,. . .as to give his daughter' in marriage to a negro–a
> *beast.*[8]

Payne could foresee only two alternatives . . . the Negro must be sent
back to Africa, or he must be re-enslaved, for this was the only way in
which Negroes would live in the presence of whites.

The views of Van Evrie and Payne were admittedly of an
extremist nature, but the polygenist interpretation which underlay their
basic positions was very much a part of the fundamental understanding
which white Americans had about race and the meaning of racial
differences in the late nineteenth century.   As the previous chapter
demonstrated, it was incorporated to varying degrees into the racial
theories of a number of reputable scientific figures during this period.
Polygenist ideas were a hallmark of the American school of ethnology in
the late 1800s and even influenced the thinking of those who would have
categorized themselves as more strictly Darwinians.

Charles Loring Brace, for example, was a New York
philanthropist who espoused a strong Darwinian perspective in his *The
Races of the Old World: A Manual of Ethnology* (1863).   Yet Brace's
understanding of the processes of natural selection led him to a view of
racial differentiation which clearly resembled that of the polygenists.
Mankind had begun as a single type, Brace argued, but as branches of
the human stock had migrated and settled in different geographic
regions, each variety had gradually become adapted to its particular
location, climate, and pursuits.   Eventually they developed into
permanent racial types, "unchanged in the historical period, each with its
own features, its habits, its peculiar diseases."[9]   Thus through a
Lamarckian process of racial adaptation, Brace's types became as distinct
as those envisioned by the polygenists.

The overlapping between polygenism and Darwinism was clearest
in Brace's discussion of race mixture.   Polygenists decried miscegenation
because of its degenerative effects in terms of physical stamina and

fertility. Brace likewise noted that there would be "a difficulty in two very diverse types crossing at first with permanent fertility," although he saw this as different from the problems encountered by the crossing of two distinct species. "If individuals of two very different races intermarried," he explained,

> their mutual differences and varying constitutions would naturally render the surviving of the first offspring somewhat doubtful . . . . Each parent is adapted to a different and peculiar condition of temperature, soil, and climate. The offspring, if it shares these adaptations equally, must be in so far unadapted to its climate and circumstances. That is, a half-blood mulatto in our Northern states, in so far as he has a negro constitution, is unfitted for our climate; in the Southern, he is equally unadapted, from his white blood, to the climate there, and it may be centuries before he becomes suited to either.[10]

Surely this was as forceful, if less passionate, an argument against amalgamation as Van Evrie and other polygenists might raise.

Brace was clearly more in the mainstream of late nineteenth-century racial thought than were extremists like Van Evrie and Payne. His attitudes reflected the interworkings of Darwinism, Lamarckianism, and underlying polygenist notions in their concern over fundamental racial traits and instincts, the processes by which they were developed, and the consequences of mixing the traits and instincts of disparate racial types. Yet the popular mainstream of racial thought always seems to have been somewhat further to the right than that characterizing the academic community. Popular attitudes, perhaps because they ultimately were tied to deep and basic social concerns, were more often inclined to slip over into extreme positions. This was especially true in the decade or so around the turn of the century, when racial attitudes, particularly in the South, took on a radically extremist cast. This was the high tide of American racism, a time when white hysteria over black retrogression, sexual assaults, and the specter of racial amalgamation reached its peak. The academic world was largely outside this trend; it was even at this time that some scientists and social scientists began moving away from traditional ideas about race and race relations. Among the general public, however, these older ideas were probably becoming more deeply entrenched than ever.

Throughout the period from Reconstruction to the First World War, white attitudes about mulattoes and race mixture encompassed a basic, rather consistent set of ideas and beliefs. These ideas were closely related to fundamental white opinions about the inferiority of the Negro and the ultimate meaning of race itself. Yet the points of emphasis within this collection of beliefs about mulattoes and race mixing fluctuated in response to changes in overall white levels of tension and concern about racial issues. Once the initial stir of Reconstruction had subsided, white racial attitudes assumed a rather conservative tone. The dominant outlook was one which emphasized place and order. Conservatives were willing to admit that the Negro had a place in American life, albeit a subordinate one. If the Negro would accept that status, race relations would be peaceful and harmonious and the entire social order would benefit. Around 1890, however, a variety of pressures within the South and within the white mind itself gradually began to aggravate white fears and anxieties. The result was a radicalizing of white racial attitudes, especially in the South. The number of lynchings ballooned, innumerable Jim Crow and disfranchisement laws were enacted, and whites generally evidenced an acute hysteria about the threat which blacks somehow represented to their traditional supremacy and way of life. Fear that blacks were "retrogressing" to a bestial state led radical thinkers to insist that there was no place for the Negro in America, that no peace could be attained as long as he continued to pollute the body politic. Yet by 1910, this radical racist spirit had begun to diminish, almost as though it had exhausted the white man's energy, and was gradually replaced by a resurgent conservatism, although the many legal proscriptions against Negroes remained on the books.

A similar cycle of conservatism, radicalism, and then conservatism was evident in white America's attitudes about mulattoes during this period. The oscillation was particularly characteristic of white feelings about the extent and threat of miscegenation. There was considerable concern in the South during Reconstruction that Radical Republican policies towards the Negro would undoubtedly lead to massive racial amalgamation. Northern Democrats even sought at times to make the threat of amalgamation into a political issue.[11] As Forrest G. Wood has noted, however, "the whole miscegenation issue was just too fantastic to be taken seriously."[12] Many Southerners did remain convinced that race mixing rose during Reconstruction due to the presence of Union occupation forces, but by the 1880s most were confident that the rate of miscegenation was clearly on the decline.

As early as 1884, Walter B. Hill, Chancellor of the University of Georgia, was explaining in *Century Magazine* that amalgamation did not realistically represent a threat to the white man. "Amalgamation of races is too abhorent to the Southern mind to seem a threatening possibility," declared Hill quite simply. "It has a natural barrier in the instinct of race."[13] Perhaps the existence of a massive number of mulattoes in the South should have led Hill to wonder about the power of the white man's racial instincts, but by the 1880s whites were regaining confidence in their mastery of Southern race relations and were not gravely worried about the issue of race mixing. In 1885, Atlanta's Henry W. Grady, spokesman of the New South, affirmed that the spirit in both the white and black races was everyday moving further away from condoning indiscriminate race mixing.[14]   The next year, W. C. Benet of Abbeville, South Carolina, made a similar point in the Augusta *Chronicle*.   "The proud race whose blood flows in our veins will never stoop to marriage with the negro, nor with any colored race," announced Benet.

> Race fusion is so abhorrent to our race instincts and so out of accord with the history of our race that we can smile at the absurd suggestion. . .There may be isolated cases of intermarriage, but they will never betoken a race movement.[15]

In later years, the most widely cited statement about the decline of racial mixing was that of Philip Alexander Bruce in his *The Plantation Negro as a Freeman* (1889).   Bruce was a Virginia historian and gentleman planter, and was generally regarded by his contemporaries as something of an expert on race relations in the South.   Although concerned about the direction that race relations were taking in the post-emancipation South (Bruce saw blacks as retrogressing, especially because of the growing gulf between the two races), Bruce was persuaded that "illicit sexual commerce between the two races has diminished so far as to almost have ceased."   The exception to this was in urban areas, he believed, "where the association, being more casual, is more frequent." On the whole, though, the rate of miscegenation was happily well below that of the ante-bellum period.   The result, Bruce contended, was that "the mulattoes are rapidly decreasing in numbers with the progress of time, and the negroes as a mass are gradually reverting to the original African type."   Whites had fortunately come to understand that in becoming involved in illicit sexual relations with Negroes, they were lowering themselves to a plane of equality with an inferior people, and any such equality represented a challenge to overall white supremacy.[16]

By the early 1890s, numerous other observers were repeating Bruce's contention.   Atticus G. Haygood, a Southern Methodist bishop and conservative defender of Negro rights, wrote in 1890 that

> it is absolutely settled that the tendencies against miscegenation increase in both races. Fewer mulattoes are born each year. The moral tone of the Negroes does improve. The white man recoils from amalgamation more than in former days; and law teaches all.[17]

The next year, William Cabell Bruce, a Baltimore lawyer and the brother of Philip Alexander Bruce, likewise declared that black/white sexual contact was much lessened from former levels.[18]   Even Tom Watson, then something of a friend to the Negro, confidently wrote in 1892 that

the "black belts" in the South are getting blacker. The race is mixing
less than it ever did. Mulattoes are less common (in proportion)
than during the times of slavery. Neither the blacks nor the whites
have any relish for it.[19]

Regardless of whether it was accurate or not, this conservative
assessment of the declining pace of racial mixing ultimately reflected a
basic feeling that the entire question of amalgamation was not one of
great concern. Certainly mixing was not to be desired, but to these
conservative observers it did not represent a valid issue about which to
be bothered. Whites in the 1880s and early 1890s were relatively
confident of their control of race relations and the Negro, and therefore
perceived no reason to be alarmed at whatever negligible mixing might
be going on among the lower sorts of each race.

By the mid-1890s, however, this sentiment had begun to change.
The issue of racial mixing became one of paramount concern. A number
of factors had gradually undermined Southern whites' sense of security
and control over race relations. Among the most important of these was
a feeling that Negroes were retrogressing to a savage state. This fact was
particularly evident in the statistics which seemed to demonstrate a
precipitous rise in Negro criminality, most importantly in the rape of
white women and girls. White fears and paranoia about this trend, and
particularly about its sexual implications, found a powerful outlet in the
subject of amalgamation of the races. Indeed, concern over this issue
took on new and frenzied dimensions as whites came to insist upon the
maintenance of racial purity while simultaneously perceiving the rate of
miscegenation as rising all about them.

An early indication of this type of thinking is found in a curious
work entitled *Anthropology for the People* which appeared in 1891. The
book was written by the Reverend William H. Campbell of Richmond
under the pseudonym of "Caucasian." Subtitled "A Refutation of the
Theory of the Adamic Origin of All Races," it attempted to resurrect
wholesale the religious argument in favor of polygenism. Like Buckner
H. Payne, Campbell insisted that the major calamities detailed in the
Bible were the result of God's wrath against racial mixing. The Negro,
he contended, was a sub-human creature, so that mixing between whites
and blacks represented "unnatural and beastly unions--unions which
always bring a curse from the Almighty."[20] Because the races of man
were not of the same origin, Campbell declared that it was "plainly
God's will that they should be kept separate and distinct. To preserve
blood purity is a paramount duty, and the corollary of universal
brotherhood is brutalizing and destructive."[21] Convinced that
"miscegenation would be the destruction of both races," Campbell
argued that

> It was to preserve blood purity that instincts against admixture and racial antipathies were implanted in all human beings. Only men who give away to brutal passions cohabit with negresses, and nothing could be more shocking to a true woman, or more repulsive to her instincts, than the suggestion of marriage to a negro.[22]

Understandably, Campbell had no patience with those who would argue for the unity of mankind, for that ultimately would mean they condoned amalgamation. "If the generally accepted dogma of 'one blood' is to prevail," he warned,

> then the end must be mongrelism and all the evils we now contemplate with horror and alarm. If the effort to bring about a healthy change of public opinion fails, the white and black races will, in one or two generations more, be brought so near the same level, by the dangerous and repulsive theory of unity and equality, that prejudices will be obliterated and opposition will be a struggle against the inevitable. God pity those exposed to so horrible a fate, and arrouse them to a sense of their danger![23]

In 1900, Campbell's ideas were essentially repeated in a bizarre and even more vicious work by Charles Carroll of St. Louis. Carroll's *"The Negro a Beast"* also subscribed to a polygenist view of racial origins and held that the Negro was in fact more an advanced ape than a human being. Miscegenation, Carroll contended, was the greatest sin of all sins, and was the true reason that God had brought on the South's defeat and the destruction of slavery. Indeed, the Bible offered one long tale of God's anger at the white man's amalgamationist tendencies, and Jesus Christ had been sent "to redeem man from atheism, amalgamation, and idolatry."

> The drift of Bible history from the Creation to the birth of the Savior clearly indicates that he came to destroy man's social, political and religious equality with the Negro and mixed-bloods and the amalgamation to which these crimes inevitably lead, and to rebuild the barriers which God erected in the Creation between man and the ape.[24]

Carroll's ideas were not important for the points which they made or for the impact which they actually had on popular racial thought. Rather, their significance lies in their tone, for while Carroll was clearly on the irrational fringe of racist thought, the maliciousness of his pronouncements about the Negro and the intensity of his fear of amalgamation are reflections of wider sentiments about blacks and the issue of miscegenation held among whites at this time. Miscegenation had become an overriding concern to whites, often to the point that their fears as to its prevalence or impendence passed the limits of credibility.

No longer were whites confident that miscegenation was on the decline. William P. Calhoun was so concerned in 1902 over the threat of massive mixing that he urged that Negroes be forcibly moved to a separate state of their own "beyond the Mississippi."[25]   Benjamin Tillman, meanwhile, was haranguing his comrades in the United States Senate with warnings against the imminent dangers of widespread racial mixing. Were the structures of racial caste weakened even slightly, he declared in 1903, the Caucasian, the "highest and noblest of the five races," would disappear in an orgy of miscegenation. Tillman cited the apparent rise in Negro rapes of white women as proof that blacks were trying, in the boldest and most horrible form possible, to break down the lines of caste and thereby effect racial amalgamation.[26]

The connection between rape and the threat of amalgamation became a stock-in-trade for demagogic Southern politicians by the early 1900s. James K. Vardaman of Mississippi, for instance, harped on the issue throughout the opening decade of the century, admonishing that when miscegenation truly took hold, the white race would inevitably deteriorate and all intellectual, social, and economic progress in America would come to an end.[27]

It was not just politicians, though, who adopted this hysterical outlook. Ellen Barret Ligon, a doctor from Mobile, Alabama, expressed the sort of paranoia that gripped most Southerners (and many Northerners as well) at this time.   In a 1903 article in *Good Housekeeping*, she censured those ignorant Northern whites who made light of the dangers confronting the Caucasian race in America. Only once they knew what it was to live "in the midst of a whelming black flood, rolling its waves aginst the bulwarks of our civilizations, overflowing our public highways and public conveyances, threatening our homes," would Northerners truly understand the enormity of the situation. Black rapes of white women were constant occurrences, she declared, despite the vigilant efforts of police. "The white woman is the coveted desire of the negro man," asserted Ligon. "The despoiling of the white woman is his chosen vengeance."   Amalgamation was the great aspiration of the entire race, and whites must stand together to oppose it. "The white woman must be saved!" she exclaimed.[28]

By 1905, radical racism had crystallized into a concrete ideology. This was evident in the spate of books which appeared around this time to justify repressive policies against Afro-Americans while refining the warnings against the dangers of race mixing. William Benjamin Smith's *The Color Line: A Brief in Behalf of the Unborn* (1905) was a major statement of this position that was cited for the next decade by those who persisted in adhering to radical ideas. Smith was concerned that the lower elements of the white race were in imminent danger of being swamped by a tide of amalgamation. After all, marriage was ultimately a matter of personal taste, and even Smith recognized that attraction across racial lines was not at all uncommon. "It is only the sense of blood superiority, the pride of race, that has hitherto protected the white labourer," he contended. "Break this down or abate it, and he sinks swiftly to the level of the mongrel."[29]   Once the purity of the white race was breached at its lowest levels, the entire race would be endangered.

> Let the mongrel poison assail the humbler walks of life, and it will spread like a bubonic plague through the higher. The standing of the South would be lost irretrievably. Though her blood might still flow pure in myriad veins, yet who could prove it? The world would turn away from her, and point back the finger of suspicion and whisper "Unclean!"[30]

It was against this threat of corruption that Smith felt the South stood alone, misunderstood and persecuted by the misguided egalitarians of the North and the rest of the world. Meanwhile, the pressures from within were rising.

> The intense, the supreme yearning of large bodies of Negroes is for social recognition among the Whites–more especially for intermarriage with their haughty, old-time despisers. Who does not know this, simply does not understand the dominant facts of Southern life.[31]

Smith saw it as his duty to enlighten the world to this threat, for there could be no middle ground. "He that is not against amalgamation is for it. Who does not oppose must *ipso facto* favour it."[32]   "If the race barrier be removed," he gravely warned, " . . . the twilights of the century will gather upon a nation hopelessly sinking in the mire of Mongrelism."[33]

If Smith's book was firm in its admonitions about the dangers facing white America, Alexander Harvey Shannon's *Racial Integrity and Other Features of the Negro Problem* two years later was bitterly strident. Whereas Smith feared impending massive mixing, Shannon, a Methodist minister and former chaplain at the Mississippi State Penitentiary, saw miscegenation going on all about him. The mulatto population was increasing at a rapid rate, and it was the white man who was to blame.[34] Further, black and mulatto women were eager to become partners in this sinful alliance. Shannon felt that Negro women believed that a mixed-blooded child would have greater advantages in life, so that they freely gave themselves to white men.[35]   Indeed, Shannon was convinced that racial purity represented "unquestionably the most important feature of the negro problem."[36] Amalgamation, he declared, "involves a degree of moral depravity which, because it affects the very foundation of all virtue and of all character, cannot be overlooked."[37]

Radicalism found its quintessential expression, however, in the viciously anti-Negro works of Robert W. Shufeldt, a physician who was a major in the Army Medical Corps.   In 1907, Shufeldt published *The Negro: A Menace to American Civilization* and followed this with an expanded version under the title *Americas Greatest Problem: The Negro* in 1915. Shufeldt seemed to pull together all of the essential threads of radical racist thought, especially with regard to the threat of amalgamation and the necessary solution. Like Shannon, Shufeldt was convinced that amalgamation was proceeding at an accelerating pace. It was the natural result of close and prolonged contact between two divergent racial groups. Negro men, Shufeldt believed, were from an early age driven by a powerful desire "to carnally possess white maidens and women." This was but one indication of the fact that "in the negro, all passions, emotions and ambitions are almost wholly subservient to the sensual instinct." It was not simply Negro men who worried Shufeldt, though, for he saw Negro women as equally sensuous and lascivious. They "readily accept the sensuous embraces of white men, with characteristic avidity, and glory in the congress."[38] Because the Negro race was so lacking in morals, it was obviously highly dangerous to the whites who might be forced to live in proximity to it.

Yet it was not only passions of the Negro race with which Shufeldt was concerned, for miscegenation was by definition a biracial act. From Shufeldt's radical point of view, the Negro could not really be held responsible for "his animal nature any more than he is for the opportunities he takes to gratify the normal impulses that are a part of him."[39]   Ultimately, it was the white man (and woman) who was answerable for the mixing of the races. On the one hand, Shufeldt's "careful, extensive and direct personal examinations" led him to conclude that there was a large class of "degraded, sensuous white women" who preferred "to copulate with black men, on account of the unusual length of time that the act commonly lasts with them [and] on account of the immensity of their parts."[40] Fortunately, most women of the higher race were too refined, sensitive, and unpassionate to find such practices anything but repugnant. Among white men, however, this was not the case.   As Shufeldt lamented,

No such sentiments control the males of the dominant or advanced and cultured race with respect to seeking the females of the savage people. The pressure or demand to satisfy the sexual appetite in the male--even if he be an individual endowed with refinement--often completely blinds him, rendering him practically irresponsible in many cases, and, the desire for variety coming into play, carries him over almost anything.[41]

It was this uncontrollable sexual drive among white men, in combination with the natural sensuality of Negro women and their great desire to bear mixed-blooded children for the advantages they would have in later life, which led Shufeldt to fear for the racial integrity of the white race in America. In this regard, Shufeldt's books offer a striking exposition of the sort of fears which seem to have underlain much of the radical racist denunciation of race mixing. Ultimately, it was not really the black man who was to be feared so much as it was the white. Negroes were not dangerous because they were going to force racial mixing on the white man, but because they threatened, by their own apparently passionate natures, to arouse inner desires which whites were striving so hard to control or suppress within themselves.[42] Certainly this sort of tension was evident in the fiction of such radical writers as Thomas Dixon, but it was also there in the radicals' obsession with sexual matters in general, as well as with the alleged sexual capabilities of Negroes and the freedom with which they were believed to exercise them.[43] Shufeldt's two books reflect this inner strain, as they are strewn with illustrative photographs (as he probably would have termed them) of naked black and mulatto men and women. There is a sense of a rising level of anxiety as the books progress, as Shufeldt's tensions found relief in an increasingly bitter and irrational denunciation of Negroes and the very idea of interracial sex.

In the end, Shufeldt, like a growing number of radicals, could conceive of no practical means of dealing with this situation. In a sense, the resolution of this dilemma was central to the irrational racial segregation that was imposed on the South during this period. Yet for Shufeldt and numerous others, even segregation was not adequate. As he wrote in 1907, "If they [whites and Negroes] are left to occupy the same geographical area, as they now do, they will continue to interbreed, in spite of anything man can do to prevent the disaster."[44] Within a few centuries, the black race would have been completely absorbed by the white, with all the evil effects which that entailed. Shufeldt consequently staunchly supported the adoption of "any rational scheme" on the part of the federal government to transport Negroes out of the country. He admitted that few would want to go, for he believed it their intention "to stay right here and do all the harm to our country they can," but he had no sympathy for any arguments to the contrary. "No," he adamantly announced,

> were it possible, I would be in favor of shipping every living one of them back to the region they came from, whether it pleased them or not. I am so loyal to anything that will sustain the purity of the best of Indo-European blood in the United States; drain it of superstition of all kinds; purge it of crime and immorality; preserve its integrity,--that I would see every negro in America at the bottom

of the Pacific Ocean, or howling in the desert of the Soudan, before I would allow them for any consideration whatsoever, to jeopardize by race intermixture the civilization it has taken us centuries to establish.[45]

Ideas like this have an irrational sound to them, but they represent a logical extension of the basic premises of radical racist thought. Indeed, Shufeldt was certainly correct in his insistence that as long as Negroes and whites continued to live together they would inevitably have sexual contact. From the perspective that such contact threatened the future of the white race, ultimately there was no other viable solution to the problem than to rid the entire nation of the black menace.

Radicals never swayed enough people to their side to achieve a program of mass deportation, but on the local level in various parts of the South, distinct efforts were made to cope with the problem of race mixing. Many white Southerners were acutely conscious of the paradox of public policies being enacted to separate the races while covert mixing was still widely condoned. In January, 1907, J. H. Currie, a district attorney in Meridian, Mississippi, spoke out forcefully against the "curse of miscegenation" which was corrupting the blood of the white South:

> The accursed shadow of miscegenation hangs over the South to-day like a pall of hell. We talk much of the Negro question and all of its possible ramifications and consequences, but, gentlemen, the trouble is not far afield. Our own people, our white men with their black concubines, are destroying the integrity of the Negro race, raising up a menace to the white race, lowering the standard of both races and preparing the way for riot, mob, criminal assaults, and finally, a death struggle for racial supremacy. The trouble is at our own door. We have tolerated this crime long enough, and if our country is not run by policy rather than by law, then it is time to rise up and denounce this sin of the earth.[46]

The *Star* of Monroe, Louisiana, likewise editorialized about the "destructive crime of miscegenation:"

> There can be no greater wrong done the people of any community than for public sentiment to permit and tolerate this growing and destructive crime of miscegenation, yet in many towns and cities of Louisiana, especially, there are today white men cohabiting with Negro women, who have sweet and lovable families. This is a crime that becomes almost unbearable, and should bring the blush of shame to every man's cheek who dares flaunt his debased and degrading conceptions of morality in the eyes of self-respecting men and women.[47]

The New Orleans *Times-Democrat* meanwhile carried on a strong campaign during the first decade of the century for laws which would punish white men who maintained illicit relations with Negroes. "No one can deny that the revolting practice exists in Louisiana," the paper editorialized on one occasion,

> or that it threatens, not alone untold damage to the living, but future disaster. The evil is repulsive enough as we see it today, but the logical consequence of its continuance and tolerance must appall even those degraded by its practice. *There is no defense for miscegenation, not even a semblance of apology.*[48]

Organized efforts to combat miscegenation developed in a number of Southern localities. In St. Francisville, Louisiana, citizens met to deal with what one speaker termed the "yellow peril" of the South. "Every man familiar with conditions in our midst," journalist Ray Stannard Baker reported the speaker saying, "knows that the enormous increase in persons of mixed blood is due to men of the white race openly keeping Negro women as concubines."[49] Citizens of Vicksburg, under the leadership of Harris Dickson, a journalist, novelist, lawyer, and municipal reformer, formed an Anti-Miscegnation League to prevent racial mixing and to punish offenders of both races. The League sought to secure evidence against these offenders by distributing to its members and other sympathetic individuals printed forms to be filled out with names and other information about persons involved in interracial sexual alliances. The League then publicized the names of the offenders, and apparently had some success in breaking up a number of particularly flagrant cases of miscegenation.[50] A similar organization also sprang up in Port Gibson, Mississippi, south of Vicksburg.

In all of these cases, the primary concern was with the white men involved in illicit interracial affairs. Responsible white leaders recognized that it was the white race itself that was actually to blame for the extent of race mixing in America. Dickson personally believed that lower-class whites viewed mixing as a matter of course, but many other critics of white racial impurity tended to emphasize that it was often leading members of the community who indulged in these dangerous and forbidden pleasures. Even Ray Stannard Baker, an otherwise sympathetic commentator in regard to race relations and Negro rights, became convinced by his survey of conditions in the South that the number of miscegenetic affairs was "appalling." Yet he too stressed the irony of the white man's role in the amalgamation of the races. Whites increasingly declaimed against amalgamation and mongrelization, he noted, while mixing continued unabated. White Southerners were "striving to keep the Negro in his place as a Negro," Baker wrote, although at the same time "making him more and more like a white man."[51]

Paradoxically, by the time Southerners began to exert concerted efforts to combat the miscegenation they saw all about them, the very radical racism which had spawned their perceptions was beginning to wane. Perhaps the viciousness of writers like Shannon and Shufledt can be explained at least in part by their sense that the message of radical racism was losing its appeal by 1908 to 1910. Conservative outlooks were reasserting themselves, possibly because radicalism had gone beyond the bounds of reality in its jeremiads about the threat of amalgamation facing the South and the nation. Certainly one sign of the conservative resurgence was the expression of new (or old) ideas about the limited extent of mixing. As early as 1904, Thomas Nelson Page, the Virginia novelist and apologist for the Old South (who had himself been radicalized around 1898-1902), was arguing that at least "intermixture between the pure negro and the pure white is growing less all the time."[52]

Perhaps the diatribes of radical racists did have some effect, for by the end of the decade numerous observers testified to a decline in racial mixing. Edwin Henderson Randle of Tennessee, otherwise a strongly anti-Negro writer, commented in 1910 that the prejudice against amalgamation was rapidly increasing while the number of mulatto children dropped. "I do not say white men are getting more virtuous," Randle explained, "but they are getting more cautious."[53] Edward Eggleston, a Virgina planter and amateur ethnologist, also evidenced a radical outlook in his 1913 volume, *The Ultimate Solution of the American Negro Problem.* Yet Eggleston was unwilling to admit that "the abomination of amalgamation" posed any real threat to the South, because whites simply would not accept it.[54] Charles H. McCord similarly affirmed that while amalgamation had once gone on to "an appreciable extent," it had not occurred to the degree that many alarmist writers claimed. Further, McCord was confident that the pace of interracial mixing was dropping even more.[55] Even Thomas Pierce Bailey's 1914 summary of Southern racial orthodoxy averred that miscegenation was declining, although he could still castigate those "substantial, sometimes educated men" who continued to indulge in "habitual concubinage." Fortunately, Bailey felt, "race prejudice, or conscientious scruples, or fear of being exposed" were working to discourage such illicit affairs.[56]

Clearly white opinions about racial amalgamation and fear regarding the threat it represented for the white race fluctuated with the tenor of overall racial attitudes and anxieties. Up to the 1890s, whites were relatively disinclined to view amalgamation as a threat because they were confident about the race relations situation. As white paranoia and tension rose in the next two decades, however, many commentators became acutely concerned about the degree of race mixing they perceived existing around them and what this evil augered for the future of the white race. By about 1910, such anxieties had begun to abate, so that most whites relaxed once more into the confident belief that miscegenation was a limited if undesirable phenomenon which was gradually ebbing as white racial pride rose.

3

Opinions and anxieties about the extent of amalgamation and the dangers it represented may have oscillated between Reconstruction and the First World War, but the same cannot be said about basic attitudes regarding the effects of race mixing. Whites throughout this period remained firmly convinced that the results of miscegenation were necessarily bad. This stand was closely linked to white attitudes about the nature of the mulatto himself, and ultimately to fundamental conceptions about the meaning of race and racial differences.

The belief that race mixing had deleterious consequences chiefly derived from notions of white superiority and black inferiority. Given this basic perspective, it was only reasonable to conclude that miscegenation was a mistake. John H. Van Evrie's contention that mulattoism represented an "abnormal or diseased condition" was but a blatant statement of the sort of thinking which pervaded white attitudes about the consequences of mixing two disparate racial groups. White Americans were generally rather pragmatic in their racial views--their sense of superiority to the Negro resulted quite directly from their immediate perception of his appearance, lifestyle, and accomplishments.[57] As a result, aversion to amalgamation seemed a natural response, for it was only a logical assumption that mixing a superior and inferior stock would not produce an individual equal to the original superior type. Thomas Underwood Dudley, the Protestant Episcopal bishop of Kentucky, caught this spirit in an 1885 article in *Century Magazine* which denounced race mixing. Dudley noted that:

> Instinct and reason, history and philosophy, science and revelation, all alike cry out against the degradation of the race by the free commingling of the tribe which is highest with that which is lowest in the scale of development. The process of selection which nature indicates as the method of most rapid progress indignantly refuses to be thus set at naught.[58]

As the intensity of white racism waxed after 1890, popular writers became more determined to demonstrate the negative effects of miscegenation. Often these warnings reflected the same interworkings of

Darwinism, Lamarckianism, and polygenism which characterized the thoughts of academicians of the period and their understanding of race traits and instincts.

John T. Morgan, for instance, was a Senator from Alabama who became increasingly radical in his racial outlook during the 1890s. He emphasized the detrimental effects the white race would suffer should race crossing become widespread. The result, he charged, "would be to lower the whites to the level of the intellectual, moral and social condition of the Negroes. It would destroy the white race."[59] Morgan believed that a mixing of the blood of the two races would "Africanize" the whites in "their social instincts and in their ideas of government."[60] Such a view rested on the idea that each race possessed distinct racial characterists or traits which, while essentially social in nature, were nevertheless transmitted biologically from one generation to the next. Like so many other whites of his time, Morgan seemed to see black traits as more powerful than white ones, since the former would overwhelm the latter if the two were combined in a single individual.

The *Independent* similarly noted that "The meaning of miscegenation is a downward drift--a fact so obvious that it scarcely needs arguing." Any white man who married a Negro was doing a great injustice to his posterity because the two strains were never intended to mix. A thorough commingling of the blood of the two races, the periodical suggested, "would take us as a nation from a place among the highest of a splendid race, and set us low among the lowest."[61]

The idea that racial mixing resulted in degeneration grew out of the belief that black racial traits were themselves inferior to those of the white man. These traits had been developed in the early stages of the Negro's evolution in Africa, yet they still marked him as a type distinct from the white man. Even those who were somewhat optimistic over the Negro race's progress under the influence and guidance of the white man remained convinced that deep inside the American Negro retained virtually all of his original African characteristics. To those less able or willing to see such progress, the explanation for the Negro's inability to function in white America was also to be found in his African heritage.

"The Negro of to-day is the product of his sad and dismal past," announced the Reverend A. W. Pitzer of Washington, D.C., at an 1890 conference on "the Negro Problem." "The wild, naked, man-eating savages of equatorial Africa are of the same blood as the Negro of this Republic."[62] Philip Alexander Bruce was likewise struck by the tenacity of the Negro's African racial traits:

> Their original spirit as a race has not been radically modified by transplantation to the American continent, the vigor and tenacity of the fundamental qualities having only grown more clearly perceptible

with the progress of time, these fundamental qualities appearing to be incapable of alteration, however favorable circumstances may be to it.[63]

To Bruce, as well as to most white Americans, there was ultimately little difference between the most and the least cultured and educated Negroes in terms of their inner traits. Cataloging these qualities, Bruce noted that:

> Both are unable to resist the solicitations of their physical instincts, both are more or less superstitious, both live wholly in the present, both show the same turbulent spirit when their vanity is inflated, the same lack of fortitude in danger, the same want of the power of concentrating their faculties in the form of continuous attention or resolution, the same respect for unscrupulous force, the same abject submissiveness when overawed, the same indifference to suffering in animals, the same callousness associated with amiability, the same harshness and tyranny when in the possession of power, the same insensibility to whatever is elevated in life and beautiful in the universe.[64]

These were the sort of characteristics which Alabama Senator John T. Morgan feared would "Africanize" the white man if they should enter his blood through race mixing. The underlying element in this view was the belief that the two races were so distinct and different that their traits could not be blended harmoniously. J. L. M. Curry, the general agent of both the Peabody and John F. Slater Education Funds, expressed this position in 1899. There were in America, he said,

> two distinct peoples, with irreconcilable racial characteristics and diverse historical antecedents. The Caucasian and the negro are not simply unlike, but they are contrasted, and are as far apart as any other two races of human beings. They are unassimilable and immiscible without rapid degeneracy.

The white man, of course, had a heritage of impressive achievements in art, literature, science, religion, and other aspects of cultural advancement. The African, however, had made little or no progress for nearly four thousand years. For thousands of years, Curry declared,

> there lies behind the race one dreary, unrelieved, monotonous chapter of ignorance, nakedness, superstition, savagery. All efforts to reclaim, civilize, Christianize, have been disastrous failures, except what has been accomplished in this direction in the United States.[65]

Contemporary race theory, at least on the popular level, held that a race's accomplishments were both cause and consequence of its basic race traits. From this perspective, whites could look at the cultural level of blacks in Africa and America and find an explanation in the race's fundamental composition. Whether operating from a Lamarckian or Darwinist hereditarian understanding of the importance and transmission of race traits (or some combination of the two), whites were convinced that Negroes were inferior and that the fault lay in their remote racial history. Paul B. Barringer, a professor of medicine and Chairman of the Faculty at the University of Virginia, put the matter quite bluntly in an address in 1900. "If you scratch a negro you will find a savage," he declared. The phrase rather summed up white understanding of the Negro, and indeed of anyone with some degree of black blood in his background. Race traits and instincts were deeply ingrained and largely impervious to change or alteration. Barringer was an avowed Darwinian, convinced that "sociological problems are in most cases biological problems," because "the ontogeny is the repetition of the phylogeny." More specifically, this meant that

> the life history is the repetition of the race history. . . .the life history of any individual, of any type, unless modified by forces of an exceptional character, will tend to conform to the lines of ancestral traits.[66]

For Barringer, this explained the nature and direction of Negro life in America--Negroes were simply acting in accordance with the natural tendencies inherent in their hereditary make-up. Most obviously, in Barringer's opinion, the young of the race were reverting or retrogressing to a savage state, but given the Negro's racial heritage, this was to be expected. "Fifty centuries of savagery in the blood," claimed Barringer,

> cannot be held down by two centuries of forced good behavior if the controlling influences which held down the savagery are withdrawn as they have been in this case. The language and forms of civilization may be maintained, but the savage nature remains. It is the nature that makes the criminal and imperils a civilization, not the language, the skin or the clothes.[67]

Barringer's particular concern was with the tendencies towards retrogression he perceived among Negroes. This was a major facet of radical racist thought, and in the years after 1900 other radical writers gave similar emphasis to the crucial role played by race traits and instincts and its meaning for the black race and its half-breed descendants. In 1907, John Ambrose Price, in a bitter denunciation of the Negro, emphasized the permanence of racial characteristics:

> Whether the white man goes to Africa or the black man comes to America, the inherited racial distinction remains, and no change of

environment can make the Anglo-Saxon descend to the African or lift the negro to the high plane of equality with the Anglo-Saxon; the hereditary racial qualities will remain under any environment.[68]

Edward Eggleston similarly linked the Negro's present status to his racial history. "The deficiencies of the Negro are racial, deep-rooted, and of long standing," he fervently declared. In his view, there was not justification

for attempts to separate his present condition from his past environment, or his natural inheritance from his long line of stupid, indifferent, savage ancestors. Past history of the Negro variety of human kind and his present-day traits and tendencies are inseparable.[69]

The overall implication of this emphasis upon racial traits was that the black man was so different from the white that he could not be treated in the same manner. John Moffatt Mecklin's *Democracy and Race Friction* (1914) provides a concise statement of this position and its meaning for social and racial policy. Mecklin was an Alabaman who taught philosophy at a number of Northern schools, including Lafayette College and the University of Pittsburgh. His thinking reflected a combination of Lamarckian and Darwinian concepts. At one point he would emphasize the distinctly social nature of cultural characteristcs, but at another explain that the capacity to absorb certain social and cultural characteristcs necessitated the right type of "hereditary instinctive tendencies." In general, though, Mecklin was convinced of the important role played by racial traits and instincts in shaping the life of an individual and his race. Most significantly for Mecklin, this meant that

The Negro is not merely an educated Anglo-Saxon with a black skin. There are peculiarities in the functioning of his instincts, impulses, emotions, and modes of response to external stimuli fundamentally different from those of the white.[70]

Any racial policy which failed to take this into consideration was doomed from the beginning.

The crux of America's race problem, Mecklin believed, lay in the fact that the racial instincts of the Negro were not suited to life in the white man's advanced civilization. The "tropical exuberance of temperament," explained Mecklin,

which makes the Negro extreme in joy or grief, in anger or affection, together with his strongly sensuous nature are his greatest handicaps in meeting the stern demands of a stable civilisation. They make him an alien in many respects in the midst of a highly rationalised social order. . . Such traits are hereditary, the result of ages of fixed group life. Hence they persist after many generations of contact with a higher civilisation and after the last vestige of social heritage from Africa has disappeared.[71]

This line of thinking stood behind most radical efforts to circumscribe or eliminate a variety of the Negro's rights and privileges. Radicals like John Ambrose Price, Edward Eggleston, and William B. Smith would have greatly eliminated educational opportunities for blacks, because, as Smith explained, education could have little real effect in elevating the race. Afro-Americans were handicapped by a fundamental intellectual inferiority, and any efforts to overcome that fact were wasteful.[72] Similar arguments could also be used to deny Afro-Americans the right to vote, serve on juries, or to hold public office. Negroes were aliens, made so by their inherent racial characteristics, and would only endanger the delicate institutions of the white man's democracy.

The notion of the importance of inherent racial differences was most manifest, however, in white sentiment opposing race mixing. Amalgamation would destroy the harmonious homogeneity of race traits in the blood of the white man, eventually with disastrous consequences. As John Moffatt Mecklin affirmed,

> Continuity of culture depends in a very profound sense upon the continuity of the racial type of which that culture is an expression. Race in its widest sense is, like the individual, a psychophysical unity. The continuity of race type, of course, can only be attained through control of marriage relations.[73]

Intermingling of the blood of the two races, he explained, meant much more than merely the union of two individuals. In time, it would bring "a profound modification of the cultural ideals of the white through the resulting transformation of the ethnic background of those ideals." If the white race should lose its "self-conscious ethnic personality," the factor which made civilization possible, calamitous results would ensue. Consequently, he insisted,

> The preservation of the unbroken, self-conscious existence of the white or dominant ethnic group is synonymous with the preservation of all that has meaning and inspiration in its past and hope for its future.[74]

Mecklin's conclusions were derived from a rather sophisticated, well-reasoned line of thinking. In the end, though, they represented the same sort of thinking characteristic of most whites of the period. More radical writers merely offered their arguments in a more strident tone,

but were still operating from essentially the same basic interpretation of
the meaning and significance of inherent racial differences. Robert W.
Shufeldt, for instance, spoke quite bluntly of the dangers involved in
mixing the "cannibalistic blood" of the Negro with the refined blood of
the white man.[75] E. H. Randle warned that the mixing of the opposing
natures of white and black races would bring "the ruin of one of the
most moral, polished, and cultured people on earth," causing "a shudder
of horror to thrill the world."[76] Similar thoughts bothered Thomas Pierce
Bailey. Convinced of the natural inferiority of the Negro, Bailey worried
that amalgamation would have a deleterious effect on the white man,
lowering the potency of white blood and weakening white cultural
characteristics.[77] A. H. Shannon stressed the destruction of the "inherent
qualities and racial characteristics" of the white race if widespread mixing
should occur. A "heritage of moral degradation" would be imposed on
the white man which would even outlast the signs of physical or mental
degeneration which would inevitably result from mixing with the inferior
Negro.[78]

By the mid-1910s, some of the spirit behind radical racism had
been shifted to the more respectable doctrine of eugenics. Eugenists
sharply disavowed the Larmarckian notion of acquired racial
characteristics. In their admonitions against indiscriminate race mixing
they nevertheless relied upon ideas about inherent racial traits which
were little different from earlier, more openly Lamarckian arguments.
Madison Grant's *The Passing of the Great Race* (1916), in some ways the
culmination of the racist arguments of the past half-century,[79] evidences
this sort of thought. Negroes, Grant maintained, quickly reverted to
their ancestral racial natures once removed from the direct supervision
and control of whites, for their basic racial traits had not been altered.
As a result, Grant emphasized the importance of "transmitting in
unimpaired purity the blood inheritance" of the white race so that the
higher races might be maintained.[80] The next year, Seth K. Humphrey, a
Massachusetts nativist and eugenist, stressed similar ideas in his
Mankind: Racial Values and the Racial Prospect, a popular treatise on
eugenist principles. Humphrey espoused a notion of the permanence of
the "germ-plasm" of individuals and races derived chiefly from the work
of the biologist August Weissman thirty years earlier. This notion lent
itself to the same view of "inheritable character traits" which marked
earlier Lamarckian thinking and therefore to a condemnation of race
mixing. Humphrey held that the mixing of unlike and conflicting
characteristics of superior and inferior races necessarily brought disastrous
results. This was especially true in the inheritance of mental qualities:

> Not only is there uncertainty as to what such an individual's [of
> mixed racial background] inheritance will be; there is no certainty

that from the mixed collection at his disposal he will draw
characteristics in sufficient harmony with each other to make a
workable inheritance. This is the crucial fact in race mixture. . . . an
individual so constituted cannot come to efficient development, for
he has not the unincumbered qualities of any one of the stock which
entered into his inheritance.[81]

Both Darwinists and Lamarckists subscribed to essentially the
same notions about race traits and inherent racial differences. From
Reconstruction to the First World War, most Americans probably fell in
the Lamarckian camp,[82] but in the end the distinction between the two
doctrines was really not too important. White Americans looked at
blacks, saw how blacks' physical appearance, intellectual capabilities, and
cultural patterns and beliefs differed from their own, and explained these
differences in terms of inherent racial characteristics. Differences were
generally seen as the result of divergent evolutionary development,
particularly disparities in the geo-climatic conditions the two races
experienced, but the overall effect was that the white race was superior
and the black race inferior. To white Americans, this was patently
evident in the comparison of the white race's impressive history with the
Negro's heritage of savagery, superstition, and immorality in Africa.

Given this basic set of racial beliefs, the unavoidable inference
was that amalgamation was a grievous mistake. It mixed and/or jumbled
the inherent traits of each race, distorting them and erasing the
distinctions which marked the blood of the white man as superior. Once
mixed with the inferior qualities of the black race, whites would no
longer be able to maintain the precious institutions and cultural
achievements which were the visible legacy of their superiority. Perhaps
most important, though, because amalgamation combined the traits of the
two races, its product was not literally a white man. The logic of
contemporary understanding of hereditary processes dictated that such a
being could not possibly be equal to its superior white progenitors, for it
also possessed some of the traits of an inferior race. It was in this vein
that white perceptions of the nature of the mulatto himself entered into
the argument against racial amalgamation.

4

If white Americans were uniformly adamant in their opposition
to racial amalgamation, they were not as consistent in their attitudes
about mulattoes. In general, overall assessments of the nation's mixed-
blooded population were negative, but the intensity and line of thought
behind this basic position varied according to whites' particular racial
perspective. Radicals were both more conscious and more disturbed

about the mulatto than were conservatives, so that the two groups tended to emphasize different aspects of the subject.

In one area, however, there was considerable agreement. Virtually all white writers were convinced that mulattoes were more intelligent that pure blacks, although still not the equal of the white man. This was almost an ineluctable conclusion, given the fundamental white belief in the intellectual superiority of the white race. The idea that mulattoes gained a degree of intellectual superiority to pure blacks through their inheritance of white abilities was an old one in white racial thought, but it had considerable popularity in this period as well. In 1889, for instance, Philip Alexander Bruce commented that,

> A transfusion of Caucasian blood seems to quicken the African mind, and as the volume of that transfusion is increased, there is a nearer approach in many important particulars, to the intellectual traits of the white people.[83]

At the Montgomery Conference on Race Conditions and Problems in the South in 1900, John Roach Straton of Mercer University in Macon, Georgia also commented that mulattoes were often "strengthened in mental vigor by infusions of white blood."[84]

The rising tide of radical racist thought did not significantly alter this idea. Paul Barringer admitted in 1900 that mulattoes did show more intelligence than pure blacks,[85] a point also emphasized by George T. Winston, President of the North Carolina College of Agricultural and Mechanical Arts. While race mixing was degrading to the white race, Winston explained, it was not entirely harmful to the Negro. Mulattoes derived from their white blood a "quicker, brighter, and more easily refined" nature which had proved to be of considerable benefit to the race as a whole.[86] Even the most extreme writers were inclined to admit this fact. William Benjamin Smith, for example, declared that "it seems vain to deny that the mixed blood is notably more intelligent than the pure black," and attributed this superiority to the mulatto's white blood.[87] A. H. Shannon likewise claimed that the infusion of white blood carried with it intellectual powers superior to the pure black, but "inferior indeed" to those of the white race. Mixing of the intellectual capabilities of the two races, he contended, resulted in a rough averaging of the two levels in the mulatto.[88] Numerous other such writers also testified to the increased intellectual powers of mulattoes, but always were careful to point out that they still fell short of the pure-blooded white.[89]

When conservative views began to reassert themselves, writers continued to hold to this traditional view. Alfred Holt Stone, a Mississippi planter widely regarded for his statements on race relations, announced in 1908 that "There can no longer be any question as to the superior intelligence of the mulatto over the Negro--of his higher average potential capacity."[90]   The historian Albert Bushnell Hart, surveying life in the South in 1910, similarly noted that while blacks were clearly inferior to whites, a considerable portion of the mulatto population approximated the white race in ability.[91]

Unanimity in recognizing the mulatto's superior mental capabilities did not carry over, however, to other assessments of his characteristics.   Whereas conservatives seemed to take a general stance that the mulatto was somewhere between the white man and the Negro in most traits, radicals loudly denounced mixed-bloods for their physical degeneracy and gross moral weaknesses.   The notion that mulattoes were physically weak was a direct outgrowth of earlier polygenist beliefs which held that crossing of two distinct species necessarily resulted in a weakened hybrid offspring.   This same thinking is evident in William H. Campbell's openly polygenist *Anthropology for the People*.   "It is a well-known fact in the Southern States," affirmed Campbell,

> that the mulatto and his progeny are more feeble than either of the parent stock, and much more predisposed to certain diseases, as consumption and scrofulous affections. . . . A race of hybrids cannot perpetuate themselves; they die out under the law of hybridity and reversion. . . .   Nature avenges the unnatural crime by excision.

Campbell repeated the oft-heard statement that mulattoes rarely lived to old age.   His own "extensive observation" had not uncovered a single mixed-blood of great age.[92]

Other radical writers were less explicitly within this polygenist school, yet they generally held similar views as to the mulatto's physical deficiencies.   W. S. McCurley, discussing the "Impossibility of Racial Amalgamation" in 1899, emphasized the physical weakness of the mixed-blood as a "perfectly natural" consequence of mating two races so unlike each other.[93]   Paul Barringer likewise noted what "fitting monuments" the frail mulattoes were to the shameful mixing of the races, for they demonstrated "the inherent physical weakness of hybridization".[94]   Citing the pronouncements of Nathaniel Southgate Shaler, James Bryce, and the studies of the Civil War Provost-Marshal-General's Bureau, William Benjamin Smith also stressed the deterioration which characterized the mulatto.[95]   A. H. Shannon reiterated the same notions, emphasizing the mulatto's short life span and his susceptibility to venereal disease and consumption which were linked to the immoral nature of his origins.[96]

Nevertheless, it was not so much physical weakness as moral depravity which radicals most associated with the mulatto.   Campbell insisted that the mixed-blood was "notoriously sensual, treacherous and brutal."   Mulattoes received none of the white man's sensitive moral nature, but were instead non-moral. As a result, they had "greater capacity for mischief, and as a class are lazy, vicious, cruel, malignant and treacherous."[97] Campbell's bitter words were echoed by others of like perspective. Edward Eggleston commented on the viciousness and criminality of mixed-bloods,[98] while A. H. Shannon cursed the mulatto as the very embodiment of immorality. Mulattoes were possessed by an "innate depravity" as a result of their conception in the sinful union of the white man and Negro. How could any sort of moral sense develop in a creature born out of a "lustful debauch"? Shannon was distraught that the federal government would give political appointments to these immoral beings, or that they would be employed as the teachers, preachers, and other leaders of the black race. This represented an "almost universal suspension of moral and ethical standards," he charged, for what type of morality could the mulatto inculcate in the race? What sort of example could he set, representing as he did the epitome of "moral degradation"?[99]

Shannon's ravings about mulatto immorality bordered on the irrational, yet they were but an extreme expression of a more widespread belief that mulattoes were indeed deficient in moral qualities. To a considerable degree, this belief derived from the white notion that mulattoes were particularly prone to criminality. Whites were much concerned with the issue of Negro criminality in general around the turn of the century, but many were convinced that mixed-bloods stood behind a disproportionate amount of this activity. E. H. Randle believed that people of mixed blood were inevitably restless, discontented, violent, and revolutionary because of their discordant racial background.[100] Perhaps this explained their criminal proclivities. William H. Campbell, on the other hand, cited the innate immorality of the mulatto as the source of trouble. Indeed, Campbell insisted that not only did mulatto criminals everywhere far outnumber black and white lawbreakers, they were also distinguished "in the atrocity and brutality of their crimes." Campbell even blamed the alledgedly greater intelligence of the mulatto for his ability to outdo his "black brethren" "in the annals of crime."[101]

Campbell's ideas about mulatto criminality were drawn in part from the writings of a Mississippian, Horace Smith Fulkerson. Fulkerson's *The Negro; As He Was; As He Is; As He Will Be* (1887) greatly emphasized the criminal nature of the Negro in general, but made a special point of noting the disproportionately large amount of crime committed by mulattoes. It was necessary, Fulkerson urged, that all individuals of Negro blood be deported so as to preserve peace and order in America.[102] Mrs. L. H. Harris, a resident of Rockmart, Georgia, struck an even more hysterical tone in 1889 when she described the dread horror under which the Southern white woman was forced to live. The threat of rape was everywhere and increasing as the "Negro brute" roamed freely over the countryside seeking out his innocent victims. "He is nearly always a mulatto," she affirmed in frenzy, and even blamed his actions upon the fact that he was of mixed blood. The mulatto, she explained, had "enough white blood in him to replace [the Negro's] native humility and cowardice with Caucasian audacity." The mulatto rapist, she believed, was

> always above average in intelligence. He is sure to be a bastard, and probably the offspring of a bastard mother. Can such a creature be morally responsible? His lust is a legacy multiplied by generations of brutal ancestors.

This "mongrel of civilization" was a "hideous monster, a possible menace to every home in the South," she warned. "He has the savage nature and the murderous instincts of the wild beast plus the cunning and lust of a fiend." Only when whites all over the nation understood this fact would they appreciate the need for dealing harshly with all Negroes who questioned their place.[103]

For many white Americans, particularly in the South, there was a fine line between overt criminal activity and agitation against the prevailing racial system. This was another sphere in which whites censured the behavior of mulattoes. Many were entirely convinced that mulattoes were the chief sources of unrest and discontent among Negroes. In 1886, for instance, W. C. Benet argued that "the mulatto class has supplied nearly all the stirrers-up of strife between the two races."[104] Mulattoes represented "a menace to the Negro race" because they awakened false desires among the masses of blacks. They were constantly dissatisfied with their own racial position and aspired to greater rights and privileges. To whites, this ultimately meant "social equality." John Ambrose Price expressed a common white sentiment in noting that

> Generally speaking, those who teach and practice social equality are the illegitimate mulatto idealists of the most erroneous type. To this class belongs the trouble of the future.[105]

The great majority of Southern Negroes, he insisted, had no desire for social equality, realizing "that such a thing is dangerous to their country and the welfare of their people." The real source of agitation in this regard was among the educated leaders of the race who were predominantly of mixed blood.[106]

Alfred Holt Stone gave the greatest attention to this facet of the race problem. Stone was highly conscious of the role played by mulattoes in American race relations:

Through the medium of race papers and magazines, the pulpit, industrial and political gatherings and associations the mulatto yields a tremendous influence over the Negro. It is here that his importance as a factor in whatever problems may arise from the Negro's presence in this country becomes manifest, and the working out of such problems may be advanced or retarded, just as he wisely or unwisely plays the part which fate–or Providence–has assigned him.[107]

Most blacks, Stone maintained, were docile, affectionate, good-natured, and largely content with their position in life. "The racial agitation for 'rights' of one kind or another," he affirmed, "is not the work of the Negro." In virtually all instances, "it is the mulatto who is the heart and soul of these complaints."[108] Stone was sure that,

If the statues of those states which have been charged with discrimination against the Negro were not in any wise enforceable against the mulatto, . . .America's race problem would speedily resolve itself into infinitely simpler proportions.

Were mulattoes only granted those rights which as individuals and as a class they felt themselves entitled by their education, culture, and attainments, he believed, there would probably be much less agitation about the denial of rights to the Negro.[109] Stone evinced little sympathy for these mulatto troublemakers. "One of the most pernicious influences", he declared,

today operating upon the general situation [of race relations] is the Northern mulatto agitator. He is generally utterly ignorant of Southern conditions, and frequently so of the Southern negro whom he would keep in constant turmoil.[110]

Stone nevertheless recognized that some sort of place needed to be made for the mulatto in American race relations. Mixed-bloods were the leaders of the Negro race–the educated, refined, substantial men who largely shaped its attitudes and orientation. This was another very common white perception of the mulatto. Indeed, whites for the most part were convinced that the only Negroes who had every evidenced particular ability or intelligence were of mixed blood. "So far," Philip Alexander Bruce noted in 1889, "the only persons of unusual capacity the Negro race has produced have been men who were sprung, either directly or indirectly, from white ancestry."[111] Two years later his brother made a similar claim:

It is certainly a most suggestive fact that the majority of the few negroes, who have attained prominence, have belonged to the shades intermediate between the white race and the pure blooded black.

> Every remove from the latter involves a distinct gain in intelligence and vivacity. . . . It is a matter of every day occurrence that, in all employments, open to the negro, that call for the exercise of something more than mere muscular vigor, the preference is given to the mulatto.[112]

George T. Winston similarly declared that,

> if you strike from [the Negro race's] records all that Mulattoes have said and done, little would be left.   Wherever work requiring refinement, extra intelligence, and executive ability is performed, you will find it usually directed by Mulattoes.[113]

Those whites most critical of the Negro were also persuaded that mulattoes represented the outstanding figures in the race. H. E. Belin of Charleston, South Carolina declared that the so-called "Negroes" who had in any way distinguished themselves were in fact of mixed blood, and that it was to their "mixed lineage that their superiority is due."[114] The eugenist Seth K. Humphrey concurred that,

> when a "Negro" attains to more than an imitative success in those matters which pertain exclusively to the White man, and through the ages were beyond the attainment of the African, it is a sensible conclusion that he is dominated by his White characteristics.[115]

Even the fair-minded journalist Ray Stannard Baker was convinced by his observation of Negro life that "most of the leading men of the race today in every line of activity are mulattoes."[116]

Baker was disinclined to generalize as to the cause of this phenomenon, but to most other whites the explanation was a simple one. The mulatto's superior attainments, they firmly believed, resulted from his inheritance of superior white qualities. Their conviction of white superiority actually allowed them no alternative to this view. Anyone possessed of white capabilities was by definition superior to the pure black.

The sum of all of these perceptions of the mulatto left most whites in a rather confused position. Their understanding of race and racial differences convinced them of the distinctness and inherent inferiority of the Negro. The mulatto, however, was clearly unlike the black man in many ways. He was obviously more intelligent than the Negro, but perhaps not as physically robust. Because he was more intelligent (thanks to his white blood), he commanded the most prestigious positions within the race. Yet the mulatto's white heritage did have detrimental effects, too. Most whites believed that the mulatto's admixture of white blood left him with many of the natural aspirations of the white man--aspirations which were often stifled by the strictures of American race relations. His consequent discontent drove him into the role of an agitator, dangerously fomenting unrest among the mass of blacks who otherwise instinctively recognized the superiority of the white race and submitted to its dominance.   Whites were inclined to understand and sometimes even sympathize with the mulatto's aspirations and unhappiness, since they saw them as reflections of their own progressive, impellent racial characteristics. Ultimately, however, these aspirations led mulattoes to want equality with whites, and equality meant intermarriage, a notion which repulsed all right-thinking whites.

Most whites were assured of the necessary progression from granting Negroes basic civil rights to social equality to eventual intermarriage of the two races and the demise of the white man and his civilization. It was essential, therefore, to maintain a division between the races, opposing all policies which hinted at the "social equality" of whites and Negroes, regardless of the virtues, abilities, or accomplishments of the latter. Was this justifiable?, William Benjamin Smith queried in 1905. Most assuredly! It was a necessary act on the part of the white race to preserve its blood and its essence:

> If we sit with Negroes at our tables, if we entertain them as our guests and social equals, if we disregard the colour line in all other relations, is it possible to maintain it fixedly in the sexual relation, in the marriage of our sons and daughters, in the propagation of our species?   Unquestionably, No!

As a race, he insisted, the Caucasian would be "irreversibly doomed."[117] Thomas Pierce Bailey was even more blunt in his assessment of the question. "Since 'social equality' can naturally and effectively mean nothing but amalgamation or 'miscegenation,'" he warned, "there must be no social intermingling of the races."[118] The only acceptable relation, whites contended, was one of white dominance and Negro subordination, with both races admitting and accepting their status.

There was essentially no discussion among whites about where the color line was to be drawn. White was white and black was black, and there was no middle ground. The issue at stake was far too crucial for equivocation, since it involved the maintenance of the racial integrity of the Caucasian people. The white race's "Ethnic purity," John Moffatt Mecklin explained, "is the bearer of its social heritage, and therefore, the ultimate guarantee of the continuity and integrity of its peculiar type of civilization."[119] Even the mulatto himself, many whites believed, recognized that he was outside the boundaries of the white ethos.   This was the real explanation of his fervent desire for intermarriage with whites. Mulattoes realized, Mecklin affirmed, that only through intermarriage could they achieve "the complete socialization" which was the prerequisite for attaining fully the white man's high cultural level.[120]

It was in this sphere that white attitudes about the mulatto and race mixture and the contempory understanding of the meaning of race and racial differences came together to shape public policy. The system of race relations in America from Reconstruction to the First World War reflected on a concrete level white efforts to legitimatize and institutionalize black/white distinctions believed to derive from the inherent racial traits of each group. Whiteness implied the possession of a certain set of racial characteristics, with the superior sensitivities and capabilities that went with them. Blackness implied the possession of a distinctly different (and inferior) set of traits. Maintaining the unblemished integrity of the white man's race traits thus was a crucial task, for only by doing so could he perpetuate his cultural superiority and his domination of the affairs of the world. Mixing his blood with that of inferior races like the Negro would pollute and transform the white man's racial qualities, jeopardizing his accomplishments and ultimately his very racial essence.

Any policies which even remotely hinted at equalizing the races had to be adamantly repelled, for equality necessarily meant ultimate intermixture. The presence of a massive mulatto populaton was striking testimony to the folly of a lax approach to interracial contacts, while the mulatto himself evidenced the detrimental effects of mixing. Admittedly he was superior in some ways to the pure black, yet the mulatto was still far from the equal of the white man. Further, the popular racial theory of the era dictated that the traits of the white man and the Negro could not be combined into a stable, harmonious type. These traits, and the cultural and evolutionary heritage which they represented, were far too disparate for an agreeable union. E. H. Randle expressed this popular notion well in describing the tension which boiled inside the mixed-blood. "Being made up of unlike and discordant elements of character," he wrote, the mulatto "has a nature warring with itself, restless and discontented. It is so with all mixed races and breeds of men and beasts."[121]

The mulatto, then, was not a fit representative of mankind. Because he was part black, he could not be all white, and anything less than all white had to be, according to the white racial thought of the period, imperfect and consequently inferior. Some conservatives, like Alfred Holt Stone, might argue for the establishment of a distinct and separate caste for mixed-bloods in America,[122] but for the vast majority of whites the issue was much simpler--an individual was white or he was not, and no one could be white, even if he physically appeared so, if somewhere in his blood lurked the race traits and instincts of the Negro and his savage, benighted African heritage. In the United States, the mulatto was a black man, even if he looked white, because popular understanding of the meaning of race left no room for someone in-between.

NOTES

[1]Edward Byron Reuter, "Racial Theory," *American Journal of Sociology*, L, 6 (May, 1945), 452.

[2]George M. Frederickson, *The Black Image in the White Mind: The Debate on Afro-American Character and Destiny, 1817-1914* (New York: Harper & Row, Publishers, 1971), p. 92.

[3]See *ibid.*, pp. 62-63, 69-70, 87, 92.

[4]The work was originally printed as a pamphlet under the title *Negro and Negro "Slavery": The First an Inferior Race: The Latter Its Normal Condition* (Baltimore: J. D. Toy, 1853).   It was later enlarged and republished as a book under the same title in 1861 in New York by Van Evrie's own publishing firm, Van Evrie, Horton & Co.

[5]John H. Van Evrie, *White Supremacy and Negro Subordination; or, Negroes a Subordinate Race, and (So-Called) Slavery Its Normal Condition* (New York: Van Evrie, Horton & Co., 1868), pp. 148, 162, 164, 167.

[6]*Ibid.*, p. 152.

[7]*Ibid.*, p. 161. See also p. 167.

[8]"Ariel" [Buckner H. Payne], *The Negro: What Is His Ethnological Status?* (Cincinnati: Published for the author, 1867), pp. 21-22, 23, 26-27, 47-48.

[9]Charles Loring Brace, *The Races of the Old World: A Manual of Ethnology* (New York: Charles Scribner, 1863), pp. 502-503.

[10]*Ibid.*, p. 490.

[11]Frederickson, *Black Image in White Mind*, p. 174; Forrest G. Wood, *Black Scare: The Racist Response to Emancipation and Reconstruction* (Berkeley: University of California Press, 1968), pp. 53-79; J. M. Bloch, *Miscegenation, Melaleukation, and Mr. Lincoln's Dog* (New York: Schaum Publishing Co., 1958).

[12]Wood, *Black Scare*, p. 75.

[13]Walter B. Hill, "Uncle Tom Without A Cabin," *Century Magazine*, XXVII, 6 (April, 1884), 862.

[14]Henry W. Grady, "In Plain Black and White (A Reply to Mr. Cable)," *Century Magazine* XXIX, 6 (April, 1885), 910-911.   Grady was castigating George W. Cable, the novelist and racial liberal, for what Grady believed was Cable's advocacy of social equality of the races and general racial amalgamation.

[15]W. C. Benet, "Is the Negro a Failure?", reprinted from the Augusta (Georgia) *Chronicle*, April, 1886, p. 6.

[16]Philip Alexander Bruce, *The Plantation Negro as a Freeman: Observations on his Character, Condition, and Prospects in Virgina* (New York: G. P. Putnam's Sons,

1889), pp. 53-55. See also Philip Alexander Bruce, "The Negro Population of the South," *Conservative Review*, II, 2 (November, 1899), 276-277.

[17]Letter from Bishop Atticus G. Haygood, in Isabel C. Barrows, ed., *First Mohonk Conference on the Negro Question, Held at Lake Mohonk, Ulster County, New York, June 4, 5, 6, 1890* (Boston: George H. Ellis, 1890), p. 85.

[18]W. Cabell Bruce, *The Negro Problem* (Baltimore: John Murphy & Co., 1891), p. 14.

[19]Thomas E. Watson, "The Negro Question in the South," *Arena*, VI (October, 1892), 543.

[20]"Caucasian" [William H. Campbell], *Anthropology for the People, A Refutation of the Theory of the Adamic Origin of All Races* (Richmond: Everett Waddey Co., 1891), p. 330.

[21]*Ibid.*, p. 267.

[22]*Ibid.*, p. 269.

[23]*Ibid.*, pp. 277, 334.

[24]Charles Carroll, *"The Negro A Beast," or "In the Image of God"* (St. Louis: American Book and Bible House, 1900), p. 221. Carroll repeated many of these ideas in a second book, *The Tempter of Eve; or, The Criminality of Man's Social, Political, and Religious Equality with the Negro, and the Amalgamation to which These Crimes Inevitably Lead* (St. Louis: Adamic Publishing Co., 1902). His notions were challenged in an equally curious book relying on Biblical explication by the Reverend W. S. Armistead of Tifton, Georgia, *The Negro is a Man, A Reply to Professor Charles Carroll's Book "The Negro is a Beast or In the Image of God"* (Tifton, Ga: Armistead and Vickers, 1903). For a summary of both Carroll and Armistead, see Idus A. Newby, *Jim Crow's Defense: Anti-Negro Thought in America, 1900-1930* (Baton Rouge: Louisiana State University Press, 1965), pp. 93-98.

[25]William P. Calhoun, *The Caucasian and the Negro in the United States* (Columbia, S.C.: R. L. Bryan, 1902).

[26]Francis Butler Simkins, "Ben Tillman's View of the Negro," *Journal of Southern History*, III, 2 (May, 1937), 163-164.

[27]See William F. Holmes, *The White Chief: James Kimble Vardaman* (Baton Rouge: Louisiana State University Press, 1970); Archibald Coody, IV, *"The Race Question" From The White Chief: A Story of the Life and Times of James K. Vardaman* (n.p., 1944).

[28]Ellen Barret Ligon, "The White Woman and the Negro," *Good Housekeeping* (November, 1903), quoted in Robert W. Shufeldt, *America's Greatest Problem: The Negro* (Philadelphia: F. A. Davis Company, 1915), pp. 135-139.

[29]William Benjamin Smith, *The Color Line: A Brief in Behalf of the Unborn* (New York: McClure, Phillips & Co., 1905), p. 11.

[30]*Ibid.*, p. 18.

[31]*Ibid.*, pp. 70-71.

[32] *Ibid.*, p. 72.

[33] *Ibid.*, p. xiv.

[34] Alexander Harvey Shannon, *Racial Intergrity and Other Features of the Negro Problem* (Nashville: Printed for the Author by the Publishing House of the M. E. Church, South, 1907), pp. 43, 76, 92-93.

[35] *Ibid.*, pp. 68-71.

[36] *Ibid.*, p. 16.

[37] *Ibid.*, p. 10.

[38] Robert W. Shufeldt, *The Negro: A Menace to American Civilization* (Boston: Richard G. Badger, 1907), pp. 112, 124-126.

[39] *Ibid.*, p. 135.

[40] *Ibid.*, pp. 103-104.

[41] Shufeldt, *America's Greatest Problem*, P. 90.

[42] The white fear of blacks arousing their own sexual passions is an underlying theme of Lawrence J. Friedman's study, *The White Savage: Racial Fantasies in the Postbellum South* (Englewood Cliffs, N.J.: Prentice-Hall, Inc., 1970).

[43] As an example of this thinking, see the article by William Lee Howard, a Baltimore physician who wrote numerous anti-Negro "scientific" studies during the turn-of-the-century period, "The Basic Causes for the Negro's Sensuality" included in Shufeldt, *Amercia's Greatest Problem*, pp. 96-106. See also Newby, *Jim Crow's Defense*, pp. 122-123, 130, 135-138.

[44] Shufeldt, *Negro: A Menace*, p. 153.

[45] *Ibid.*, pp. 154, 161. Efforts to colonize Negroes outside the United States did in fact revive around the turn of the century, often through an ironic alliance between discontented Afro-Americans and radical white racists. This became the thrust of the colonization movement for the rest of its active existence, especially under the guidance of John Sevier Cox.

[46] Quoted in Ray Stannard Baker, *Following the Color Line: American Negro Citizenship in the Progressive Era* (New York: Doubleday, Page & Company, 1908), p. 167.

[47] Quoted in *ibid.*

[48] Quoted in John James Holm, *Holm's Race Assimilation, or the Fading Leopard's Spots* (Napierville, Ill., J. L. Nichols & Company, 1910), p. 266.

[49] Baker, *Following the Color Line*, pp. 167-168.

[50] This information is largely derived from Holm, *Race Assimilation*, pp. 263-271.

[51] Baker, *Following the Color Line*, pp. 165-166.

[52]Thomas Nelson Page, *The Negro: The Southerner's Problem* (New York: Charles Scribner's Sons, 1904), p. 290.

[53]Edwin Henderson Randle, *Characteristics of the Southern Negro* (New York and Washington: Neale Publishing Company, 1910), p. 117.

[54]Edward Eggleston, *The Ultimate Solution of the American Negro Problem* (Boston: Richard G. Badger, 1913), p. 256. Eggleston's "ultimate solution" involved the gradual extinction of the Negro race in America because of its inherent inability to compete with the white man in a modern society.

[55]Charles H. McCord, *The American Negro as a Dependent, Defective and Delinquent* (Nashville: Press of Benson Printing Company, 1914), p. 50.

[56]Thomas Pierce Bailey, *Race Orthodoxy in the South, and Other Aspects of the Negro Question* (New York: Neale Publishing Company, 1914), pp. 139-140.

[57]In this regard, see Wood, *Black Scare,* pp. 10-11.

[58]Thomas Underwood Dudley, "How Shall We Help the Negro?", *Century Magazine,* XXX, 2 (June, 1885), 275.

[59]John T. Morgan, "Shall Negro Majorities Rule?", *Forum Extra,* I, 1 (March, 1890), 17.

[60]*Ibid.,* p. 20.

[61]Quoted in "Caucasian," *Anthropology for the People,* p. 272.

[62]A. W. Pitzer, Remarks on an address by Miss D. E.. Emerson on "Home Life of the Negroes," in Barrows, ed., *First Mohonk Conference,* p. 70.

[63]Bruce, *Negro as Freeman,* p. 126.

[64]*Ibid.,* pp. 126-127.

[65]Jabez L. M. Curry, "The Negro Question" *Popular Science Monthly,* LV (June, 1899), 178-179.

[66]Paul B. Barringer, *The American Negro: His Past and Future* (3rd. ed.; Raleigh, N.C.: Edwards & Broughton, 1900), pp. 13, 3.

[67]*Ibid.,* p. 15.

[68]John Ambrose Price, *The Negro: Past, Present and Future* (New York and Washington, D.C.: Neale Publishing Company, 1907), p. 102.

[69]Eggleston, *Ultimate Solution,* pp. 60, 231.

[70]John Moffatt Mecklin, *Democracy and Race Friction: A Study in Social Ethics* (New York: Macmillan Company, 1914), p. 30.

[71]*Ibid.,* p. 48. See also pp. 60-61.

[72]See Price, *The Negro,* p. 199; Eggleston, *Ultimate Solution,* pp. 242-246; Smith, *Color Line,* pp. 159-172. Such thinking was in part responsible for James K. Vardaman's closing of Mississippi's Negro schools while he was Governor of the state.

[73]Mecklin, *Democracy and Race Friction*, p. 143.

[74]*Ibid.*, pp. 146, 148.

[75]Shufeldt, *Negro: A Menace*, p. 135.

[76]Randle, *Characteristics of Southern Negro*, p. 122.

[77]Bailey, *Race Orthodoxy*, pp. 224-227.

[78]Shannon, *Racial Integrity*, p. 265.

[79]Mark H. Haller, *Eugenics: Hereditian Attitudes in American Thought* (New Brunswick, N.J.: Rutgers University Press, 1963), p. 149. Haller provides an excellent description of the origin and development of the eugenics movement, including its ties to the overall pattern of racial thought in the early twentieth century. See also Newby, *Jim Crow's Defense*, pp. 8-9, 33-37; Thomas F. Gossett, *Race: The History of an Idea in America* (New York: Schocken Books, 1965), pp. 157-163.

[80]Madison Grant, *The Passing of the Great Race, or The Racial Basis of European History* (New York: Charles Scribner's Sons, 1916), pp. 77, 60.

[81]Seth K. Humphrey, *Mankind: Racial Values and the Racial Prospect* (New York: Charles Scribner's Sons, 1917), pp. 157-158.

[82]For statements as to the widespread acceptance of a Lamarckian doctrine of acquired characteristcs by the American public, see Henry Fairfield Osborn, "The Present Problem of Heredity," *Atlantic Monthly*, LXVII (March, 1891), 354, and Humphrey, *Mankind*, p. 11.

[83]Bruce, *Negro as Freeman*, p. 143. See also Bruce, "Negro Population," p. 277.

[84]Address by John Roach Straton, in Southern Society for the Promotion of the Study of Race Conditions and Problems in the South, *Race Problems in the South: Proceedings of the First Annual Conference . . . at Montgomery, Alabama* (Richmond: B. F. Johnson Publishing Company, 1900), p. 149.

[85]Barringer, *American Negro*, p. 10.

[86]George T. Winston, "The Relation of the Whites to the Negroes," *Annals of the American Academy of Political and Social Science*, XVIII (July, 1901), 108.

[87]Smith, *Color Line*, p. 44. Smith based his belief partly on the findings of Sanford B. Hunt, the Civil War era anthropometrist. See *ibid.*, pp. 82-83.

[88]Shannon, *Racial Integrity*, pp. 82, 263-264.

[89]See Price, *The Negro*, pp. 128-129, 198; Randle, *Characteristics of Southern Negro*, p. 117; Eggleston, *Ultimate Solution*, pp. 249-250; McCord, *Negro as Dependent, Defective and Delinquent*, p. 50.

[90]Alfred Holt Stone, *Studies in the American Race Problem*, with an intro. and three papers by Walter F. Willcox (New York: Doubleday, Page & Company, 1908), p. 401.

[91]Albert Bushnell Hart, *The Southern South* (New York: D. Appleton and Company, 1910), p. 104.

[92]"Caucasian," *Anthropology for the People*, pp. 69, 268-269, 274.

[93]W. S. McCurley, "Impossibility of Racial Amalgamation," *Arena*, XXI, 4 (April, 1899), 453-454.

[94]Barringer, *American Negro*, p. 10.

[95]Smith, *Color Line*, pp. 52-69.

[96]Shannon, *Racial Integrity*, pp. 83, 95.

[97]"Caucasian," *Anthropology for the People*, pp. 261-262, 269, 288.

[98]Eggleston, *Ultimate Solution*, p. 250.

[99]Shannon, *Racial Integrity*, pp. 62-64, 82-83, 90-94, and *passim*.

[100]Randle, *Characteristics of Southern Negro*, pp. 117-118.

[101]"Caucasian," *Anthropology for the People*, pp. 288-292.

[102]Horace Smith Fulkerson, *The Negro; As He Was; As He Is; As He Will Be* (Vicksburg, Miss.:   Commercial Herald, Printers, 1887).

[103]Mrs. L. H. Harris, "A Southern Woman's View," *Independent*, LI (May 18, 1899), 1354-1355.

[104]Benet, "Is the Negro a Failure?", pp. 6-7.

[105]Price, *The Negro*, pp. 57-58.

[106]*Ibid.*, p. 139.

[107]Stone, *American Race Problem*, p. 433.

[108]*Ibid.*, p. 405.

[109]*Ibid.*, pp. 433, 339-340.

[110]*Ibid.*, p. 411n.

[111]Bruce, *Negro as Freeman*, p. 244.

[112]Bruce, *Negro Problem*, p. 14.

[113]Winston, "Relations of Negroes to Whites," p. 108.

[114]H. E. Belin, "A Southern View of Slavery," *American Journal of Sociology*, XIII, 4 (January, 1908), 518.   See also, as examples, Eggleston, *Ultimate Solution*, pp. 187, 202-203; McCord, *Negro as Dependent, Defective and Delinquent*, p. 50; Shufedlt, *Negro: A Menance* p. 153.

[115]Humphrey, *Mankind*, p. 165.

[116]Baker, *Following the Color Line*, p. 173.

[117]Smith, *Color Line*, pp. 7-8.

[118]Bailey, *Race Orthodoxy*, p. 98.

[119]John Moffatt Mecklin, "The Philosophy of the Color Line," *American Journal of Sociology*, XIX, 3 (November, 1913), 356.

[120]Mecklin, *Democracy and Race Friction*, p. 12. See also Smith, *Color Line*, p. 71n.

[121]Randle, *Characteristics of Southern Negro*, p. 117.

[122]See Stone, *American Race Problem*, pp. 339-340 and 397-437, *passim*. Stone developed his ideas from observing race relations in Latin America and the Caribbean, where mulattoes represented a distinct third caste in-between the white minority and the black majority.

CHAPTER IV

MULATTO IMAGES IN TURN-OF-THE-CENTURY
AFRO-AMERICAN FICTION

In the late nineteenth and early twentieth centuries, the dynamics of racial thought essentially denied the very existence of the mulatto. Particularly from the white perspective, deeply rooted beliefs in inherent racial traits and instincts dictated that anyone possessing the slightest degree of black blood was necessarily a Negro. The popular turn-of-the-century minstrel song, "All Coons Look Alike to Me," quite succinctly caught the basic white sentiment towards people of mixed blood--for all intents and purposes they were as black as a full-blooded Negro. Yet racial theory, both at the popular and the more sophisticated academic levels, was largely denying reality, for America did possess a sizable mulatto population, many of whose members themselves recognized certain distinctions between mixed-bloods and pure blacks. Consciousness of color gradations was firmly established among Afro-Americans. Further, despite his efforts to thrust the mulatto into the Negro race, the white man was also aware that many Afro-Americans were not entirely black. He might not grant the mulatto any status other than that of a Negro, but he did often sense that the mulatto was somehow different from pure blacks. Somehow whites had to accommodate themselves to this dual perspective of seeing the mulatto as a Negro yet still somewhat different from Negroes.

A similar task confronted Afro-Americans. The basic intellectual patterns which shaped racial thought among whites were well entwined in Afro-American thought as well. Few Negroes accepted the wholesale condemnation of black traits which was so characteristic of white racial attitudes, but many did subscribe to similar notions about the distinctiveness of black and white racial traits and instincts, the backbone of contemporary racial theory. Inevitably, this belief shaped the way Afro-Americans, including mulattoes themselves, perceived the nature of the mixed-blood and his role in the American racial system.

One means of assessing how Americans viewed the mulatto and his role in race relations in the half-century between Reconstruction and the First World War is through an analysis of the fictional literature of the period. Creative writings generally convey telling images of culture and social relations while revealing the motivations of human personality within the socio-cultural complex. Consequently, because the treatment of mulattoes in fiction was conditioned by the social and historical background out of which the authors wrote, the resultant images of mulattoes--personality characteristics, behavior patterns, socioeconomic roles, etc.--provide reflections of how blacks, whites, and mulattoes themselves viewed the status of mixed-bloods in America, especially with regard to the changing nature of race relations.[1]

Fiction thus offers a potential index to the depth of public adherence to the racial attitudes propounded in books and articles by academics and popularizers of academic theories. While such works found their most likely audience among molders of community opinion like preachers and newspaper editors, fiction was consumed by a wider group. Often, of course, fiction dealing with the Negro and/or the problem of race relations was itself overtly propagandistic, designed to sway popular attitudes towards one view of the issue or another. At the same time, however, it seems reasonable to assume that many writers, both white and Afro-American, wrote of the racial situation as they actually perceived it, or on occasion as they wished it one day might be. Therefore, by investigating the fiction of the period it is possible to develop a sense of how Americans viewed a variety of questions involved with the subject of race, including how they felt about the mulatto and issue of race mixture.

2

During the turn-of-the-century period, Afro-American fiction was overwhelmingly concerned with "the Race Question." The precipitous deterioration of black/white relations was a dominant fact of life for Negroes in America, because it affected all aspects of their existence. Disfranchisement, segregation, peonage, the convict lease system, and mob violence undermined the security of Afro-Americans in the South, while those in the North faced similar, though generally less severe, manifestations of increasing prejudice. Much more significant than intermittent racial violence against Northern Negroes was the development of economic and residential discrimination which greatly circumscribed their lives and kept them, for the most part, at the bottom of the socioeconomic ladder.[2]

Afro-American writers inevitably responded with intensity to this crisis confronting their race, and their fiction therefore provides a valuable means of measuring the response of one segment of the Negro population to the major racial issues of the day. Further, from their descriptions of Negro life, one can formulate a picture of life and social interrelationships within the Afro-American community itself, including the role of the mulatto.

Much of this fiction represented a deliberate rejoinder to various forms of racist literature and the American racial system. Unavoidably, then, it often took on grossly propagandistic characteristics.[3] It also reflected divisions within Afro-American thought as to how best to deal with the situation. This division was particularly acute for most Afro-American authors. They were generally members of a rising middle class which since emancipation had gradually become differentiated from the Negro masses. As a result, they were deeply imbued with the goals and ideals inherent in the traditional notion of the American dream, i.e., that success and upward social mobility resulted from thrift, industry, perseverance, and an upright moral character. Unfortunately, they found themselves effectively excluded from the supposed fruits of their hard earned middle-class status as discrimination and segregation spread throughout virtually every facet of the nation's social and economic system.[4]

This Negro middle class developed two prospective solutions to this dilemma, both of which found expression in various fictional works and in the way mulattoes were treated within those works. Some urged an assimilationist stance which was, after all, the underlying motivation behind their struggle to become middle-class in the first place. By becoming more like white, middle-class America--by making their color seem less important a trait than their social refinement and economic position--they hoped to be accepted as individuals on their own merit. Such a proposal offered little real hope for the race as a whole, however, since it involved mobility on an individual rather than a mass basis. Further, it often meant a rejection of many things black, a belief in the inherent superiority of the white, bourgeois lifestyle and ultimately, perhaps, of the white race itself.

Other Afro-Americans argued instead for greater racial pride and unity. Barred from white institutions, they would have Afro-Americans create their own social and economic system. Segregated black schools, churches, businesses, and social organizations would allow the race to develop at its own pace, free from the rebuffs, insults and constrictions of life among the dominant race. Such institutions would provide opportunities for the bright young men and women of the race who found themselves excluded from positions in the white world to which their education and upbringing had naturally suited them.

One can perceive these patterns of thought in the works of virtually all Afro-American authors of the turn-of-the-century period. Their fiction had a strong "inspirational" emphasis, reflective of a desire to spur the ambitions of the youth of the race. The values of middle-class success were constantly being urged upon the readers, but there was uncertainty as to the ultimate purpose of the individual's efforts. Should he be working for his own advancement or for that of the race as a whole? What responsibility does the individual Negro have to his race, especially in the light of the racial oppression of the era? The manner in which mulatto characters were treated is indicative of the trials the Negro middle-class writers themselves encountered in attempting to resolve these issues.[5]

Three primary images of mulatto figures emerge from a reading of the Afro-American fiction of this period:

1. the "tragic mulatto," a stereotyped image with a long literary history, designed to evoke the sympathy of the reader;

2. a stout-hearted hero or heroine who epitomizes middle-class virtues and who sees his/her role as a leader of the Negro race, despite the possibility, in many cases, of passing for white; and

3. a more complex individual who is sensitive to his position between the two races and who is more likely to opt for passing into the white world.

Although they overlapped at times, each of these images served, in its own way, as a vehicle by which Afro-American authors protested the injustices of the American caste system. Each image also provides the historian with clues as to how blacks and mulattoes viewed the relationship of mixed-bloods to their darker (and lighter) brothers.

According to one student of Afro-American literary characters, the "tragic mulatto" is an *archetype*, i.e., a character type which embodies cultural beliefs, values, aspirations, and fears which are accepted uncritically, entirely apart from the character's actions as an individual. An archetype possesses a life of its own resulting from a tradition of stereotyped use.[6] The tragic mulatto itself represents "a visible symbol of lust and what the culture deemed, pejoratively, miscegenation."[7] It is one of the oldest archetypes in American literature, with a history dating back to the propaganda novels of abolitionist writers. Authors like Richard Hildreth, Harriet Beecher Stowe, and William Wells Brown saw in the near-white victim of slavery a valuable tool for pricking the conscience of white America. Playing upon the sentiments and race pride of whites, they employed the mistreated mulatto to argue repeatedly about the injustice of a system which could promote miscegenation and then literally enslave the children of the dominant race. The result was a well-defined stereotyped figure, explains Penelope L. Bullock, a student of mulatto characters in fiction.

> He is the son or daughter of a white Southern aristocratic gentleman and one of his favorite slave mistresses. From his father he has inherited mental capacities and physical beauty supposedly superior to that of the white race. Yet despite such an endowment, or rather because of it, his life is fraught with tragedy. What privileges and opportunities he may enjoy are short-lived; for he is inevitably a

slave. Suffering the degrading hardships of bondage, he becomes miserable and bitter. The indomitable spirit of his father rises up within him, and he rebels. If he is successful in escaping to freedom, he becomes a happy, prosperous, and reputable citizen in his community. But even if his revolt against slavery fails, he meets his tragic defeat nobly and defiantly.[8]

It is clear that despite their antislavery proclivities, these authors were writing from within the perspective of nineteenth-century racial thought, which demeaned the characteristics of the black man while lauding those of the white. Their mulatto characters are intransigent, resentful, and intelligent for biological, not social reasons. Their desirable traits, especially those which lead them to rebel against their bondage, result from their white blood.[9] It was an attitude which inevitably found expression in the post-Civil War period as well, even among a number of Afro-American writers.

The tragic mulatto reappeared during the turn-of-the-century period in the works of Negroes who felt it was necessary to defend the correctness of emancipation against racist white arguments to the contrary. In effect, they became abolitionist writers once again, arguing the manifold injustice of the peculiar institution.

Frances Ellen Watkins Harper's novel, *Iola Leroy, or Shadows Uplifted* (1892), was one of the first works published by an Afro-American author (and the first by an Afro-American woman) after the Civil War. Herself a former member of the abolitionist ranks, she was quick to employ the tragic mulatto image to restate her earlier opposition to slavery. Iola Leroy has all of the characteristics of the tragic mulatto stereotype. Her father was a wealthy Creole planter who had even married her mother, the beautiful mulatto, Marie. When he suddenly dies, however, scheming relatives reduce Marie and her children to slavery, and Iola is sold away from her mother when she refuses the lustful advances of her new owner. Indeed, she is repeatedly sold from planter to planter because despite her enticing beauty, she is a "reg'lar spitfire," according to a fellow slave, in defense of her maidenly virtue. It is a difficult task, however, considering Iola's shapely figure, long, wavy hair, blue eyes, and white skin. The tragedy of her predicament leads a fellow slave (himself light in color, refined in nature, and unknowingly Iola's uncle) to lead her to the safety of Union lines, where she immediately captivates the hearts of the Union officers and men:

The beautiful, girlish face was full of tender earnestness. The fresh, young voice was strangely sympathetic, as if some great sorrow had bound her heart in loving compassion to every sufferer who needed her gentle ministrations.[10]

Even the Union general is much impressed by Iola's modest demeanor and

> surprised to see the refinement and beauty she possessed. Could it be possible that this young and beautiful girl had been a chattel, with no power to protect herself from the highest insults that lawless brutality could inflict upon innocent and defenseless womanhood? Could he ever again glory in his American citizenship, when any white man, no matter how coarse, cruel, or brutal, could buy and sell her for the basest purposes?[11]

The beautiful mulatto girl and her plight have come to epitomize, for Harper's characters and for the author herself, much of the evil inherent in the slave system.

Similar characters are to be found in the works of other Afro-American fictionists of this period. Pauline E. Hopkins, a Boston writer, singer, and lecturer who was herself of mixed blood, created a number of such figures.[12] In a story entitled "A Dash for Liberty," published in 1901, she describes the escape of a group of slaves who seize the slaveship on which they are being transported. Among the human cargo is Susan, a beautiful octoroon whose grandfather had been a Revolutionary War hero and member of Congress. Having been a lady's maid, she is well-educated and can sing and dance, but more important are her physical attractions which make her prey to the desire of licentious white men:

> She lay stretched at full length with her head resting upon her arm, a position that displayed to the best advantage the perfect symmetry of her superb figure; the dim light of a lantern played upon the long black ringlets, the finely-chiselled mouth and well-rounded chin, upon the marbled skin veined by her master's blood--representative of two races, to which did she belong?[13]

In *Winona, A Tale of Negro Life in the South and Southwest*, which was serialized in the *Colored American Magazine* beginning in May, 1902, Hopkins wrote of another beautiful young near-white slave. Winona, the daughter of a fugitive mulatto slave woman and a white man living as an Indian near Buffalo, New York, is carried back to Missouri and slavery by vicious slave-catchers. There lustful whites attempt to assault her virtue before she is rescued by a noble Englishman. With the aid of John Brown's band, he eventually helps her to flee to Canada and then England, where her racial background is no longer a bar to true happiness. In typical melodramatic form, Hopkins has it revealed at the end that Winona's father is actually a long-lost British nobleman, and with this new status she can now marry her handsome, white rescuer.[14] Similar trials befall Grace Montfort, a beautiful mixed-blood, and her son, Jesse, in Hopkins' novel, *Contending Forces* (1900). When her husband, an immigrant planter from the West Indies, is killed by his white South Carolina neighbors, the two are forced into slavery by an unscrupulous white lawyer.[15] A like fate befalls Hagar Enson, the mulatto wife of a Virginia planter in *Hager's Daughter*, another novel serialized in the *Colored American Magazine*.[16]

Yet by the mid-1890s, when Afro-American fiction began to appear in significant numbers, the ordeal of slavery was a largely unknown experience to young Afro-Americans. Growing to maturity in the shadows of an increasingly rigid caste system, they were more concerned with the difficulties they had to face on a daily basis. Consequently, a variation of the tragic mulatto stereotype--the individual who was brought up thinking himself white only to discover in later life that one of his parents had some degree of black blood--was developed to underscore the irrationality of a caste system which ultimately measured all people by their race. Just as the abolitionists' near-white characters had been designed to enable white readers to identify with the plight of the slave, so now this new stereotype would hopefully make white America more conscious of the unjust discrimination being suffered by Afro-Americans in their own time.

The bizarre turns of fate so characteristic of the melodramatic plots employed by these early Afro-American writers made such developments far from uncommon. In William M. Ashby's *Redder Blood* (1915), Zelda Marston Birch has long been passing for white and is happily married to a wealthy New York social figure. When a childhood lover jealously reveals Zelda's true racial identity to her husband, he viciously denounces her, despite his earlier liberal pronouncements about racial matters. Their twenty-year-old son, Adrian, leading student and star football player at Pemberton (Princeton?), suddenly finds his life shadowed by the specter of black blood, although he in no way resembles a Negro. He nevertheless stands by his mother, declaring that his blood is "redder blood, redder blood,--the corpuscles of which are not hate, envy, prejudice, but respect and kind feeling for others."[17] Unwilling or unable to hide the truth of his racial heritage from himself, Adrian finds his romance with a beautiful white girl destroyed when he tells her of his fate.

> You leper! [she excoriates him] You cancer in a man's form, you imp let loose from limbo! You deceived me. Acid-like you ate into my pure soul, knowing all the time what you were, knowing that you were black as midnight. Let me wipe away your kisses, let me tear my flesh from my frame. I was pure; your black skin has corrupted me, polluted me. Get out of my sight forever.[18]

Even when she reconsiders and admits to Adrian and herself that she cannot live without him, Adrian, within hours having adopted the frame of mind of a Negro, will not allow their relationship to continue. Law and custom forbid intermarriage, he tells her, and she would find herself a social outcast. More important, however, is the fact that he is now somehow inherently different from her because of his black blood:

> We can never know each other perfectly, Wanda, could never get into each other's soul. Thousands of years of training have made us different. In me there is something Negroid that you could never understand, in you there is something Caucasian that I could never fully understand and know. We could never get into each other's souls.[19]

This is an expression of the very heart of contemporary race theory--the notion of distinct racial "geniuses" reflecting well-established sets of racial traits and instincts. But Adrian has yet another objection. Beyond this sense of basic psychological and spiritual differences between members of disparate races, Adrian fears that a child might show evidence of his black blood, i.e., be "atavistic."

> They say, Wanda, that the offspring of a quagga and a mare will have its mark,--will be striped. . . .Some people call me a quagga. . . .We must live apart, dearest; I cannot ruin your life because mine is ruined.[20]

Adrian's life has been "ruined" because he has discovered himself to be of mixed blood. Similar consequences befall Aurelia Madision, a beautiful Washington socialite in *Hagar's Daughter*. When her black blood is made known, she is rejected by her lover and sinks into disgrace, poverty, and madness. In Charles W. Chesnutt's "Her Virginia Mammy," a mulatto ex-slave refrains from telling her long-lost daughter of their true relationship because she realizes how the knowledge would ruin the girl's life.[21] Even children can suffer intensely from the discovery of their racial background. James Weldon Johnson describes with particular poignancy the devastating effect of this knowledge on his young hero in *The Autobiography of an Ex-Coloured Man (1912)*. Having always thought of himself as white, one day at school his white teacher almost inadvertently forces the truth of his mixed blood upon him. It was, he explains, "a sword-thrust. . . which was years in healing."

> Since I have grown older [he reflects] I have often gone back and tried to analyze the change that came into my life after that fateful day in school. There did come a radical change, and,

young as I was, I felt fully conscious of it, though I did not fully comprehend it . . .

And so I have often lived through that hour, that day, that week, in which was wrought the miracle of my transition from one world into another; for I did indeed pass into another world. From that time I looked out through other eyes, my thoughts were coloured, my words dictated, my actions limited by one dominating, all-pervading idea which constantly increased in force and weight until I finally realized in it a great, tangible fact [that blacks in America must see everything in terms of their blackness].[22]

Because he alone among the Afro-American writers of this period moved well beyond the contrived devices and constricting form of melodrama, it is Johnson who most clearly makes his readers feel the almost tangible significance of the mixed-blood who learns the painful truth that will forever shape his life. Regardless of his literary skills, however, each of these writers was using such mulatto characters for a dual purpose: to emphasize the chasm which existed between whites and blacks in America because of irrational white prejudice, and to underline the difficulties faced by Negroes (and particularly those with essentially white, middle-class tastes, refinement, and sensibilities) in a nation whose social system was based upon racial caste.

4

These points were made even more vividly through the second major (and by far the most common) mulatto image found in the Afro-American fiction of this period--the respectable, middle-class mulatto who must suffer the indignities of the American caste system. Men and women of this type were consistently cast as the heroes or heroines of these early Afro-American novels and short stories, and there was little variation from one work to the next in the nature of the characterizations involved. However, there were paradoxes in the depictions of such characters which reveal uncertainties in the minds of these middle-class, often mulatto writers about their own relationship to the black race.

On the one hand, these characters served as models for individual and thereby ultimately race advancement. These fictional works often had a clearly inspirational emphasis, reflecting a desire to encourage ambition in the race. The bourgeois characters, especially the men, embodied the range of property-acquiring virtues necessary for getting ahead in an expanding American economy. A premium was placed on education. Equally important was a strict Protestant asceticism which stressed the strength of character necessary to withstand temptations which might interfere with the accumulation of property or the achievement of middle-class status.   Home ownership was an important goal, as were outward signs of respectability like neatness, good manners, and conservative dress.   Through such efforts one would become "cultured" or "refined" or a member of "the bettter class of colored persons."[23]

Consequently, the men were generally portrayed as aspiring young professionals, well educated, socially refined, and of impeccable demeanor.   Indeed, they epitomized the Victorian notion of ideal manhood described by Peter Gabriel Filene in his study of sex roles in America:

> Ideally, a man was self-reliant, strong, resolute, courageous, honest--traits which people summed up simply as *character*.   At home he governed absolutely but justly, chivalrous toward his wife and firm toward his children, defending them against all adversity.   He provided a benevolent patriarchy.   Outside the home, he worked to earn the income that would feed, clothe, and shelter his family in happy comfort.   As breadwinner he must struggle against his fellow men and natural forces, but with enough determination he would succeed.[24]

Dr. Adam Miller in Charles W. Chesnutt's *The Marrow of Tradition* (1901) typifies this idealized hero.   Handsome, well educated, cultured, and refined, he is a flawless man and a model of reason and intelligence.   "The mulatto's erect form," Chesnutt comments, "broad shoulders, clear eyes, fine teeth, and pleasingly moulded features showed nowhere any sign of that degeneration which the pessimist so sadly maintains is the inevitable heritage of mixed races."   He has been to school in the North and in Europe, is known by top medical authorities, and is rising quickly in his profession.   Indeed, the novel offers no white men who are his equal.[25]

Sutton E. Griggs' *Imperium in Imperio* (1899) offers a similar character in Bernard Belgrave, the near-white son of an important Senator and a beautiful mulatto.   Handsome and well-bred, he is brilliant and eloquent as well.   Having graduated with highest honors in both classics and the law from Harvard (where his popularity won him the presidency of his class), Belgrave quickly becomes a leading lawyer and politician in Norfolk, Virginia and a prominent social figure.[26]

Other such figures abound in fiction of the period.   Baug Peppers is a distinguished mulatto lawyer and political leader in Griggs' *Pointing the Way* (1908).[27]   Captain Paul Dale is a dashing American officer assigned to duty in Liberia in *The American Cavalryman* (1917) by Henry Francis Downing.   He is described as "a well set-up, light-brown colored man about thirty years of age, with straight black hair, somewhat prominent, well-shaped lips, and dark brown eyes."   His bravery and genuine concern for the welfare of the Liberian people win him the hand of the President's beautiful daughter.[28]   Pauline Hopkins portrays an aspiring young Boston mulatto along similar lines in her *Contending Forces (1900)*:

> Will Smith was tall and finely formed, with features almost perfectly chiseled, and a complexion the color of almond shell. His hair was black and curly, with just a tinge of crispness to denote the existence of Negro blood. His eyes were dark and piercing as an eagle's.[29]

Although forced by the death of his father to assume a position in a leading Boston hotel, Will nevertheless proves to be an invaluable employee and maintains his hopes of attending college. He demonstrates his keen intelligence in discussions of race issues at public gatherings and at a leading club for white men to which he is invited.[30]   Other mixed-blood characters in the same mold include physicians such as Lotus Stone in *Hearts of Gold* (1896) and Dr. Latimer in *Iola Leroy* (1892), teachers such as Russell Woodleigh in "A Georgia Episode" (1901) and Harry Leroy in *Iola Leroy*, and journalists such as Clement St. John in *Hearts of Gold.*[31]

Robert Bone, a leading student of Afro-American fiction, has noted that all of these characters are driven by the property-acquiring urges inherent in a middle-class society. Indeed, the notion of manliness which dominated the period recognized such drives as a central part of the male sex role. Yet in a society where racial prejudice placed marked limitations on a Negro man's ability to compete in the economic world, he might find his sense of manliness severely challenged by powers beyond his control.[32]   One means of sidestepping the restrictions imposed by the American caste system was through a recognition of one's obligation to serve the race. The middle-class characters in many of these novels demonstrate an extreme sense of *noblesse oblige*, a recurrent tendency to identify their interests with those of the race as a whole. According to Bone, this was also a way of dealing with the guilt generated by the confrontation of individual competitiveness and natural in-group loyalties.[33]

To a degree, of course, this attitude is simply a manifestation of the idea of racial unity combined with Booker T. Washington's preaching of middle-class virtues. These fictional characters served as models for the race. In their business and professional activities, as well as in the home life, they evidence the respectability, industry, and honesty which Washington hoped would bring the race greater acceptance by white America. As each individual improved his socioeconomic position, the race as a whole would rise a bit. The activities of the Negro middle class, then, were the key to undermining the racial caste system. "Greater industry, skill, the sticking quality, honesty and reliability will open the way," explains one character in G. Langhorne Pryor's *Neither Bond Nor Free* (1902).

> . . . If we will only cultivate the saving spirit, cut loose from extravagant habits, work the year round, encourage and assist one another in business, we will acquire wealth, and this will effectively dissipate race prejudice.[34]

There was considerably more to this attitude than simply the role of modeling bourgeois respectability and success. These middle-class mulatto characters were to be the leaders of the race, the men (and women) who would guide it through difficult times until it reached an economic and cultural level which would cause whites to reconsider their prejudicial attitudes and grant the race an equitable position in American society. It was their responsibility to be actively involved in working out the problems which currently beset all Afro-Americans.

Frances Harper's *Iola Leroy* (1892) presented an early yet clear-cut statement of this point of view, a position which would be reiterated in Afro-American novels for the next twenty-five years.[35] Three near-white mulatto characters explicitly illustrate Harper's feeling that such people are the natural and necessary leaders of the Negro race. Harry Leroy, Iola's brother, finds himself confronted with the decision of choosing his status when he seeks to enlist in the Union army--he must decide between joining a white regiment (by passing for white, since he shows no real evidence of Negro blood) or a Negro regiment.

> He winced when the question was asked. He felt the reality of his situation as he had not done before. It was as if two paths had suddenly opened before him, and he was forced to choose between them. On one side were strength, courage, enterprise, power of achievement, and memories of a wonderful past. On the other side were weakness, ignorance, poverty, the proud world's social scorn. He knew nothing of the colored people except as slaves [having been raised as a white], and his whole soul shrank from equalizing himself with them. He was fair enough to pass unchallenged among the fairest in the land, and yet a Christless prejudice had decreed that he should be a social pariah. . . . [Yet it] was more than a matter of choice where he should stand on the racial question. He felt that he must stand where he could strike the most effective blow for freedom.[36]

That, of course, was as a Negro. Harry goes on to become a successful   teacher   in a black school in the Reconstruction South. When a Northern white man notes that Harry could have prospered far more had he cast his lot with the white race, Harper, speaking through Iola, counters that, in fact,

> he has greater advantages as a colored man. . . . To be leader of a race to higher planes of thought and action, to teach men clearer views of life and duty, and to inspire their souls with loftier aims, is a far greater privilege than it is to open the gates of material prosperity and fill every home with sensuous enjoyment.[37]

Harper herself explains that while some have pitied or criticized Harry for choosing to acknowledge his black blood,

> he knows that life's highest and best advantages do not depend on the color of the skin or the texture of the hair. He has his reward in the improved condition of his pupils and the superb manhood and noble life which he has developed in his much needed work.[38]

Robert Johnson, Harry and Iola's uncle, is also a near-white mulatto, but he too has chosen to live as a Negro. When a Northern white friend asks Johnson, who is an escaped slave, why he does not pass for white, Johnson replies that he would prefer a lower rank in the Union army as a Negro than to be an officer as a white man:

> When a man's been colored all his life, it comes a little hard for him to get white all at once. Were I to try it, I would feel like a cat in a strange garret. Captain, I think my place is where I am most needed. You do not need me in your ranks, and my company does. They are excellent fighters, but they need a leader.[39]

Even Dr. Latimer, the man Iola eventually marries, is a light mulatto who has deliberately chosen life as a Negro despite his white grandmother's promises of a life of riches "if he would ignore his identity with the colored race." Still, he proves to be "a man of too much sterling worth of character to be willing to forsake his mother's race for the richest advantage his grandmother could bestow."[40]

Such decisions to work for the welfare of the race are widespread in the Afro-American fiction of the period. Dr. Adam Miller, the mulatto hero of Chesnutt's *The Marrow of Tradition* (1901), had the option of pursuing his medical career in the North or in Europe where he would be free from the strictures of Southern race prejudice, but he chose to return to the South to build a hospital where "his people" needed such facilities more.[41] Lucius Storms in John Wesley Grant's *Out of the Darkness* (1909) is another near-white physician, who after studying at Harvard, returns to the South to practice among the Negro population. In the same novel, Julius Jarnigan decides to practice law in the South in hopes of uniting Negroes in their struggle for equal opportunities.[42] Even James Weldon Johnson's nameless hero gives up a lucrative position traveling in Europe as the companion of a millionaire, returning to America with the dream of making a positive contribution to his race by collecting and transcribing Afro-American folk music.

This determination on the part of middle-class mulatto characters to work for the betterment of the race was not limited to men, however. Indeed, female mulatto characters were drawn as even more idealized bouregeois figures in the fiction of this era. Perhaps this was reminiscent of the use of female figures in the tragic mulatto stereotype to underscrore the evils of slavery. Surely, though, it also reflects a sensitivity to Victorian ideas about womanhood and recognition of how the treatment of Afro-American women contradicted those ideas.

These characters clearly epitomized many of the virtues Victorian Americans traditionally connected with the image of "true womanhood." It was a concept which involved a number of characteristics--most important of which were piety, purity, domesticity, and submissiveness-- all captured in the popular notion of what it meant to be a "lady." The lady stood as the foundation of the home and the family, as the teacher and exemplar of proper social conduct and moral principles, as a symbol of all that was held sacred in middle-class American culture.[43]

Victorian ladies were common figures in the literature of the period, of course, but they were portrayed with particular intensity in the fiction of the early Afro-American writers. Virtually all were of a light complexion and notably beautiful. Sutton E. Griggs, for instance, a popular Negro preacher, lecturer, and writer of the period, peopled his five novels with mulatto women of remarkable character and attractiveness. Morlene Dalton, the light-skinned heroine of his 1902 novel *Unfettered*, is a typical example:

> A wealth of lovely black hair crowning a head of perfect shape and queenly poise; a face, the subtle charm of which baffles description; two lustrous black eyes, wondrously expressive, presided over by eyebrows that were ideally beautiful; a neck which, with infinite regard for the requirements of perfect art, descended and expanded so as to form part of a faultless bust; as to form, magnificently well proportioned; when viewed as a whole, the very essence of loveliness. Such was the picture of Morlene, who, once seen, left an image that never again passed from the mind of the beholder.[44]

Similarly, Erma Wysong, the mulatto heroine of *Overshadowed* (1901), is described as a "queen of beauty":

> Her hair, slightly coarse of thread, glistening as if in pride of its extreme blackness, was combed away from a brow that was exceedingly pretty and formed a part of a head that forewarned you

to expect the possessor thereof to have an intellect of high order. . . . tender brown eyes so full of soul; . . . a row of pearls even and gleamingly white; . . . a cheek the tenderness and ruddiness of which were standing invitation for gentle pressure.

Firma, nearly tall, a happy medium between the plump and lithe, the perfection of symmetry, her whole frame a series of divinely fashioned curves.[45]

Amid his bombastic phrases, Griggs is attempting to describe a type of beauty which transcends the race of the woman herself. Other authors, however, found a special beauty in the peculiar color of the mulatto. Delphine, in George Marion McClellan's tragic tale, "Old Greenbottom Inn," is especially beautiful because of her mixed blood:

She was too beautiful and of a beauty that cannot be well described. The jetty splendor of her hair, the lustre of her eyes, the blending of yellow and pinkish hues of her skin, her lithesome and perfect form and face might have been thought a contribution from all the beautiful women of the ages and of all climes.[46]

David B. Fulton, author of *Hanover*, a 1900 novel about the Wilmington race riot, also stresses the uniqueness of the mixed-blood's beauty in his description of Molly Pierrepont:

Though vulgarly called a "negress," her skin was almost as fair as a Saxon's; and because of the mingling of Negro blood--more beautiful in color . . . No one will deny that among the women of mixed blood in the South, there are types of surpassing beauty. The inter-mixture of Negro and Saxon, Negro and Spanish and Indian blood gives the skin a more beautiful color than exists in the unadulterated of either race. While the mulatto and octoroon may reveal the Saxon in the fairness of the skin, the Negro reinforcement shows itself generally in the slight inclination of the lips towards thickness, the lustrious [sic] black of the eye and hair which is generally abundant and slightly woolly in texture.[47]

Physical beauty, then, was a common element among the female mulatto characters of this fiction. However, it was not the true hallmark of these mulatto women. More important was exemplary character, a combination of piety, compassion, intelligence, unquestioned chastity, and modest demeanor which in essence defined the middle-class lady. These bourgeois traits are continually emphasized by the early Afro-American authors, presumably to provide guidance to the younger women of the race. As Frances Harper comments,

> I do not think that we can begin too early to teach our
> boys to be manly and self-respecting, and our girls to be useful and
> self-reliant .   .   .
>
> We must instill into our young people that the true
> strength of a race means purity in women and uprightness in men.[48]

The heroine of Otis M. Shackelford's didactic novel, *Lillian
Simmons* (1915), for example, embodies all of the virtues of the true
Victorian woman. The daughter of a civil servant and leading figure in
the Afro-American life of a Northern community, she lives a comfortable
life not unlike that of white, middle-class young women. Naturally she is
very attractive, with "a beautiful brown skin" and

> eyes that sparkled and wavy black hair that glistened in the sunlight,
> falling in a thick cluster of curls about the girlish neck, she looked
> more like the nymphs or fairies of the woods than she did the
> ordinary mortal at home.[49]

Nevertheless, Shackelford notes, "she was not spoiled." Rather, Lillian is
shown to be poised, kind, and unselfish in her dealings with others:

> A lovable, beautiful, sensible, accomplished girl. A girl full of health
> and vigor and buoyancy of spirit. A girl whose training had not
> been neglected in any line. Cooking, sewing and piano playing were
> her accomplishments . . . . No young woman would have a greater
> asset to character or a greater aid to future life and happiness than
> she, with qualifications like these.[50]

Similar attributes characterize most other female figures in the
Afro-American fiction of the period,[51] yet these mulatto women differ
from the conventional patterns of white middle-class behavior in their
determination to work for the betterment of their race. Like their male
counterparts, they feel a strong responsibility to help those of the race
less fortunate than they. Generally well educated, one finds them
repeatedly going South as teachers among the ignorant black masses, or
less often, becoming involved in campaigns to alleviate racial mistrust
and discrimination.

Frances Harper's heroine Iola Leroy set an early example in
following this pattern of behavior. Rejecting a handsome Northern
doctor who has asked for her hand in marriage, she resolves instead "to
cast my lot with the freed people as helper, teacher, and friend." "I
don't think I could best serve my race by forsaking them and marrying
you," she tells her white suitor. When he protests that her education has
"unfitted" her for social life among lower-class Negroes, Iola replies that

"I did not choose my lot in life, and the simplest thing I can do is to accept the situation and do the best I can."[52]

Similarly, Regina Underwood in J. McHenry Jones' *Heart of Gold* (1896), Lillian Simmons in Otis M. Shackelford's *Lillian Simmons* (1915), Rena Walden in Charles W. Chesnutt's *The House Behind the Cedars* (1900), and Lizzie Story in George Marion McClellan's story, "A Creole From Louisiana," all determine to devote themselves to teaching careers in the South, often at the expense of more comfortable lives elsewhere. Ernestine DeShon, the beautiful mulatto heroine of John Wesley Grant's *Out of the Darkness* (1909), offers the most forceful arguments for making such a decision to work for the betterment of the race. "When a little girl at my mother's knee," she explains to a friend at college, "I made a resolve to do all I could for my darling mother's people; to do whatever I could to correct that public opinion which doomed me and my poor mother to obscurity and disgrace."[53]

> I love my people the more because they are ignorant, poor and cast off; because they are being ground to powder between the upper and nether millstones. I feel the more the duty resting upon me to help them in whatever way I can. By reason of the opportunities I have enjoyed in this and other schools I am better prepared to go out and teach and lead my people on to better things; to encourage them to look up and toil up, while I and others who love the race lift up. If this short, eventful life were all we hope for, we of the dark race would be of all creatures the most miserable. But we trust, hope, and pray for a better, brighter day--for rewards that perish not, neither are snatched away from us.[54]

She was convinced that because Negroes had been downtrodden and abused for so long, they needed "some loving heart and gentle hand to guide and help them," and through her work in the South she subsequently became to them "ever a source of solace in sorrow; of courage in times of doubt and fear; and strength in weakness."[55]

Other mulatto women became involved in campaigns to lessen racial tensions. In *Pointing the Way* (1908), Sutton E. Griggs described the efforts of Eina Rapona, a beautiful light-skinned Northerner, to convince a liberal Southern politician of the need to work for greater harmony between the two races in the town of Belrose. Erma Wyson, in Griggs' *Overshadowed* (1901), promotes a plan whereby the better young men of the white race might come in contact with refined young Negro women, in the hopes that mutual understanding of racial matters might ensue. Elsa Mangus, the daughter of a conservative Methodist bishop, becomes an ardent supporter of the Union of Ethiopia, an organization stressing Afro-American unity, in *Ethiopia, The Land of Promise* (1917) by Charles Henry Holmes, while Beulah Jackson, an escaped slave, is renowned as an abolitionist speaker in Charles H. Fowler's *Historical Romance of the American Negro* (1902).[56] In Griggs' *Unfettered*, Morlene Dalton is so concerned with the sad state of race relations in America that she refuses to marry her lover until he can develop a suitable plan for bringing about greater harmony between the races.[57]

This great concern about racial matters and the persistent inclination to work for the uplift of the race demonstrated by both male and female mixed-blood characters are reflections of certain key attitudes held by early Afro-American writers. It is clear that they envisioned the role of the educated mulatto as that of a race leader--culturally, socially, politically, and economically. Edward Byron Reuter's 1918 study of the mulatto's role in the Negro race did in fact find that in the late nineteenth and early twentieth centuries, mixed-bloods did compose a disproportionately large number of the race's most prominent figures.[58] Yet this fictional picture was more than a mere representation of Afro-American life as these authors saw it. It involved a second line of reasoning which argued that mulattoes must necessarily identify with the black race rather than with the white, regardless of how white their actual physical appearance (or sociocultural outlook) might be.

This concept of racial identification itself involved a cluster of ideas which provides insight into how people of mixed blood were perceived by blacks and by mulattoes themselves. (In point of fact, there seems to have been little difference between the viewpoints of these two groups in this regard.) First, there was little or no challenge to the widely held notion among whites that "one drop of Negro blood" was enough to make an individual black. Mulatto characters of the most Caucasian appearance unquestioningly accept their classification as black, despite the social and economic handicaps which they realize such a classification necessarily involves.[59] Even people who have been raised as white show no defiant feelings about changing their racial affiliation upon learning of their black background. Adrian Birch immediately assumes the attitude of a Negro in William M. Ashby's *Redder Blood*.[60] Similarly, Freda Waters, the beautiful heroine of F. Grant Gilmore's 1915 novel, *The Problem*, although raised by an aristocratic Virginia family and showing no physical trace of black ancestry, upon discovering her true racial history (her mother was of mixed blood) instantly becomes a Negro, both in her own eyes and those of her white and Negro friends. There is no thought that because of her actual appearance and social background she might desire or even be allowed to continue life as white.[61] Romantic involvement with whites must cease, not only because of social restrictions upon racial intermarriage, but because of the possibility that the offspring of even a white mulatto might show definite black physical characteristics. Thus, Iola Leroy feels that she must refuse her white suitor, for she knows that one day he would surely reject her because of her black blood, especially if "little children in after years should nestle in our arms, and one of them show unmistakable signs of color."[62]   Likewise, Adrian Birch cannot marry his white sweetheart because their children might show the mark of color, although he himself does not.[63]

The idea of atavistic children resulting from interracial marriages was a common notion in contemporary racial thought. It was closely linked to the belief that mulattoes carried in their blood various distinct black racial traits, ready to assert themselves at any moment. This was, of course, merely one expression of the general cluster of ideas which emphasized the importance of distinctive racial traits and instincts. In Afro-American fiction, it appeared somewhat more vividly in references to inherent psychological differences between the races, perhaps because Negroes did not accept the general white assessment of the inferiority of black racial traits. When Iola Leroy tells her white suiter, Dr. Gresham, that "there are barriers between us that I cannot pass," she is getting to the core of the racial thought of the period and its explanation of why a mulatto was ultimately a Negro. Afro-Americans seem to have been as firmly convinced as whites that the two races were fundamentally different because of basic inner qualities. Hence mulattoes, because they had some degree of black blood in them (and therefore black traits as well), could not ever be truly white, regardless of their appearance or socioeconomic background. They would always be closer to blacks in an inner, psychic sense, and their identification should therefore be with the black race.[64] As among white racial thinkers, there was no suggestion by Afro-Amercian authors that a mulatto's proportionately greater admixture of white blood might be the cause of psychic/spiritual alienation from blacks, i.e., that "one drop (or usually many drops) of white blood" made an individual white. It was as though "black blood" involved an almost tangible ingredient which was not present in "white blood," and its possession guaranteed one's sense of blackness.

This vein of thought was most obviously manifested during this period in the writings of W. E. B. Du Bois. Although light of color, highly educated, and of refined cultural tastes, Du Bois passionately identified with the black race. Indeed, one might say he became the prophet of the uniqueness of the black experience based upon a belief in the value and the distinctiveness of inherent black characteristics.

The notion of distinctive black racial traits, instincts, and/or "genius" permeated Du Bois' lyric *The Souls of Black Folk* (1903) and underlay the development of the Afro-American characters in his 1911 novel, *The Quest of the Silver Fleece*.[65] However, perhaps Du Bois' most overt statement of this attitude appeared in a paper published in 1897 by the American Negro Academy. In this essay, he noted that racial differences ran far deeper than mere physical distinctions. Ultimately, the cohesiveness and continuity of racial groups derived from spiritual and psychic bonds which, while "undoubtedly based" on physical qualities, actually were of a more transcendent character. "The whole process," Du Bois explained,

> which has brought about these race differentiations has been a growth, and the great characteristic of this growth has been the differentiation of spiritual and mental differences between great races of mankind and the integration of physical differences.[66]

Each separate race had its own special spirit or gift which it would eventually bequeath to the progress of mankind.

Du Bois' thought was thus very much in tune with the basic patterns of contemporary racial thought. He believed very deeply in the importance of innate and distinguishing racial qualities, but broke with most white thinkers by insisting that the qualities of the Negro race were valuable and worthwhile. At the same time, he believed that these traits left the black man somehow apart from his white neighbor, and the racial pressures generated within American society further hampered spiritual integration of the two races.

Such circumstances left the Negro in a peculiar dilemma. As Du Bois observed in his essay, *The Conservation of Races,*

> No Negro who has given earnest thought to the situation of his people in America has failed, at sometime in life, to find himself at these crossroads; has failed to ask himself at some time: what, after all, am I? Am I an American or am I a Negro? Can I be both? Or is it my duty to cease to be a Negro as soon as possible and be an American? If I strive as a Negro, am I not perpetuating the very cleft that threatens and separates black and white America? Is not my only possible practical aim the subduction of all that is Negro in me to the American?[67]

These probing queries, of course, were at the very heart of the issues Du Bois sought to confront in *The Souls of Black Folk.* The central concept was that of two-ness--of being simultaneously black and American--with the white world incessantly forcing the Negro to be conscious of this fact. "It is a peculiar sensation, this double-consciousness," he wrote,

> the sense of always looking at one's self through the eyes of others, of measuring one's soul by the tape of a world that looks on in an amused contempt and pity. One ever feels his twoness--an American, a Negro; two souls, two thoughts, two unreconciled strivings; two warring ideals in one dark body, whose dogged strength alone keeps it from being torn asunder.

The history of the American Negro is the history of this strife,--this longing to attain self-conscious manhood, to merge his double self into a better and truer self. He would not Africanize America, for America has too much to teach the world and Africa. He would not bleach his Negro soul in a flood of white Americanism, for he knows that Negro blood has a message for the world. He simply wishes to make it possible for a man to be both a Negro and an American, without being cursed and spat upon by his fellows, without having the doors of Opportunity closed roughly in his face.[68]

Perhaps more than he personally recognized, Du Bois here caught most specifically the plight of the refined and educated mulatto in America--the individual whose social and cultural horizons reached far beyond those of the bulk of the Negro race. The mulatto was most acutely caught in the middle between identifying with the black race or with the larger world of white America and its way of life. The "double-consciousness" of which Du Bois spoke was the mixed-blood's peculiar dilemma, imposed upon him by a racial system which refused to recognize him as anything but black.[69]

This general pattern of thought--that even distant black ancestry made one a Negro, and that being a Negro, one was inherently different from white people because of the very nature of fundamental race traits-- led to the widely held conclusion that attempting to pass for white was a tragic mistake, both for the individual and for the race. The mulatto characters in Frances Harper's *Iola Leroy* (1892) voice these sentiments (and hers) quite clearly. Harry Leroy's uncle, himself a light mulatto, applauds Harry's own decision to stand as a member of the black race: "I think it would be treason, not only to the race, but to humanity, to have you ignoring your kindred and masquerading as a white man."[70] The choice of the word "masquerading" seems important, for it reveals just how strongly Harper believed that even the lightest mulatto still remained essentially a Negro. Iola also refuses to bow to the temptations to pass, even though she finds difficulty in keeping good jobs when her racial identity is discovered. "I see no necessity for proclaiming the fact on the house-top," she declares, "yet I am resolved that nothing shall tempt me to deny it. The best blood in my veins is African blood, and I am not ashamed of it." "I am not willing to live under a shadow of concealment which I thoroughly hate as if the blood in my veins were an undetected crime of my soul," she defiantly announces.[71] Understandably, Iola is proud of young Dr. Latimer (whom she eventually marries) who refused his white grandmother's offer of riches if he would forget his black background. His decision, Iola contends, was "the grandest hour of his life," although he sees it only as his natural "duty." While the inducements to pass are great in America, particularly because of the discriminations practiced against Afro-Americans, "even these advantages," Iola notes,

> are far too dearly bought if they mean loss of honor, true manliness, and self-respect. He could not have retained these had he ignored his mother and lived under a veil of concealment, constantly haunted by a dread of detection. It were better that he should walk the ruggedest paths of life a true man than tread the softest carpets a moral cripple.[72]

In like tones of racial pride, Oscar Micheaux ridicules light mulattoes who marry white women and thereby pass into the white race. As time passes, such people develop "a terror of their race; disowning and denying the blood that coursed through their veins; claiming to be of some foreign descent; in fact, anything to hide or conceal the mixture of Ethopian [sic]." It was, he felt, far too dear a price to pay to escape "a race that is hated."[73]

Sutton E. Griggs' *The Hindered Hand* (1905) treats the question somewhat more sympathetically, but nonetheless shows clearly that passing can only bring harmful results. Arabelle Seabright, an ambitious mixed-blood who shows no evidence of black ancestry, forces her family into a scheme of passing, even at the expense of casting off one daughter who does show Negro features. Predictably, the consequences are tragic, as her son, Percy Marshall, is murdered by a jealous black man for meeting with his own rejected sister. Arabelle subsequently commits suicide, and her other daughter, Eunice, goes mad when it is revealed in court that she is of mixed blood. She is unable to cope with the pressure inherent in being recognized as an Afro-American. "I declare to you all to-day that I am a white woman," Eunice frantically cries to those around her, unwilling to admit the truth to herself.

> My blood is the blood of whites, my instincts, my feelings, my culture, my spirit, my all is cast in the same mold as yours, That woman [her darker sister] who talked to you a few moments ago is a Negro. Don't honor her word above mine, the word of a white woman. I invoke your law of caste. Look at me! Look at my boy! In what respect do we differ from you?
>
> . . . in the name of heaven I ask you, send not my child and me into Negro life. Send us not to a race cursed with petty jealousies, the burden bearers of the world. My God! the thought of being called a Negro is awful, awful![74]

In a sense, Griggs here seems to be arguing against the idea of race traits, since he apparently sympathizes with Eunice's position, but her eventual defeat may signal that Griggs recognized that popular beliefs are often much stronger than logic.

Given the clearly negative attitude with which most of the early Afro-American writers viewed attempts at passing for white, it is understandable that there were few examples in the fiction of the period of the third type of mulatto image--that of an individual who is sensitive to his position between the two races and who is more likely to choose to pass into the white world. In *The Hindered Hand*, Griggs demonstrates a degree of insight into why such people would decide to pass. Tiara Merlow, the daughter who was cast aside because of her color, tries to defend her mother's misguided efforts:

> . . . do not judge her too harshly. You people who are white do not know what an awful burden it is to be black in these days of the world. If some break down beneath the awful load of caste which you thrust upon them, mingle pity with your blame.[75]

In Earl Bluefield, Eunice Seabright's mixed-blood husband, Griggs had another vehicle for portraying the plight of the mulatto. He is also sensitive about his white blood: "am I not as much of an Anglo-Saxon as any of them?" Earl queries. "Does not my soul respond to those things and those things only to which their souls respond?"[76] Not truly a part of either race, he is "Humanity's Ishmaelite."

> Non-existent was I [he soliloquized] until the whim of a Southern white man, trampling upon the alleged sacred canons of his race, called me into being and endowed me with the spirit of his kind. In the race into which I was thrust, I sought to manifest my martial spirit, but met with no adequate response from men grooved in the ways of peace.[77]

Only in his wife did he find someone able to understand his situation, for she too was "a victim of the bloods," a true member of neither race.

> He looked upon himself as a sort of exotic in the non-resisting Negro race and considered himself a special object of scorn on the part of the white people of the South, who seemed to him to resent his near approach unto them in blood, and to mistrust *his* kind more than all other elements of Negro life.[78]

Ultimately, however, Griggs' fiction was designed to serve a propagandistic purpose; his primary goal was to attack racial prejudice and discrimination in America. He was consequently writing from the perspective of the race as a whole, and therefore tended to view passing and the mulatto's complex status in that light. Passing might well indeed be viewed as an index of the state of race relations, with increased degrees of passing being seen as reflective of greater racial repression. Yet in the end passing represents an individual decision on the part of the person of mixed blood.   When he sees whites in possession of privileges denied him because of his status as a Negro; when he is aware of the argument that blacks' physical differences from whites are proof of racial inferiority; and when he himself is free from these differences, it becomes an understandable response to wish to escape the burden of race inherent in being a Negro and to merge in the identity of the white group.[79] It is those Afro-American writers who deal with the mulatto and the question of passing on an individul basis, then, who demonstrate the greatest insight into the difficult position faced by the mixed-blood in America.   Prior to World War I, only Charles W. Chesnutt and James Weldon Johnson offered such treatments of mulatto characters.   Perhaps it is not coincidental that theirs are the only Afro-American fictional works of this period which have proved of lasting literary worth.

5

Carl Van Vechten called Charles Chesnutt's *The House Behind the Cedars* (1900) "perhaps the first authentic study on the subject of passing."[80]   It is the story of John and Rena Walden, the light-skinned children of a Southern aristocrat and his mulatto mistress.   As a youth, John, the elder of the two, had decided to leave the community where he was classified as an inferior human being, change his name, and enjoy elsewhere the privileges accorded to white men.   In his new home he married a refined white woman.   After giving birth to their son, she died, leaving John the sole heir to her large estate and a respected man in the community.   He demonstrates no reservations about his decision.   Indeed, in *The House Behind the Cedars* there is little doubt expressed about the worth of the goal of passing:

> Once persuaded that he had certain rights [Chesnutt says of John Walden], or ought to have them, by virtue of the laws of nature, in defiance of the customs of mankind, he had promptly sought to enjoy them. This he had been able to do by simply concealing his antecedents and making the most of his opportunities, with no troublesome qualms of conscience whatever.[81]

The only true reservation is the fear that the passing might be detected.
John risks the chance of detection by returning to his home to take his beautiful sister away with him, for she too is restless in a town where she has no future save as a Negro. This is in essence the dilemma both of them feel--the notion that they cannot remain as they are, but must either become blacker or whiter.[82]   John (and Chesnutt) realized

that the light mulatto, though so close to breaking into the white mainstream, still must suffer a particular stigma:

> Of course she [Rena] will have no chances here, where our story is known. The War has wrought great changes, has put the bottom rail on top, and all that--but it hasn't wiped *that* out. Nothing but death [a foreshadowing of Rena's fate] can remove that stain, if it does not follow us even beyond the grave. Here she must forever be--nobody.[83]

At all costs, they must minimize their past and the stigma of being connected to the black race. When Rena becomes engaged to a young white man, George Tryon, her brother warns her to keep her racial origins a secret:

> It is a matter of the future, not of the past. . . . We are under no moral obligation to inflict upon others the history of our past mistakes. . . . Still less are we bound to bring out from this secret chamber the dusty record of our ancestry.[84]

Rena, however, is of a somewhat different frame of mind than her brother. While she wishes to escape from the proscriptions of the lower-class life of Southern blacks, she nevertheless tends to view passing as an act of deception. She is tortured by the possibility of being found out, especially by her lover:

> I am afraid to marry him, without telling him. If he should find out afterwards, he might cast me off, or cease to love me. If he did not know it, I should be forever thinking of what he would do if he *should* find out; or, if I should die without his having learned it, I should not rest easy in my grave for thinking of what he would have done if he *had* found out.[85]

Inevitably, of course, Tryon does discover the truth, then repudiates Rena as his prospective bride. He does, however, want her as his mistress. To escape him, she flees to a teaching job in a Negro school, where she is crudely molested by Jeff Wain, an unscrupulous school principal and one of Chesnutt's few dissolute mulatto characters. She eventually dies of a delirious illness, unable to cope with the sexual and racial pressures confronting her Victorian sense of womanhood.

What Chesnutt seems to be saying in *The House Behind the Cedars* is that passing (and therefore assimilation of the races) by deception is perhaps morally wrong, but without deception it is impossible. It is tragic that Rena's goal was crushed, but the aim itself was not wrong. The most important consideration facing the mulatto as an individual is that of self-survival, and the demands inherent in such considerations are those which Chesnutt seeks to have his mixed-blood characters meet.[86]   It was a situation which he confronted in his own lifetime, a decision which he himself had to make.   Able to pass for white quite easily, he also felt the isolation of the refined mulatto trapped in the dismal world of lower-class black life in the South. Quite naturally, it would seem, he also considered passing into the white world, yet he ultimately rejected that path, choosing instead to abandon his teaching job in the South for a professional career in the North (first in New York, then in Cleveland).   There he hoped to be able to escape the racial repression and personal frustrations he felt so sharply in the South.[87]   The choices facing the Waldens, and the mental torment that was involved in the decisions they had to make, were well understood by Chesnutt.   As a result, unlike most other Afro-American writers of the period, he could deal with such characters, and with their decisions to pass for white, in a sympathetic and yet realistic manner.[88]

James Weldon Johnson's *The Autobiography of an Ex-Coloured Man* (1912) is at once the most artistic, subtle, yet poignant Afro-American portrayal of race relations in the United States written prior to the Harlem Renaissance of the 1920s.   Through the exploits of his unnamed hero, Johnson provides vivid pictures of numerous facets of Afro-American life.   As the novel opens, he moves with his mother, the mulatto mistress of a young Southern gentleman, from agricultural Georgia to urban Connecticut where he grows up, attending school with whites and demonstrating considerable talent as a pianist.   Thwarted in his plans to attend Atlanta University, he moves on to Jacksonville, Florida, where he works in a cigar factory. Later he returns to the North, settling in New York's Tenderloin District where he becomes a gambler, ragtime pianist, and an accepted member of cabaret society. A murder forces him to travel to Europe as the companion of an eccentric millionaire.   Eventually, however, he grows dissatisfied with this "exile" and resolves to return to the South to study and transcribe Afro-American folk music.   While in Georgia, though, he is revolted by the sight of a Negro being lynched and concludes to join the white race. Within a few years he has become financially secure, married a respectable white woman, and fathered two children.

As with Chesnutt, Johnson does not censure his hero's decision to pass for white.   It represents an individual step, reflective of this one man's inability to copy with the pressures of being black.   Indeed, the novel itself is the story of the narrator's search for self-identity and fulfillment, which necessarily involves a gradual realization of just what it means to be black (and white) in America.   Because he is not wholly of either race, he vacillates in terms of racial identity.   Originally he enrolls in Atlanta University, a Negro school, determined to reject his white ancestry and to identify with those who are more likely to accept him.

Yet the lynching compels him to change his identity. "A great wave of shame and humiliation swept over me," he explains. "Shame that I belonged to a race that could be so dealt with." He rejects the black race (although not truly accepting the white one), because he no longer wants to be identified with a group that "could with impunity be treated worse than animals."

> I finally made up my mind that I would neither disclaim the black race nor claim the white race, but that I would change my name, raise a mustache, and let the world take me for what it would; that it was not necessary for me to go about with a label of inferiority pasted across my forehead.[89]

This is obviously the easy way out, a self-rationalization of racial "neutrality," but more deeply it reflects the cowardice and selfishness which Johnson shows to be the tragic flaw of his hero. Yet given the racial climate of the times and this individual's social and cultural background, it is a choice which we can nevertheless understand. As one student of Afro-American fiction has noted:

> It is to be expected that a man who is so sensitive to "the dwarfing, warping, distorting influence" of race prejudice, who has no powerful urge towards the reform and betterment of a race in which he has no real belief, and who possesses the same white complexion as that of the dominant group, should not feel hindered from changing races, when circumstances fostered that desire.[90]

Nevertheless, it does prove difficult to live with this decision, for although the narrator is now free from economic troubles and the flagrant persecution, insults, and circumscribed rights which Negroes must suffer, he is not freed from internal suffering, "a vague feeling of unsatisfaction, of regret, of almost remorse."[91] His anguish is compounded when he must decide whether to tell his white fiancée the whole truth about himself. Perhaps deception can be condoned in certain relationships, but not when it involves such a powerful issue as marrying a Negro. Yet his uneasiness goes deeper than this, for even once he is happily married and raising a family as a white man, he feels dissatisfaction and a rising sense of guilt. Watching self-sacrificing Negroes struggling for the betterment of their race, he sometimes feels himself "a coward, a deserter," "possessed by a strange longing for my mother's people."[92]   In comparison to such men, he laments,

> I feel small and selfish. I am an ordinarily successful white man who has made a little money. They are making history and a race. I, too, might have taken part in a work so glorious.[93]

Such shifting sentiments of repulsion and attraction are expressions of a chronic restlessness. On the one hand, shame, a feeling of superiority to the mass of blacks, and an intense individualism drive him from the black race, while on the other a vague sense of affinity and a desire to help naggingly pull him back. In the end he must live with both fear and guilt--fear that his children will one day discover their true ancestry, and guilt because in denying his own blackness, he has lost the opportunity to publish the musical manuscripts he had hoped would demonstrate black contributions to American culture. "A vanishing dream, a dead ambition, a sacrificed talent," he notes remorsefully. "I cannot repress the thought that after all, I have chosen the lesser part, that I have sold my birth-right for a mess of pottage."[94] This is the true burden born by the middle-class mulatto who is identified with both races and with neither, who is torn between two dichotomous positions with no real hope for finding complete contentment in either.[95] Johnson, more than any other Afro-American writer of his time, understood the tragedy of the mixed-blood in a severely biracial caste system like that of America.

6

The sense of isolation experienced by many mulatto characters involved both their relations with whites and with the mass of Negroes. It was also, to a certain degree, self-imposed, for while their relations with whites depended almost entirely upon the attitudes of the dominant group, their affiliation with the black masses was greatly affected by their own attitudes and actions. Further, their interactions with both groups involved not only considerations of caste (including basic notions about blackness and whiteness), but more importantly, elements of class consciousness as well.

It would seem that a considerable part of the problem of isolation stems from the ambivalent attitudes of many mulatto characters (and many of the authors themselves) towards blacks and blackness. Admittedly, most mulatto figures acquiesce to being identified as Negroes. Passing, as one option of responding to the state of race relations, was in reality open only to the relatively few mulattoes who possessed very light complexions and no distinguishing Negro features. Most mulattoes, then, thought of themselves as black and, as noted above, demonstrated a certain sense of responsibility toward the race. Because they were often characterized as having had educational and cultural advantages denied to most Negroes, they were expected to be leaders of the race and models of the bourgeois success which was seen as the key to the race's eventual acceptance by white America. Yet despite seeing themselves as black and recognizing their roles as race leaders, many mulatto characters evidenced disdain about actually becoming a "part" of the race. Their class consciousness and color prejudice inhibited their racial loyalty.

With few exceptions, these mulatto characters, like the writers who created them, were staunch members of the middle class.[96] As such, they had little in common with the masses of the race in terms of lifestyles or socio-cultural outlook. Consequently, in their functional depictions of Afro-American life, these early authors portray marked degrees of social stratification within the race, often reflective of distinctions of skin color as well (with mulattoes congregating for the greater part in the higher social classes).

These color and class distinctions are reflected in the different manners in which mulattoes and black characters are portrayed. Virtually all mulattoes are middle-class, models of Victorian demeanor, and essentially indistinguishable from whites of the same socio-economic status. They evidence no trace of Negro dialect in their speech, nor any inclination toward the unrefined tastes and habits attributed by both white and Afro-American authors of the period to the lower classes of Negroes.

This is not to say that there were no virtuous, middle-class black characters in the Negro fiction of this era. On the contrary, many Afro-American authors seem to have taken great pains to develop noble characters of markedly black complexions. Most were male figures. Sgt. William Henderson, the hero of F. Grant Gilmore's *The Problem* (1915), is characterized as a handsome, very black man of great courage, integrity, intelligence, and patriotism. Abe Overly, in Robert L. Waring's *As We See It*, (1910), is described as having come

> of a stock of nature's noblemen. He was tall, straight, broad of shoulder, strong limbed, good featured and very black—a typical African—but the kind of man that inspires trust and confidence at a glance.[97]

Charles Henry Holmes portrays Allan Dune, the founder of an organization for racial unity in *Ethiopia, The Land of Promise* (1917), as a paragon of Victorian manhood. "Of athletic build, black in color, and possessing a very intelligent face," he is a natural leader of men, "indomitable of will" yet "generous and unselfish to an absurd degree" and unflinchingly chivalrous in his respect for and defense of women.[98] Female black characters of this type are far fewer in number, although some do exist. In *Iola Leroy* (1892), for instance, Henry Leroy marries a young black schoolteacher. "She is medium height," he says of her, "somewhat slender and well formed, with dark, expressive eyes, full of thought and feeling. Neither hair nor complexion show the least hint of blood admixture."[99]   In *Hearts of Gold* (1896), J. McHenry Jones depicts a similar young black woman of refined tastes and attractive features in the character of Lucile Malone.

Nevertheless, when these authors wished to portray the lower orders of Afro-American life, they almost always chose black-skinned characters.   Comic characters throughout the fiction of the period were universally of a black complexion, e.g., Jerry, Sandy, and Mammy Jane in Charles Chesnutt's *The Marrow of Tradition* (1901) and Peter in his *The Colonel's Dream* (1905), Whreabo in Henry Francis Downing's *The American Cavalryman* (1917), and Pete in F. Grant Gilmore's *The Problem* (1915).[100]   More significantly, however, numerous writers assembled groups of uncouth lower-class blacks to emphasize the refined mulatto's superiority.   Indeed, as Robert Bone has noted, it became almost a stock scene in the early Afro-American novels for a "refined Afro-American" to have to share a Jim Crow railroad car with a group of dirty, boisterous, and drunken Negroes.[101]   Dr. Miller, in Chesnutt's *The Marrow of Tradition*, is subjected to such an experience among a crowd of "noisy, loquacious, happy, dirty, malodorous" lower-class blacks.   He tries to concentrate on his sense of racial brotherhood with them, but in the end is forced from the car because he finds them too "offensive."[102]   Otis M. Shackelford describes the ordeal of Lillian Simmons on a Jim Crow car in similar terms.   She was outraged at having to ride with "disrespectful, loud mouthed, foolish Negroes."   One "vile, uncouth idiot of a Negro," a dirty, impudent, "depraved animal" even accosted her so that she was forced to seek the aid of the white conductor.[103]

The point of such episodes, however, was not merely to criticize the behavior of lower-class blacks, although, as Bone contends, there was considerable feeling during the period that "the bad Negro keeps the good Negro back."[104]   More important, they served as devices for showing white readers that in fact all Negroes were not alike, and that many felt as much disdain for the lower classes of the race as whites did. Indeed, the ultimate purpose of all the exaggerated characterizations of mulatto figures as paragons of middle-class (white) virtues was the desire of bridging *caste* distinctions with *class* affinities.   By drawing extreme distinctions between bourgeois mulatto figures and the distasteful black masses, the early Afro-American writers, and the class they represented, hoped for greater acceptance by the white, middle-class majority. In their novels, as in their own lives, they hoped that by eliminating virtually all traces of blackness they might convince whites that they were better assimilated, both biologically and culturally, than the Negro masses, and consequently deserving of integration into American life.   Cultural uniformity based upon similarity of tastes and lifestyles hopefully would win the mulatto middle class a more equitable social and economic status, even if it came, for the time being, at the expense of the rest of their race.[105]

This disengagement from the black masses was not necessarily an easy direction to make, nor was it universally accepted as the proper course of action. The work of Charles Chesnutt is indicative of the conflicting sentiments that were involved. Markedly assimilationist in tone, his fiction nevertheless argues for greater racial justice for all Afro-Americans. As one student has noted, however, his pleas for racial equality are undercut by the nature of the characters he develops most fully.[106] The counter-stereotypes Chesnutt created to challenge negative images of Negroes in racist white literature of the day often reinforce unfavorable attitudes about blacks. His primary characters are not black at all, either in color or outlook. They emulate white standards of behavior, of cultural refinement, and even of skin color. The characteristics which stand out about them are those which make them white-like, not those which make them a part of the Negro race. Chesnutt's black figures, on the other hand, generally reflect widely held popular notions about Afro-Americans. They remain, for the most part, simple character types--superstitious, flattering of white quality, lacking in intellectual depth, seemingly incapable of true equality with whites. They serve only to heighten the contrast between the refined mulatto figures and the rest of the race. Is it Chesnutt speaking through Dr. Miller when the physician wonders why Jim Crow cars cannot be operated on the basis of class rather than caste?[107]

It is as though Chesnutt, perhaps because of his personal history, was unable to decide just where the refined mulatto fit in the scheme of race relations in America. His fiction included a number of condemnations of the harmful effects of color and class prejudice among Negroes.[108] Yet at the same time his major characters convey a sense of superiority to the black masses, a superiority which is vaguely related to their white blood. Chesnutt's private life offers evidence of similar confusion. Although always an active and outspoken critic of racial injustice, he nevertheless found life among lower-class Negroes in the South personally distasteful and subsequently moved to the urban North.[109] In Cleveland, he and his family were involved with leading social groups, including the Cleveland Social Circle, which his daughter and biographer described as "a very exclusive organization--membership in it was the *sine qua non* of social standing among the better-educated people of color."[110] His professional position and literary renown also allowed him to mix in cultured white circles in the North. It was a sphere that was far removed from the way of life of the majority of Negroes in America, yet it was one which understandably led to a desire for greater white acceptance of himself and his kind.

Robert Bone has criticized Chesnutt's outlook as being "assimilationist," an attitude which he views as "a means of escape, a form of flight from 'the Problem.'"

> It involves a denial of one's racial identity, which may be disguised by such sentiments as "I'm not a Negro but a human being."–as if the two were mutually exclusive. This denial is accompanied by a contrived sense of race consciousness and a belittling of caste barriers. By minimizing the color line, the assimilationist loses touch with the realities of Negro life. Ultimately, he identifies with the white group. Assimilationism, viewed as a personal adjustment to being a Negro in America, is a kind of psychological "passing" at the fantasy level.[111]

The fiction produced by Chesnutt and other Afro-American writers of his day must, however, be considered in the light of the racial situation as they themselves experienced it. At a time of burgeoning white racial prejudice, perhaps individual advancement on the part of middle-class mulattoes was the most obvious and realistic means of personally dealing with the situation. In a society still engulfed in primitive notions of race, heredity, and "blood" which together emphasized the inherent superiority of the white race, is it inconceivable that mulattoes would point with pride to their white heritage, especially if they felt that that might win them greater acceptance from the dominant group? Certainly this could be, and was, carried to unnecessary extremes by some of the Afro-American writers of the period, first in their exaggerated employment of aristocratic whites as the forebears of the mulatto characters, and secondly in their not infrequent tendency to attribute the character strengths of these mulatto figures to their white blood.[112] But these faults must be seen within the context of contemporary popular and scientific notions about race and as personal statements of individuals who were often, in actuality, more white than black themselves, both in terms of physical appearance and socio-cultural outlook.

With all of their praise for mixed-blooded characters, though, surprisingly little sentiment existed in favor of further racial intermixture. Indeed, numerous authors make vigorous statements against such a course of action, viewing both legal and extra-legal sexual relations between whites and Negroes as detrimental to the cause of more harmonious race relations. Because many saw Afro-American unity and racial pride as essential to the growth and prosperity of the race, amalgamation represented a significant threat. All of the mulatto characters in Frances Harper's *Iola Leroy* (1892) speak out against racial mixing, as do Will Smith in Pauline Hopkins' *Contending Forces* (1900), Ensal Ellwood in Sutton Griggs' *The Hindered Hand* (1905), and Bernard

Belgrave in Griggs' *Imperium in Imperio* (1899). Oscar Micheaux attacks marriage to whites in his semi-autobiographical work, *The Conquest* (1913), because it tended to make Negroes denigrate their connections with their own race.[113]   Robert L. Waring criticized most intermixture as bad for the black race because it too often involved whites of the lower order, or "crackers." The mulatto offspring of such unions, he felt, were invariably inferior to pure blacks.[114]

Defenders of racial amalgamation, on the other hand, were few. Charles Chesnutt and James Weldon Johnson seem to imply at least partial approval in allowing certain very light mulatto characters to pass and marry whites. William M. Ashby similarly contends that intermarriage is acceptable from a sentimental standpoint between two people truly in love, while prohibitive legislation only promotes "subterfuge and illicit dealings."[115]   Joel Augustus Rogers also saw baneful effects in prohibitive legislation, since it went against the natural human inclination toward interracial mixing and drove this inevitable activity underground, depriving it of its rightful moral sanctions.[116]

While further racial amalgamation met with widespread disapproval among these Afro-American authors, they recognized that the mulatto's future itself was not in jeopardy. In their reflections of social attitudes and practices within the Afro-American community, many writers gave attention to the common practice (or desire) of choosing a marriage partner of a lighter complexion than oneself. This was particularly true of dark men marrying lighter women. Indeed, although a number of these authors were critical of such an inclination among the race, it was a frequent occurrence even within their own fictional works. Sutton Griggs, for example, expressed considerable disdain for the practice in *Overshadowed* (1901). Josiah Nerve, a disgruntled black preacher who has been rejected by his middle-class congregation because he is too much darker than they, gives expression to Griggs' own views:

> Nowadays you never hear of two coal-black persons marrying each other. The black man is pushing the black women aside to grab the yellow woman; and the black woman is pushing the black man aside to grab the yellow man. I know of black mothers with black daughters that have sworn they will poison their daughters if they attempt to marry black men.[117]

When the light-skinned heroine, Erma Wysong, marries dark-hued Astral Herndon, Griggs notes the two-sided reaction among the Afro-American community:

> Astral was criticized by some on the score that he had chosen a wife of mixed blood when there were so many girls in the city of pure Negro extraction. Others insisted that he had acted

wisely, on the theory that each succeeding generation should be as far removed as possible from the original color which had so many ills chargeable to it.[118]

In *Pointing the Way* (1908), Griggs likewise emphasizes the folly of Letitia Gilbreath's color prejudice. She considers it "a shocking crime for two dark persons to marry each other" and consequently plots, although unsuccessfully, to have her niece Clotille marry Baug Peppers, a light mulatto lawyer, rather than the dark-skinned Conroe Driscoll.[119] In *Contending Forces* (1900), a black woman similarly complains of the disadvantages her type faces in finding a spouse: " . . . a good wholesome-lookin' colored woman with kinkey hair don't stan' no livin' chance ter git a decen' lookin' man fer a husban'."[120] Even Chesnutt derides such color consciousness in "A Matter of Principle," wherein Mr. Clayton's great concern over the color of his daughter's potential suitors leads him to reject meritorious young men who are too dark.[121]

The depth of this color prejudice which placed a premium on whiteness is evidenced by the nature of the physical descriptions of female characters of mixed blood in the fiction of this period. Invariably they are praised for those attributes which are most white-like--long, flowing hair, unblemished, light complexions, finely chiseled noses and other facial features, etc. With fictional images emphasizing the beauty of such white features, actual social attitudes among Negroes were only reinforced.

A predilection for light-skinned mates was but one manifestation of the color prejudice seen in Afro-American fiction which hindered intraracial harmony among the nation's Negro population. More significant was the inclination of middle- and upper-class members of the race, who were disproportionately of mixed blood, to segregate themselves socially from the rest of the race. Charles Chesnutt's portrayals of this class are the most vivid,[122] but rigid social stratification within the race was dealt with by a number of other writers as well. The staunchly bourgeois character of the great majority of mulattoes has already been noted, but social stratification involved more than merely physical lifestyles. Middle- and upper-class Negroes often shunned contact with the masses of the race because of color prejudice itself, a fact which engendered antipathy, distrust, and perhaps even envy on the part of the darker majority.

The conflict is seen in Griggs' treatment of Josiah Nerve. Speaking of the upper-class group which discharged him from his pastorial duties, he complains:

> . . . all of the mulattoes, whose skins are such that their blue blood shows, have decided to form an aristocracy. If you are yellow and don't work any with your hands, you are all right . . . If you are

black and don't work any with your hands and are smarter than the
whole lot of them blue-veiners put together, you will be accepted
until they get something on you . . . .The color line is drawn tighter
within the race than ever it was on the outside, and the original
bona fide members of the race didn't draw the line. It is the first
time that I ever knew of a people who slipped into a race through a
backdoor sitting on the front piazza and hollowing to the honest-
born chaps to stay in the kitchen.[123]

Griggs clearly perceived that the problem centered around the inclination
of mulattoes, and of the race as a whole, to identify whiteness with
goodness. There was an obvious tendency within all segments of the
race to ape the ways of the white man, although it was most noticeable
among those who were closest to him in physical appearance. As long as
blackness symbolized evil and ugliness in the minds of Afro-Americans,
the race could generate little of the self-respect so essential to its
development. This explains the importance of virtuous black characters
in the literature of the period, but the fact that they were greatly
outnumbered by mixed-bloods is indicative of the outlook of many
members of the race, both black and mulatto. Griggs caught the point
quite succinctly in the words of Josiah Nerve:

I really think what makes blue-veiners so aristocratic is that we
blacks like them, the white folks like them, and they like themselves;
leaving us nobody to like us blacks. If we ever turn to liking black
faces it will only be after the whites turn that way. The whites
regulate all of our tastes, even to telling us who are our greatest men
among us.[124]

Herein lay the crucial dilemma confronting Negroes during this
period--how to find a place for themselves in a nation totally dominated
by another race, while at the same time coming to grips with the issue of
their own blackness. For those whose ancestry mixed the blood of two
races, the problem was surely even more acute, especially given the
manner in which the majority of Americans understood the meaning of
race and racial differences. This largely explains the overwhelming
concern of the era's Afro-American fiction with the race problem.
Indeed, it seems evident that the manner in which the early Afro-
American writers dealt with mixed-blood characters mirrored, to a
considerable degree, the actual situation in which many mulattoes found
themselves at this time. They did compose a disproportionately large
segment of the Negro middle and upper classes, but despite their
bourgeois lifestyles still found themselves shunned by the white
majority.[125]   That they should have sought through their literature to
ameliorate racial tensions and convince their white counterparts of their
socio-cultural refinement in hopes of bettering their own status seems an

understandably human goal. That they failed in their efforts to breach caste with class is an indication of the depth of American racial prejudice in the early decades of this century.

NOTES

[1] In this regard, see Penelope L. Bullock, "The Treatment of the Mulatto in American Fiction from 1826 to 1902" (unpublished M.A. thesis, Atlanta University, 1944), pp. ii-iv; Penelope L. Bullock, "The Mulatto in American Fiction," *Phylon*, VI, 1 (Spring, 1945), 78-79; Catherine Juanita Starke, *Black Portraiture in American Fiction: Stock Characters, Archetypes, and Individuals* (New York: Basic Books, Inc., 1971), p. 18; and Rebecca Chalmers Barton, *Race Consciousness and the American Negro: A Study of the Correlation Between the Group Experience and the Fiction of 1900-1930* (Copenhagen: Arnold Busck, 1934), pp. 9-16, 70-72.

[2] This is not to say that blacks in the North had had an easy life prior to this time. For evidence of earlier Northern prejudice and discrimination by whites, see Leon F. Litwack, *North of Slavery: The Negro in the Free States*, 1790-1860 (Chicago: University of Chicago Press, 1961) and Jacque Vogeli, *Free But Not Equal: The Midwest and the Negro During the Civil War* (Chicago: University of Chicago Press, 1967). For a thorough summary of prejudice, discrimination, and violence disrupting Afro-American life in the late nineteenth and early twentieth centuries, see Rayford W. Logan, *The Betrayal of the Negro from Rutherford B. Hayes to Woodrow Wilson* (London: Collier-Macmillan, 1965).

[3] The nature of propaganda in black fiction has been treated in Nick Aaron Ford, "The Negro Author's Use of Propaganda in Imaginative Literature" (unpublished Ph.D. dissertation, State University of Iowa, 1945). Ford classified these efforts into five main techniques, all visible in the Afro-American fiction of this period:

1. exalting the character and achievements of the race;
2. debunking the "legend" of white supremacy;
3. threatening revolt;
4. appealing for justice, equality, and fraternity;
5. criticizing unfavorable attitudes held by Negroes themselves.

[4] For a summary of the changing patterns in Afro-American social structure during this period, see August Meier, "Negro Class Structure and Ideology in the Age of Booker T. Washington," *Phylon*, XXIII, 3 (Fall, 1962), 258-266.

[5] For a fine discussion of the essential patterns of thought found in this early Afro-American fiction, see Robert Bone, *The Negro Novel in America* (Rev. ed.: New Haven: Yale University Press, 1965), pp. 11-28. Bone contends that a division between assimilationist and nationalist attitudes has characterized most of Afro-American life and writing since emancipation. The general intellectual/ideological currents of the period are thoroughly treated in an indispensible study by August Meier, *Negro Thought in America, 1880-1915: Racial Ideologies in the Age of Booker T. Washington* (Ann Arbor: University of Michigan Press, 1963).

[6] Starke, *Black Portraiture*, pp. 24-25.

[7] *Ibid.*, p. 88.

[8] Bullock, "Mulatto in American Fiction," p. 79. See also Bullock, "Treatment of Mulatto in American Fiction," pp. 25-55; Starke, *Black Portraiture*, pp. 89-107; David W. Levy, "Racial Stereotypes in Antislavery Fiction," *Phylon*, XXXI, 3 (Fall, 1970),

272-278; and Jules Zanger, "The 'Tragic Octoroon' in Pre-Civil War Fiction," *American Quarterly*, XVIII, 1 (Spring, 1966), 63-70. Zanger gives a description of the character similar to that of Bullock:

> " . . . . a beautiful young girl who possesses only the slightest evidences of Negro blood, who speaks with no trace of dialect, who was raised and educated as a white child and as a lady of the household of her father, and who on her paternal side is descended from 'some of the best blood of the "old Dominion."' In her sensibility and vulnerability she resembles, of course, the conventional ingenue 'victim' of sentimental romance. Her condition is radically changed when, at her father's unexpected death, it is revealed that he has failed to free her properly. She discovers that she is a slave; her person is attached as property by her father's creditors. Sold into slavery, she is victimized, usually by a lower-class, dialect-speaking slave dealer or overseer--often, especially after the Fugitive Slave Act, a Yankee--who attempts to violate her; she is loved by a high-born young Northerner or European who wishes to marry her. Occasionally she escapes with her lover; more often, she dies a suicide, or dies of shame, or dies protecting her young gentlemen."
> (pp. 63-64)

[9]See Sterling A. Brown, "A Century of Negro Portraiture in American Literature," *Massachusetts Review*, VII, 1 (Winter, 1966), 79; and Hugh M. Gloster, *Negro Voices in American Fiction* (Chapel Hill: University of North Carolina Press, 1948), p. 17.

[10]Frances E. W. Harper, *Iola Leroy, or Shadows Up-lifted* (Philadelphia: Garrigues Brothers, 1892), pp. 39-40.

[11]*Ibid.*, p. 39.

[12]Pauline Hopkins' varied career is described in Anne Allen Shockley, "Pauline E. Hopkins, A Biographical Excursion into Obscurity," *Phylon*, XXXIII, 1 (Spring, 1972), 22-26. Hopkins' picture, showing her to be of a medium complexion, may be found in the *Colored American Magazine*, III, 1 (May, 1901), 52.

[13]Pauline E. Hopkins, "A Dash for Liberty," *Colored American Magazine*, III, 4 (August, 1901), 246.

[14]Pauline E. Hopkins, *Winona, A Tale of Negro Life in the South and Southwest*, serialized in the *Colored American Magazine*, beginning in V. 1 (May, 1902), 29.

[15]Pauline E. Hopkins, *Contending Forces: A Romance Illustrative of Negro Life* (Boston: Colored Co-Operative Publishing Company, 1900).

[16]Sarah A. Allen (Pauline E. Hopkins), *Hagar's Daughter, A Story of Southern Caste Prejudice*, serialized in the *Colored American Magazine*, beginning in II, 5 (March, 1901), 337.

[17]William M. Ashby, *Redder Blood, A Novel* (New York: Cosmopolitan Press, 1915), pp. 169-170.

[18]*Ibid.*, p. 178.

[19] *Ibid.*, p. 181.

[20] *Ibid.*, p. 182.

[21] Charles W. Chesnutt, "Her Virginia Mammy", in *The Wife of His Youth, and Other Stories of the Color Line* (Boston and New York: Houghton, Mifflin and Company, 1899), pp. 25-59.

[22] [James Weldon Johnson], *The Autobiography of an Ex-Coloured Man* (Boston: Sherman, French and Company, 1912), pp. 19-21.

[23] Bone, *Negro Novel in America*, pp. 13-14.

[24] Peter Gabriel Filene, *Him/Her/Self: Sex Roles in Modern America* (New York: Harcourt Brace Jovanovich, Inc., 1974), p. 78.

[25] Charles W. Chesnutt, *The Marrow of Tradition* (Boston and New York: Houghton, Mifflin and Company, 1901), p. 49.

[26] Sutton E. Griggs, *Imperium in Imperio* (Cincinnati: The Editor Publishing Co., 1899), esp. pp. 83-110.

[27] Sutton E. Griggs, *Pointing the Way* (Nashville: Orion Publishing Company, 1908).

[28] Henry F. Downing, *The American Cavalryman: A Liberian Romance* (New York: Neale Publishing Company, 1917). p. 22.

[29] Hopkins, *Contending Forces*, p. 90.

[30] *Ibid.*, pp. 263-273, 287-302.

[31] J. McHenry Jones, *Hearts of Gold, A Novel* (Wheeling, W. Va.: Daily Intelligencer Steam Job Press, 1896); Harper, *Iola Leroy;* A. Gude Deekun, "A Georgia Episode," *Colored American Magazine,* III, 1 (May 1901), 3-8.

[32] Peter Filene contends that white men as well were confronted with great difficulties, socially, economically, and psychologically, in meeting the demands of the traditional ideas of manliness in the late Victorian period. In part, this explains the enthusiastic response of American men to the challenging opportunities they perceived as being offered by the Great War. See Filene, *Him/Her/Self,* pp. 77-127.

[33] Bone, *Negro Novel in America*, p. 15.

[34] George Langhorne Pryor, *Neither Bond Nor Free. (A Plea)* (New York: J. S. Ogilvie Publishing Company, 1902), p. 81. This strong pro-Booker T. Washington position is evident in a number of fictional works by Afro-Americans in this period. See especially Otis M. Shackelford, *Lillian Simmons, or, The Conflict of Sections* (Kansas City, Mo.: Published by the Author by the press of R. M. Rigby Printing Co., 1915); Hopkins, *Contending Forces;* and three works by Oscar Micheaux, *The Conquest: The Story of a Negro Pioneer* (Lincoln, Nebr.: The Woodruff Press, 1913); *The Forged Note: A Romance of the Darker Races* (Lincoln, Nebr.: Western Book Supply Company, 1915); and *The Homesteader, A Novel* (Sioux City, Iowa: Western Book Supply Company, 1917).

[35]Both Hugh Gloster and Robert Bone, the leading students of Afro-American fiction, have been quick to dismiss Harper's book as grossly sentimental and too similar to earlier abolitionist works to be of much value in understanding Afro-American attitudes in the late nineteenth/early twentieth century period. See Gloster, *Negro Voices in American Fiction*, pp. 30-31, and Bone, *Negro Novel in America*, pp. 31-32. Quite the contrary, however, would seem to be the case. Although she does employ stock characters found in earlier works, and although the novel is exaggerated melodrama, her characterizations of different mulatto and black figures and the racial attitudes they expound are clearly patterns which numerous Afro-American fictionists also employed in the next twenty-five years. This includes the ideas about the value of middle-class manners and ideals, about the restrictions blacks suffer in the racial caste system, and about the role of educated mulattoes and the necessity of their identifying with the Negro race rather than trying to pass for white. It also involves underlying notions about Negroes and whites themselves.

[36]Harper, *Iola Leroy*, p. 126.

[37]*Ibid.*, pp. 218-219.

[38]*Ibid.*, p. 280.

[39]*Ibid.*, pp. 43-44.

[40]*Ibid.*, p. 240.

[41]Chesnutt explains of Dr. Miller: "His people had needed him, and he had wished to help them, and had sought by means of this institution [the hospital] to contribute to their uplifing." Chesnutt, *Marrow of Tradition*, p. 57.

[42]John Wesley Grant, *Out of the Darkness, or Diabolism and Destiny* (Nashville: National Baptist Publishing Board, 1909).

[43]Barbara Welter, "The Cult of True Womanhood: 1820-1860," *American Quarterly*, XVIII, 2 (Summer, 1966), 151-174; Filene, *Him/Her/Self*, pp. 8-9; David M. Kennedy, *Birth Control in America: The Career of Margaret Sanger* (New Haven: Yale University Press, 1970), chapter 2.

[44]Sutton E. Griggs, *Unfettered* (Nashville: Orion Publishing Company, 1902), pp. 10-11.

[45]Sutton E. Griggs, *Overshadowed* (Nashville: Orion Publishing Company, 1901), pp. 9, 10.

[46]George Marion McClellan, *Old Greenbottom Inn and Other Stories* ([Louisville]: George M. McClellan, 1906), pp. 28-29.

[47]Jack Thorne [David Bryant Fulton], *Hanover; or The Persecution of the Lowly, A Story of the Wilmington Massacre* (n.p.: [M. C. L. Hill, 1901]), p. 33.

[48]Harper, *Iola Leroy*, pp. 253, 254.

[49]Shackelford, *Lillian Simmons*, pp. 27-28.

[50]*Ibid.*, p. 28.

[51]See, for instance, Erma Wysong in Griggs, *Overshadowed*; Dora Smith in Hopkins, *Contending Forces*; Janet Miller in Chesnutt, *Marrow of Tradition*; Zelda Marston in Ashby, *Redder Blood*; Merna Attaway in Pryor, *Neither Bond Nor Free*; and Elsa Mangus in Clayton Adams, [Charles Henry Holmes], *Ethiopia, The Land of Promise: A Book with a Purpose* (New York: Cosmopolitan Press, 1917).

[52]Harper, *Iola Leroy*, pp. 114, 234-235.

[53]Grant, *Out of the Darkness*, p. 65.

[54]*Ibid.*, p. 84.

[55]*Ibid.*, pp. 119-120.

[56]Charles H. Fowler, *Historical Romance of the American Negro* (Baltimore: Press of Thomas & Evans, 1902).   Fowler even provides a photograph of his fictional heroine, showing her to be a seemingly model Victorian lady of light complexion and Caucasian features.

[57]The proposed solution, partly devised during a balloon ride, is appended to the novel as *"Dorlan's Plan:* Sequel to *Unfettered:* A Dissertation on the Race Problem." The essay contends that the major need in alleviating the race problem in America is the substitution of merit for color as the standard for preferment. Afro-Americans are advised to combat conservatism and to cease relying solely on the Republican Party. Griggs emphasized a number of factors as important in preparing the race for a better future: character development, worthy home life, public school education for the masses, technical training for industrial workers, and universities for educating wise and capable leaders of the race.   Land ownership and a back-to-the-farm movement are recommended.   The replacement of race supremacy and partisan patronage with good government and simple justice is seen as a desirable goal of political action. Also stressed as essential to an enlighted racial policy is cultivation of the friendship of the Southern white man as well as of the people of other sections of the country and of other nations.   As Hugh Gloster has noted, as a statement of desirable procedures for blacks in America, *Dorlan's Plan* was a significant precursor of James Weldon Johnson's *Negro Americans, What Now?* (1934) and of numerous other guides to interracial harmony.   See Gloster, *Negro Voices in American Fiction*, pp. 61-62. For a longer statement of Griggs' position, see Sutton E. Griggs, *Wisdom's Call* (Nashville: Orion   Publishing   Company, 1911).

[58]See Edward Byron Reuter, *The Mulatto in the United States, Including a Study of the Role of Mixed-Blood Races Throughout the World* (Boston: Richard G. Badger, 1918), pp. 183-397. Also note, for instance, the overwhelmingly large percentage of mulattoes among the one hundred contributors to D. W. Culp, comp., *Twentieth Century Negro Literature, or A Cyclopedia of Thought on the Vital Topics Relating to the American Negro by One Hundrerd of America's Greatest Negroes* (Napierville, Ill. and Atlanta: J. L. Nichols & Co., 1902) an anthology of essays by "prominent members of the race" on important aspects of the race question.

[59]There is only one real exception to this rule.   John Calvert, in Downing, *American Cavalryman*, is an important New York financier who refuses to admit that his slight Negro blood is of any significance. He lives as a white man, because being at most one-sixteenth black, he insists that he *is* a white man.   When his sister, who publicly acknowledges her mixed blood and lives as a wealthy mulatto, says that his friends would not view him as white if they knew the truth, Calvert replies, "Possibly not;

but they don't know and never will. If a person was possessed of a quality, good or bad, or indifferent, which, if his fellows knew of it, would prevent him from living his life fully and usefully he wouldn't advertise the fact."

This is the sort of individualistic response to the question of passing which characterized the earlier works of Charles W. Chesnutt and James Weldon Johnson. Calvert's sister, however, cannot see him as anything other than a Negro, despite the preponderance of white blood in his background. To her, his course is sinful deception, to which Calvert counters, "Well, if I'm a sinner, I guess there's any number of sinners just like me. America is a Bleachery, and I am one of its peculiar outputs. The country is full of my kind." (p. 15)

[60] Ashby, *Redder Blood*, pp. 161-170 and *supra*, pp. 252-253.

[61] F. Grant Gilmore, *The Problem, A Military Novel* (Rochester, N.Y.: Press of Henry Conolly Co., 1915).

[62] Harper, *Iola Leroy*, p. 117.

[63] Ashby, *Redder Blood*, p. 182.

[64] Harper, *Iola Leroy*, p. 109. This notion is most clearly stated in Ashby, *Redder Blood*, p. 181. One might also note the strange force which draws Freda Waters to her black paramour, Sgt. William Henderson. When it is later revealed that Freda is actually of mixed blood, one gets the sense that a vague racial affinity has been involved all along. See Gilmore, *The Problem*.

[65] W. E. Burghardt Du Bois, *The Souls of Black Folk: Essays and Sketches* (Chicago: A. C. McClurg & Co., 1903); W. E. Burghardt Du Bois, *The Quest of the Silver Fleece* (Chicago: A. C. McClurg & Co., 1911). The novel dealt with white exploitation of Southern black agricultural workers and the need for cooperative effort among Afro-Americans to combat this situation.

[66] W. E. Burghardt Du Bois, *The Conservation of Races*, American Negro Academy, *Occasional Papers*, No. 2 (Washington, D.C.: By the Academy, 1897), pp. 8-9.

[67] *Ibid*, p. 11.

[68] Du Bois, *Souls of Black Folk*, pp. 3-4.

[69] On this notion, see Everett V. Stonequist, *The Marginal Man: A Study in Personality and Culture Conflict* (New York: Charles Scribner's Sons, 1937), pp. 25-26.

[70] Harper, *Iola Leroy*, p. 203.

[71] *Ibid.*, pp. 208, 233.

[72] *Ibid.*, pp. 265, 263, 266.

[73] Micheaux, *The Conquest*, pp. 157-163.

[74] Sutton E. Griggs, *The Hindered Hand: or, The Reign of the Repressionist* (Nashville: Orion Publishing Company, 1905), pp. 241-242.

[75] *Ibid.*, p. 238.

[76] *Ibid.,* p. 52.

[77] *Ibid.,* p. 256.

[78] *Ibid.,* p. 258.

[79] See Barton, *Race Consciousness and American Negro,* pp. 58-59.

[80] Quoted in Gloster, *Negro Voices in American Fiction,* p. 39, n. 12.

[81] Charles W. Chesnutt, *The House Behind the Cedars* (Boston: Houghton, Mifflin and Company, 1900), p. 72.

[82] See William McCrea Ramsey, "Character Stereotypes in the Novels of Charles Waddell Chesnutt" (unpublished M.A. thesis, University of North Carolina at Chapel Hill, 1969), p. 30.

[83] Chesnutt, *House Behind the Cedars,* p. 24.

[84] *Ibid.,* p. 73.

[85] *Ibid.,* p. 72.

[86] Ramsey, "Character Stereotypes in Chesnutt," p. 32. Thirty years after the appearance of *The House Behind the Cedars,* Chesnutt still considered the position of the mulatto one of particular complexity and hardship. "The problems of the people of mixed blood," he wrote in 1931, "while in the main the same as those of the true Negro, are in some instances and in some respects much more complex and difficult of treatment, in fiction as in life." Chesnutt, "Post-Bellum--Pre-Harlem," *The Crisis,* XXXVIII, 6 (June, 1931), 194.

[87] See Helen M. Chesnutt, *Charles Waddell Chesnutt, Pioneer of the Color Line* (Chapel Hill: University of North Carolina Press. 1952), pp. 1-17 on his early life in North Carolina, esp. p. 13 on his being taken for white and considering passing. His picture (Frontpiece, opposite p. v) shows Chesnutt to have evidenced no Negro features. At least one other member of his family had already crossed the color line, and his own father had once intended to do so. See Sylvia Lyons Render's introduction to Charles W. Chesnutt, *The Short Fiction of Charles W. Chesnutt,* ed. by Sylvia Lyons Render (Washington, D.C.: Howard University Press, 1974), p. 4.

[88] To Chesnutt, passing was an ordeal which actually required great personal courage, although few members of either race truly appreciated the considerations involved. This view was clearly stated in *House Behind the Cedars,* pp. 127-128.

[89] [Johnson], *Autobiography of Ex-Coloured Man,* p. 190.

[90] Barton, *Race Consciousness and American Negro,* p. 139.

[91] [Johnson], *Autobiography of Ex-Coloured Man,* p. 3.

[92] *Ibid.,* p. 210.

[93] *Ibid.,* p. 211.

[94] *Ibid.*

[95]See Eugene Levy, *James Weldon Johnson: Black Leader, Black Voice* (Chicago: University of Chicago Press, 1973), pp. 140-141. This is, of course, the same dichotomy to which W. E. B. Du Bois spoke in *The Souls of Black Folk*, pp. 3-4.

[96]See Bone, *Negro Novel in America*, pp. 12-15, esp. p. 15, n. 4, wherein he notes that of the early Afro-American novelists writing between 1890 and 1920, eighty percent were professionals and the remaining twenty percent white collar workers.

[97]Robert Lewis Waring, *As We See It* (Washington, D.C.: C. F. Sudwarth, 1910), p. 12.

[98]Adams [Holmes]. *Ethiopia, Land of Promise*, pp. 13, 27, 28, 40. Other such virtuous, bourgeois black figures include Charles Christopher in Shackelford, *Lillian Simmons*; Dorlan Warthell in Griggs, *Unfettered*; Ensal Ellwood in Griggs, *Hindered Hand*; and Conroe Driscoll in Griggs, *Pointing the Way*. In "A Dash for Liberty," Pauline E. Hopkins even drew a courageous black slave along such lines, perhaps to counter notions that rebellious bondsmen were invariably of mixed blood. Madison, the slave, "was an unmixed African, of good physique, and one of the handomest of his race. His dignified, calm and unaffected bearing marked him as a leader among his fellows. His features bore the stamp of genius. His firm step and piercing eye attracted the attention of all who met him." (p. 246) Madison feels very acutely the injustice of slavery, especially in denying Negroes the right to protect and hold their wives, and he eventually leads a successful slave rebellion aboard a slave trader's ship.

[99]Harper, *Iola Leroy*, p. 199.

[100]For a discussion of Chesnutt's use of blacks in comic roles, see Ramsey, "Character Stereotypes in Chesnutt." pp. 24-29, 53-56.

[101]Bone, *Negro Novel in America*, p. 18.

[102]Chesnutt, *Marrow of Tradition*, pp. 60-61.

[103]Shackelford, *Lillian Simmons*, pp. 138-139.

[104]Bone, *Negro Novel in America*, p. 18. In Chesnutt's *Marrow of Tradition*, for instance, after the murder of a prominent white woman, for which a black is blamed (although unjustly), Dr. Miller expresses such sentiments:

> The whole thing is profoundly discouraging. Try as we may to build up the race in the essentials of good citizenship and win the good opinion of the best people, some black scoundrel comes along, and by a single criminal act . . . neutralizes the effect of a whole year's work." (p. 190)

Direct criticism of lower-class blacks was not unknown, however. Sutton Griggs, for example, referred to "colored people of the lower order–besotted men and slovenly women, denizens of the slums." *Pointing the Way*, p. 125. Paul Lawrence Dunbar similarly described the sinful way of life of the black urban masses in his *The Sport of the Gods* (New York: Dodd, Mead and Company, 1902).

[105]See Bone, *Negro Novel in America*, p. 19.

[106]Ramsey, "Character Stereotypes in Chesnutt," pp. 13-19, 25-29.

[107]Chesnutt, *Marrow of Tradition*, p. 61.

[108]Note, for instance, his criticism of the color prejudice of Miss Alice Clayton and her father in "A Matter of Principle" and of Professor Revels in "The Sway-Backed House." "The Wife of His Youth" ridicules the standards of "the Blue Vein Society" of Groveland (patterned after the Social Circle of Cleveland to which Chesnutt actually belonged), while "Uncle Wellington's Wives" underscores the foolishness of marrying whites because they are somehow "superior" to Negroes. All stories are found in Chesnutt, *Wife of His Youth*.

[109]Speaking of the uneducated blacks with whom he was forced to associate in the South, he termed them

> "the most bigoted, superstitious, hardest-headed people in the world.
> . . . These people don't know enough words for a fellow to carry on
> a coversation with them. He must reduce his phraseology several
> degrees lower than the first reader. . . . They are the most
> superstitious people in the world, etc."

See diary entries for August 13 and 20, 1875 in H. Chesnutt, *Charles Waddell Chesnutt*, pp. 14-15.

[110]*Ibid.*, pp. 61-62.

[111]Bone, *Negro Novel in America*, p. 4. For his specific comments on Chesnutt, see pp. 35-38.

[112]The mixed-blood characters who were not derived from aristocratic white stock are extremely rare in the Afro-American fiction of this era. Further, such individuals often lack the personal virtues generally attributed to those mulattoes whose white ancestors were of the upper class. The inclination to explain mulattoes' finer qualities by reference to their white blood was much more common. In explaining the gradual rise of the Negro race, for instance, Pauline E. Hopkins (herself a mulatto), evidenced such a belief in the superiority of white blood:

> "Then again, we do not allow for the infusion of white blood, which
> became pretty generally distributed in the inferior black race during
> the existence of slavery. Some of this blood, too was the best in the
> country. . . . Surely the Negro race must be productive of some
> valuable specimens, if only from the infusion which amalgamation
> with a superior race must eventually bring."

Hopkins, *Contending Forces*, p. 87. Similar sentiments are found elsewhere, e.g., in Griggs, *Hindered Hand*, p. 141 and Chesnutt, *House Behind the Cedars*, p. 163.

[113]Micheaux, *The Conquest*, pp. 155-163.

[114]The inevitable continuation of race mixing, he felt, would eventually lead to the obliteration of the line between the two races in the South. See Waring, *As We See It*, pp. 48, 180, 192-196. Pauline Hopkins also saw negative results in the mixing of

black and "cracker" blood. John Pollock Langley, an unscrupulous lawyer and politician, is a mixed-blood of such background:

> "Natural instinct for good had been perverted by a mixture of 'cracker' blood of the lowest type on his father's side with whatever God-saving quality that might have been loaned the Negro by pitying nature. This blood, while it gave him the pleasant features of the Caucasian race, vitiated his moral nature and left it stranded high and dry on the shore of blind ignorance, and there he seemed content to dwell, supinely self-satisifed with the narrow boundary of the horizon of his mental vision."

Hopkins, *Contending Forces*, p. 221.

[115]Ashby, *Redder Blood,* [p. 5].

[116]Joel Augustus Rogers, *From "Superman" to Man* (Chicago: M. A. Donohoe & Co., Printers, 1917), pp. 78-89. Rogers was somewhat unique in his contention that amalgamation actually held the promise of building a stronger race of men in the South, since the vitality of the Negro would up-grade the diminishing energy of the native whites:

> ". . . what the Caucasian needs as a rejuvenator particularly in the South--where the vitiation of the Caucasian stock is glaringly apparent--is an infusion of blood from some primitive stock, with nerves and tissues unspoiled by the greed of civilization, like the magnificent Zulu; that is, if this primitive stock would stand for it, which I very much doubt. The Negro with his fresher, more buoyant mentality can do a great deal toward relieving the tension on the nerves of the Caucasian. . . . I think it is for this reason then--repairing the ravages made by civilization, that Nature has with its usual prevision, deposited this balance from its reserve fund--the Negro--here in America." (p. 106)

[117]Griggs, *Overshadowed*, p. 69. (I have here omitted the hyphens which Griggs placed between virtually every word of Nerve's speeches as an indication of the ignorant preacher's pretentious attempts to control his language and to sound dignified and refined.)

[118]*Ibid.*, pp. 183-184.

[119]Griggs, *Pointing the Way*, p. 31.

[120]Hopkins, *Contending Forces*, p. 187.

[121]Chesnutt, "A Matter of Principle," in *Wife of His Youth*, pp. 94-131.

[122]See especially Chesnutt's "The Wife of His Youth' and "A Matter or Principle," in *Wife of His Youth*, pp. 1-24 and 94-131, respectively.

[123]Griggs, *Overshadowed*, pp. 63-64.

[124]*Ibid.*, p. 71. The final sentence of the quotation seems to imply criticism of Booker T. Washington's position as the recognized "leader of the race." Taken as a whole, Griggs' works indicate a basic opposition to Washington's policies, although by the second decade of the century Griggs had shifted his personal attitudes regarding race relations to a considerably more conservative position. For more on Griggs' life and work, see David M. Tucker, *Black Pastors and Leaders: Memphis, 1819-1972* (Memphis: Memphis State University Press, 1975), pp. 71-86, the most recent and thorough assessment of Griggs' efforts to influence race relations. More directly concerned with his fiction are Robert E. Fleming, "Sutton E. Griggs: Militant Black Novelist," *Phylon*, XXXIV, 1 (Spring, 1973), 73-77, and Hugh Gloster, "Sutton Griggs, Novelist of the New Negro," *Phylon*, IV, 4 (1943), 335-345.

[125]Joel Augustus Rogers contended that whites simply could not think of Afro-Americans in anything other than lower-class roles. "Very many whites seem unable to imagine a Negro, however decent, as being anything else but a minstrel." he remarked. Popular jokes ridiculing Afro-Americans as principally chicken-stealers and filanderers, Rogers held, were thought to portray "the full depth of Negro character, cultured and uncultured. The desire, throughout the United States, is to degrade the highest Negroes to the level of the lowest in the mass." Much of the problem, he felt, resulted from the fact that most whites had little conception of the better sort of Afro-Americans, drawing their entire opinion of the race from their encounters with lower-class Negroes. Rogers, on the other hand, insisted that there existed a great number of respectable Afro-American families, who were "white in everything but color." Rogers, *From "Superman" to Man*, pp. 65, 75.

CHAPTER V

MULATTO IMAGES IN WHITE FICTION

Contemporary racial theory and the changing patterns of American race relations together shaped whites' fictional treatments of mulattoes in the years between Reconstruction and the First World War, just as they did those of Afro-American authors. Indeed, because the rising tide of prejudice, racial violence, and legal discrimination found expression in a variety of fictional works during this period, there is considerable evidence of how whites interpreted the nature of the mulatto and his place in the racial system. Although there are certain similarities in the treatment of mulattoes by both white and Afro-American writers, ultimately their differences are more important, for they reveal not only divergences in perceptions of the mulatto but in basic outlooks towards the course of black/white relations during this crucial fifty-year period.

As with Afro-American writers, a number of white authors saw the mulatto as a tragic figure, the unfortunate victim of his heritage and circumstances beyond his control. A few whites emphasized the mulatto's role as leader of the Negro race, but others portrayed him as a malcontent, unable to adjust to the demands of the racial system which denied him any status other than that of a Negro. To this extent, images developed by white and Afro-American authors paralleled each other. There was nevertheless a separate, highly conspicuous group of white writers who viewed the mixed-blood in a negative perspective. This position, which was perhaps the dominant attitude towards the mulatto by the turn of the century, was part of the overall shift in white racial attitudes in the 1890s towards a more radical posture. From this perspective, the mulatto was the "embodiment of the worst qualities of both races and hence a menace to the dominant group." The mulatto woman was seen as the seducer of otherwise virtuous white aristocrats, while the mulatto man was "the besmircher of white virginity and the most dangerous intruder in the political scene."[1] For such radical racists, the mixed-blood was inextricably linked to the issue of racial amalgamation; he was a visible symbol of a major threat to white society. Although Afro-American writers thought of race mixing as of only minor significance, whites believed it to be a crucial issue. In fact, among whites, feelings about mulattoes seem to have been a function of feelings about the issue of race mixture itself. Some saw white blood as a definite advantage for the mulatto, setting him off from the mass of darker Negroes and making him a somewhat superior if nevertheless pitiable character. To the growing number of radical thinkers, though, the mulatto represented a menace to be dealt with forcefully before he could further undermine the purity of the white race.

In this sense, as with Afro-American fiction of this era, the white fiction which dealt with mulatto characters and the subject of interracial sexual contact was of strongly propagandistic nature. Robert Ezra Park, the eminent sociologist of race relations, once wrote that

> Literature and art, when they are employed to give expression to racial sentiment and form tᴑ racial ideals, serve, along with other agencies, to mobilize the group and put the masses *en rapport* with their leaders and with each other. In such a case art and literature are like silent drummers which summon into action the latent instincts and energies of the race.[2]

It is not unlikely that, as racial propaganda, many of the fictional works discussed below contributed significantly to a solidification of white attitudes regarding the Negro, race relations, and the inflammatory question of racial amalgamation. The ideas and attitudes expressed cover the spectrum of prevailing positions on race relations, from radically racist to strikingly liberal. At the same time, certain fundamental notions display a marked consistency. To this extent, fictional treatments of the mulatto and more general racial questions were linked to contemporary race theory and probably served more to reinforce than to reshape regnant attitudes and images. In this capacity, however, they offer historians one means of ascertaining how white Americans between Reconstruction and the First World War understood race and their relationship to blacks and mulattoes.

2

Sympathetic attitudes towards mulattoes generally characterized those who held essentially liberal position in race relations. These liberals, while not believing in racial equality, felt that the black man deserved to have his basic political and economic rights recognized, and that given time, white support and understanding, and relatively equal opportunity, he might one day approach the civilized position of the white man. Few of these thinkers believed that blacks could ever equal the white man, particularly on a race-wide basis, yet they were willing to reserve judgment about the Negro's ultimate destiny and to give him a chance to develop to the extent of his capabilities.

Conservatives also exhibited a sympathetic attitude toward mulattoes, although their view of the nation's system of race relations was less optimistic. Convinced of the Negro's inferiority and seeing little hope that condition would change, conservatives, unlike radicals, were nevertheless willing to admit the inevitability of the black man's presence in America, and consequently sought to adjust to it. They adopted a paternalistic stance towards Afro-Americans, emphasizing the "childlike" nature of the race and its need for firm and understanding guidance by their class of whites. They supported limited educational opportunities for Afro-Americans, particularly in the vein of Booker T. Washington's industrial training, but were insistent that the Negro recognize and accept his properly subordinate "place."[3]

The liberal position was particularly evident in the ten or fifteen years after Reconstruction. Perhaps it was a lingering manifestation of the optimistic spirit which had prompted the egalitarian efforts of the Reconstruction era or the earlier fervor of the abolitionists. Such sentiment is clearly seen in Rebecca Harding Davis' *Waiting for the Verdict*, an 1867 novel which set the tone for later liberal depictions of the mulatto as a tragic figure. Focusing on the Civil War struggle and the contributions made by both free and enslaved Afro-Americans to the Union effort, the book includes the story of John Broderip, whose professional career and romance are destroyed by his painful (but to Davis, heroic) decision to disclose his mixed blood. Broderip had become a respected surgeon in Philadelphia by passing as white with the help of a sympathetic Quaker. Nevertheless, his social and professional status dissolve when his true racial heritage becomes known. To Davis, the injustice of this situation marked the real tragedy of the mulatto. Broderip, despite the meager amount of black blood in his veins, was blocked "from all the hopes, the ambitions, the enjoyments of other men."[4]

> . . . he stood alone, shut out from every human relation with the world to which he belonged. A negro--no wealth, no talent, no virtue could wash out that stain or put him on a level with the meanest servant in his house again.[5]

That indeed was the problem--that in the eyes of white American, any person of mixed blood, regardless of how infinitesimal the degree of his black blood might be, still remained a Negro. All of the white fiction of this era which dealt with mulattoes reflected this fundamental attitude, although virtually none saw any reason to challenge the basic premise involved. Whether liberal, conservative, or radical, white authors, and the audience for whom they were writing, saw the mulatto as a black man, regardless of how distant his black ancestor might be. Even the vaguest *suspicion* of black blood might relegate an individual to the status of a Negro. Such is the plight of the beautiful, white-skinned Lily in Margaret Deland's short story, "A Black Drop" (1908). Her white lover becomes infected with the idea that Lily is of mixed blood and in actuality the daughter of the mulatto woman who has raised her as white.   Unable to live with the uncertainty of not knowing if Lily is in fact white or black, he must leave her. The racial instinct which Deland pictures as overwhelming will not let him risk the chance of marrying someone of an inferior race.[6]

The most liberal white writers could not divorce themselves from the inevitable inclination to see mulattoes as black.   Although many would draw distinctions between mixed-bloods and pure Negroes, whom they considered obviously inferior, ultimately there could be no exceptions to this rule.   It is this fact which underscores the tragedy of the mulatto's position in the eyes of these white authors.   Walter Hines Page expressed this sentiment in his 1909 novel, *The Southerner.* Nicholas Worth, his narrator, reflects on the lamentable status of the mulattoes he sees in the choir of a Negro industrial school:

> Here were three hundred half-white faces before me--three hundred
> tragedies--the white man calling out in every one of them to the life
> of his kinsmen and the black man holding him to the plane of the
> African.[7]

Even Thomas Dixon, perhaps the most radical racist writer of this period, seemed to be aware of the pathos of the mulatto's unusual position.   In *The Leopard's Spots* (1902), his portrait of George Harris, a refined and educated young mulatto, is essentially that of a tragic figure.   Led to aspire to political and social goals far beyond those which whites would allow him, he is crushed by the burden of his Negro heritage, ultimately ending in a life of gambling and crime.[8]

Liberal authors, however, evidenced a more sympathetic view of the plight of the mixed-blood.   George Washington Cable's descriptions of the *gens de couleur* of ante-bellum Louisiana indicate a particularly sensitive feeling for the mulatto's problems.   Unlike many other authors of his era, Cable was able to avoid much of the gushing sentimentality which often characterized fictional treatments of the tragic mulatto. Consequently, his figures are less stereotyped, yet still reflective of the problems encountered by mixed-bloods.

In "'Tite Poulette," Cable tells the story of two women, mother and daughter, trying to deal with the problems of their mixed blood. Madame John, the mother, had been the mistress of a kind white man whose property she inherited.   Her octoroon daughter, 'Tite Poulette, is characterized by the physical beauty so often attributed to mulatto women:

> . . . tall, straight, lithe, her great black eyes made tender by their
> sweeping lashes, the faintest tint of color in her Southern cheek, her
> form all grace, her carriage a wonder of simple dignity.[9]

Although both are virtually indistinguishable from white, their few drops
of black blood, being publicly known, make them Negroes and
consequently miserable. Madame John agonizes over their misfortune.
"You will be lonely, lonely, all your poor life," she tells her daughter.
"There is no place in this world for us poor women. I wish we were
either white or black! . . . if we were only real white!--both of us."[10]

Her one desire is to see her daughter married to a white man,
and she urges 'Tite Poulette to keep parentage a secret from any white
man who might be attracted to her. Seeing herself as the product of the
white man's sins, Madame John feels justified in retaliating against the
white race, through silence, if possible. 'Tite Poulette, however, is more
inclined to see herself as the product of God's will, and therefore tends
to assume the role of a martyr. Since she is legally prohibited from
marrying a white man, she resigns herself to an unfulfilled life, refusing
the proposal of her Dutch neighbor, Kristian Koppig, although he is
fully aware of her racial background.[11] At this point Madame John steps
in, frantically declaring that 'Tite Poulette is in reality not her daughter
but the child of a Spanish family for whom she once worked. By
renouncing her motherhood, she hopes to erase the drop of black blood
which threatened to deny 'Tite Poulette her happiness. As one student
has noted, though, had Cable given 'Tite Poulette the opportunity to
respond, she would probably have exposed her mother's deception,
reiterated the impossibility of her marrying Kristian, and thus brought
unnecessary grief upon all three.[12]

The theme of a mulatto mother making a supreme sacrifice for
her child's welfare is repeated in "Madame Delphine." The octoroon
daughter in this tale is Olive, whose beauty rivals that of 'Tite Poulette:

> From throat to instep she was as white as Cynthia.
> Something above the medium height, slender, lithe, her abundant
> hair rolling in dark, rich waves back from her brows and down
> from her crown. . . . The forehead and temples beneath her loosely
> bound hair were fair without paleness, and meek without languor.
> She had the soft, lack-lustre beauty of the South; no ruddiness of
> coral, no waxen white, no pink of shell; no heavenly blue in the
> glance; but a face that seemed, in all its other beauties, only a
> tender accompaniment for the large, brown, melting eyes, where the
> openness of child-nature mingled with the sweet mysteries of maiden
> thought. We say no color of shell on face or throat; but this was no
> deficiency, that which took its place being the warm, transparent tint
> of sculptured ivory.[13]

Lacking the lofty notions of self-renunciation which characterized 'Tite
Poulette, Olive readily accepts the proposal of a white man. When the
prejudices of his relatives threaten their marriage, Madame Delphine is

forced to act, dramatically renouncing her motherhood to insure Olive's future.

Madame Delphine represents a different type of mulatto from Madame John. She refused to be crushed by the burdens which her condition of birth forced upon her, the conditions which drove Madame John to despondency. With Madame Delphine,

> there was this quiet evidence of a defiant spirit hidden somewhere down under her general timidity, that, against a fierce conventional prohibition, she wore a bonnet instead of the turban of her caste, and carried a parasol.[14]

Further, she is determined that her child's happiness shall not be frustrated by the unjust laws of the white man which would prohibit interracial marriages and keep the races separate. She mocks the notion of separating the races with a defiant tone:

> Separate! No-o-o! They do not want to keeep us separated; no, no! But they *do* want to keep us despised! But, very well! from which race do they want to keep my daughter separate? She is seven parts white! The law did not stop her from being that; and now, when she wants to be a white man's good and honest wife, shall that law stop her? On, no! No; I will tell you what that law is made for. It is made to--punish--my--child--for--not--choosing--her--father! . . . but . . . dey *shall not* punizh my daughter! She shall marrie oo she want![15]

It is this forceful spirit which sets Madame Delphine apart from her predecessors in the tragic mulatto stereotype, for where they generally evoke pity, she commands the reader's respect.[16]

Similar attributes are evident in Cable's portrait of Palmyre Philosophe in *The Grandissimes* (1880), a novel about ante-bellum New Orleans. Like Madame Delphine, she refuses to be overwhelmed by the difficulties of her racial position. "This woman had stood all her life with dagger drawn," Cable says of her, "on the defensive against what certainly was to her an unmerciful world."[17] Like so many other mulatto characters, she is cursed with a physical beauty which makes her irresistably appealing to men of the dominant race, yet Cable emphasizes what to him were the animal characteristics inherited from her black ancestors as well as the more traditional attributes of white beauty:

> While yet a child she grew tall, lithe, agile; her eyes were large and black, and rolled and sparkled if she but turned to answer her name. Her pale yellow forehead, low and shapely, with the jet hair above it, the heavily pencilled eyebrows and long lashes below, the faint red tinge that blushed with a kind of cold passion through the clear lips and the roundness of her perfect neck, gave her . . . a barbaric

and magnetic beauty that startled the beholder like an unexpected drawing out of a jewelled sword. . . . Such a type could have sprung only from high Latin ancestry on the one side and--we might benture--Jaloff African on the other. To these charms of person she added mental acuteness, conversational adroitness, concealed cunning and noiseless but visible strength of will; ..nd to these, that rarest of gifts in one of her tincture, the purity of true womanhood.[18]

The united grace and pride of her movement was inspiring but--what shall we say?--feline?   It was a femininity without humanity, -something that made her with all her superbness, a creature that one would want to find chained.[19]

It is as though Cable sensed in Palmyre that forbidden animal sensuality, that "untamable beauty," which whites so long imagined characterized women with some portion of black blood. He admires her for her personal strengths in the face of adversity, but she remains somehow different and less acceptable than the white women with whom one would associate on a social basis. She is, he explains, a "monument of shame of two races," since her origins are in the illicit act of miscegenation. For many whites, it was this simple association between mulattoes and an illicit deed which served to guarantee the mixed-blood an ignominious status.[20]

Cable's most sympathetic portrait of a mixed-blood was that of Honoré Grandissime, free man of colour. He was a "remarkable figure" with

a strong, clear, olive complexion; features that were faultless (unless a woman-like delicacy, that was yet not effeminate, was a fault); hair *en queue*, the handsomer for its premature streakings of gray; a tall, well knit form, attired in cloth, linen and leather of the utmost fineness; manner Castilian, with a gravity almost oriental,--[which] made him one of those rare masculine figures which, on the public promenade, men look back at and ladies inquire about.[21]

His position in New Orleans society is one of particular poignancy. His white father, Numa Grandissime, was a Louisiana grandee. After an affair with Honoré's quadroon mother, he was forced by his family to enter into a social marriage with the daughter of another prominent Creole family. To this marriage was born a son who, too, was named Honoré. But Numa felt that his main obligation was due his first-born son--when the white Honoré was sent to Paris for his education, his half-brother accompanied him; in his will Numa left the greater portion of his estate to his elder son. While Honoré, f.m.c., becomes a *rentier* in New Orleans, his white brother must enter a commercial business. There exists little or no antagonism between the two men, for the white Honoré acknowledges his brother's rights as the true elder son, while Honoré, f.m.c., saves his brother from bankruptcy by consolidating their two businesses into the firm of Grandissime Fréres.

Despite his father's sincere interest in him and the absence of feelings of malice on the part of his white brother, Honoré remains a supremely tragic figure.   As Sterling Brown once noted, he is "an ineffectual victim of caste" regardless of his wealth and the social standing of his father.[22]   These attributes, which would ordinarily have gained him access to the highest social circles among whites, are invalidated by the meager amount of Negro blood in his veins. The plight of Honoré and men like him, "the saddest slaves of all," emphasized for Cable the gross inequity of the American system of race relations, for they were paralyzed by the white man's will and were withering under the hypnotic "glare of the white man."[23]   Cable recognized that the present pattern of race relations offered little hope for the man of mixed blood, when "whatever was not pure white was to all intents and purposes pure black."[24]

> The quadroons want a great deal more than mere free papers can secure them. Emancipation before the law, though it may be a right which man has no right to withhold, is to them little more than a mockery until they achieve emancipation in the minds and good will of the . . . ruling class.[25]

3

Cable's mulatto characters were considerably more realistic than most other fictional treatments of mixed-bloods.   Perhaps this was because he drew his characters from a real life situation,[26] yet equally important was his ability to avoid excessive sentimentality or over-idealization of the mulatto. Indeed, in *The Grandissimes* he was harsh in his denunciation of the mulatto caste's fawning acquiescence to white injustices, indicative of a desire for greater acceptance by whites:

> Your men, for a little property, and your women, for a little amorous attention, let themselves be shorn of even the virtue of discontent, and for a paltry bait of sham freedom have consented to endure a tyrannous contumely which flattens them into the dirt like grass under a slab. I would rather be a runaway in the swamps than content myself with such a freedom.[27]

Few other writers, however, were able to approach the apparent tragedy of the mulatto's position free from the sentimentality so characteristic of popular Victorian fiction.   An especially appealing emotional device employed by such authors was the shock of an individual's discovering, after having been raised as a white person, that he actually possessed some small degree of Negro blood. Even to a liberal writer, there could be few notions more devastating than the thought of being suddenly thrust into the Negro race. In Payne Erskine's *When the Gates Lift Up Their Heads* (1901), for instance, the common fictional contrivance of a baby switch was used to have the child of an ex-slave raised by its father's white wife as her real son. When in later life he learns the truth, he feels himself compelled to renounce his inheritance and break off relations with his fiancée, hoping that by fleeing to Japan he can escape the shame of his past.[28] Madeline Capelle, the beautiful heroine of Matt Crim's short story, "Was This An Exceptional Case?"(1892) goes through even greater torment when she inadvertently learns that she is really the illegitimate child of a Louisiana aristocrat and his quadroon lover. Having been instilled with a deep sense of racial prejudice by the aunt who raised her as her own daughter, Madeline finds it impossible to cope with the thought that she herself possesses some black blood:

> Could it be true, or only a hideous nightmare out of which she would presently awake? Her mother a quadroon, her grandmother a slave! She wondered that the very thought of it did not kill her. Her name, her pride, everything that she had cherished, had been torn from her, and she—she had been hurled down into a black abyss where she must grovel and suffer until death set her free. Strange visions seemed to come before her our of the remote past—visions of African jungles, of black half-naked savages. . .
>
> There were her ancestors; their blood, degraded by generations of slavery, flowed in her veins. Her education, her refinement, her prejudices would only be instruments of torture now, with that secret conciousness of shame and degradation underlying them. It was as cruel as complete, as if it had been planned with Machiavellian art to this end. . .[29]

She too flees from her lover, although he, being the scion of an old New England family of abolitionists, is willing to love and marry her regardless of her true racial background. She later dies after becoming a nun and working diligently to teach, nurse, and elevate Negroes in New Orleans. In "The Little Convent Girl" (1893) by Grace King, the tale is equally sorrowful, as a twelve-year-old girl returns to New Orleans from a Northern convent to find that her mother, whom she has not seen since she was a baby, is a mulatto. Her only recourse is to drown herself, for she also cannot live with the shame of black blood.[30]

Even statesmen were not immune to such startling revelations. In *"The Nigger,"* a 1910 play by Edward Sheldon which sharply attacked the idea of racial prejudice, the progressive governor of a Southern state, Philip Morrow, discovers that his grandmother was of mixed blood.

Although he had always held that regardless of the degree of blood admixture, "either a man's a niggah or he isn't,"[31] Morrow at first hopes to hide the truth. "Why, I'm the same as I was b'fo'–" he tells his fiancée,

> I haven't changed a mite–I'm the man you've been in love with all these yeahs. I tell you I'm white--I'm all Morrow--theah's ha'dly a drop o' the othah! We'll hush it up–you love me–we'll go right on as if nothin' had happened--it's been kept all this time--it'll go on bein' kept.[32]

The girl initially reacts with horror to the idea, and Morrow eventually comes to realize the impossibility of his scheme. The races are too far apart, and must remain so:

> theah's a black gulf between us--[he tells her] an' it's filled t' the brim with sweat an' hate an' blood! We can stretch out our hands from eithah side, but they won't meet! An' even while we're tryin', don't we heah from down theah--miles down–comin' up through the centuries–the crack of a white man's whip an' the scream of a [black slave.][33]

The proclivity of writers of melodramatic Victorian fiction for highly contrived plot devices partially explains the popularity of this trick of sudden discovery of a character's mixed racial background. However, the fact that its use extended throughout the period, from Rebecca Harding Davis' *Waiting for the Verdict* in 1867 well through the turn of the century, and the fact that it was employed by good writers as well as bad,[34] indicates that this literary tool was reflective of something more than simply a convenient plot device. Rather, it seems to indicate that many Americans were uneasy about their identity--unsure about who they were and, perhaps more importantly, about who their neighbor was. In a land being inundated by hordes of immigrants, having its social structure revolutionized by the rise of new wealth associated with the growth of a new urban-industrial order, the individual American's position and very identity seemed insecure. Further, in a race-conscious age, what threat could be more dire than that of the blood of the inferior races of the world secretly slipping into that of the mighty civilizing race of Anglo-Saxons? Perhaps this psychological unrest resulting from massive social and economic change can partly explain the peculiar direction American racial thought took in the late nineteenth century, particularly in terms of ideas about mulattoes and race mixing. The surety that black was black and white was white may have offered something of a palliative to the troubled minds of white Americans who had difficulty comprehending the changes overwhelming their society.

Philip Morrow, the unfortunate hero of Sheldon's *The Nigger,"* gives voice to this uneasiness early in the drama. Race mixing is a crime, he says,

> it's demo'alizin' the South! Things have chanaged some since the wah, an' if we want t' keep our blood clean, we've got to know that *white's white* an' *black's black*–an mixin' 'em's damnation![35]

How could one know about the purity of his neighbor's blood if he could not even be sure about his own? Surely the quickness with which each of these newly-discovered mixed-bloods is relegated to the Negro race is indicative of white America's desire for certitude. "Black's black, an' white's white," Morrow firmly announces. "If yo' not one, yo' the othah."[36] There could be no middle ground in America as there was in Latin America, for white Americans needed to be sure about who they were and where they stood in reference to others around them. That this meant that race overrode class affinities was of little concern to them.[37] The important thing was to be able to be sure about who was who, and to guarantee that the purity of the white race was not threatened.

This sharp black/white division between the races, then, only made the mulatto's status that much more tragic in the eyes of sympathetic white authors. Such was the case with two of the novels of Albion Winegar Tourgée, despite the fact that he was an out-spoken champion of equal rights for Afro-Americans throughout his life.[38]   In both *A Royal Gentlemen* (1881) and *Pactolus Prime* (1890), he introduced mulatto characters who, while making important points about the inequities of the American system of race relations, nevertheless fell largely within the traditional mold of the tragic stereotype.

Toinette, the beautiful mixed-blood heroine of *A Royal Gentleman,* like her mother before her, becomes involved in an illicit affair with her handsome young master.   Each of the two humane masters is deeply in love with his mistress, but he cannot overcome the barriers of race to fulfill his love properly.   Toinette's mother, inadvertently victimized by the slave system, mistakenly blames her lover and murders him. The daughter's owner, Geoffrey Hunter, a carefree yet intelligent young man, seeks to educate Toinette in preparing her for eventual freedom only to discover that she possesses extraordinary intellectual capabilities. Tourgée portrays Toinette as a tender creature who voraciously consumes the lessons of her master, who emulates him completely, and who permits him to manipulate her in a benevolent and instructive manner. While she is clearly not the equal of her master at this point, Tourgée is implying that her rapid progress will lead to a state of eventual equality, his purpose being to urge the benefits of education for all Afro-Americans.[39]   Inevitably, Hunter comes to love his young charge, yet despite his critical views of slavery, he cannot conquer his prejudices enough to marry her and thereby legitimatize their relationship. Toinette is soon freed and travels to the North with their son just prior to the Civil War. As a Union nurse she again encounters her lover and nurses him back to health, dreaming all the while of a happy future together. Upon recovering, Hunter is shocked to find Toinette passing as white and brutally exposes her in a powerful episode:

> She deserved all he could make her feel for trying to pass for a white woman and a lady. This rushed through his brain in an instant, and then, with a voice hoarse with excitement, he cried out, imperiously: "I say, you girl, Toinette! Toinette!" Five years were brushed away in a second. Their months of toil and study were in vain. . . . The free, white, intelligent, interesting, beautiful Mrs. Hunter [as she had been calling herself] was lost for the moment. In her stead was the poor, abject, timid, pretty, "nigger gal." . . . She started like a guilty loiterer, and answered instantly, with that inimitable and indescribable intonation of the slave: "Sir?" That was all she said. It was enough. It revealed all. The brand showed. The one drop of base admixture had overtopped all else, and marred the fairest hopes.[40]

Sobered by the realization of his own cruelty and by his real love for Toinette, Hunter later pleads that she return to her ante-bellum relationship with him. But the free Toinette, true to the precepts of Victorian womanhood, refuses to be sullied by such sin. "I demand nothing from others," she announces, "but I must, I will, respect myself."[41] Indeed, it is the sin of interracial cohabitation as a natural outgrowth of the evil slave system which Tourgée seeks to condemn in this novel, although he is actually more concerned with its effects on the Southern white man than on the mulatto characters involved. In the original version of the book,[42] love and need finally do conquer Hunter's prejudice after he suffers a stroke and becomes blind, and the work ends with a reconciliation and the implication of an intended marriage. In *A Royal Gentleman*, as the revised and more widely read version was titled, Tourgée drew back from this position, and the novel ends, as one critic has noted, "more effectively with no solution at all."[43] Toinette has been able to break away from the subordinate attitude of her days as a slave, but Hunter is bound by the prejudices of an earlier era. This peristence of pre-war attitudes into the post-bellum period, Tourgée contended, was the most obvious example of "those unconscious influences which shape and mold mental and moral qualities, and through which Slavery *still lives and dominates*."[44]

In her beauty and her irrepressible spirit, Toinette clearly resembles the tragic mulatto stereotype so well developed in abolitionist fiction. Both characteristics are the product, it would seem, of the infusion of white blood in her veins.   Indeed, after her introduction to the white world of her master, she soon comes to loathe the black blood which was "transforming and degrading all the nobler blood."[45] As the novel ends and Toinette, having moved to the North and passed for white, reflects upon her new status, she is conscious of the loneliness involved in being between the two races, a deceptive member of one, yet not truly at home in the other. For Tourgée, this was the dilemma the refined mulatto faced in the United States:

> Just sufficiently connected with the menial race to be spurned by the dominant one, her position as associated with the one was always liable to suspicion and detection, and to identify herself with the other was to step down the ladder of development to a level which she shuddered to contemplate. She had risen far above the mass of the lately subject race. By education and culture the equal, aye, the superior, of thousands of the master race. She felt this, and the sting of her destiny was all the sharper for its knowledge. She was not a missionary. She did not care to devote herself to the elevation of the freed people. She loved the good things of life, her own enjoyments, light, love, music, pleasant and agreeable surroundings. She was not wide in her views. She did not care to make the world so much better for her having lived it it. She did not think she was called to do it, perhaps scarcely thought of it at all.[46]

Here Tourgée captured the confusion of the mulatto's position in much the same manner as many Afro-American writers of the period did, but in having Toinette opt for a life as a white woman, with no particular concern for the plight of the newly-freed black race, he made a major departure from the sort of patterns typical of most liberal interpretations of the mulatto's role in the racial system.

In his other portrait of a tragic mulatto, however, Tourgée reverted to this more common position. Eva Collins in *Pactolus Prime* (1890), a novel set in post-bellum Washington, D.C., reflects the sort of embittered resignation typical of the tragic mulatto figure.   Eva is unaware that Pactolus Prime, an old mulatto who has reared her as the child of his former master, is in reality her father. Although a bootblack in a leading hotel, Prime has made shrewd investments in real estate which allow the girl to grow up well-educated and refined, with the promise of a future of comfort as a well-to-do white woman. On the eve of Prime's death, however, she learns of their true relationship, and the knowledge is horrifying to her.   She cries out to Lawyer Phelps, the executor of her father's will:

> Would you not rather see your daughter dead than in my place? Would you not rather be dead yourself than suffer the contamination of a single drop of colored blood?   Talk about Christ!   What was the agony of the Cross to the humiliation of a colored man in a

> white world? For the world is white--I know that--*my* world--the
> world of ambition, art, literature, society, the world that contains all
> that one loves to enjoy--the world which it is life to be a part of,
> and worse than death to be shut out from--this is white–all white--
> pure white! All else is foul, inferior--tolerated only![47]

Once again, through the device of a sudden discovery of an individual's
mixed blood, a liberal writer underlined the pathos of the refined
mulatto's position.

Through the lawyer's surprised reaction, though, Tourgée was
able to move beyond the problems of the mulatto to the difficulties
confronting all Afro-Americans. "It was the first time he had ever
realized the process through which the intelligent young colored
American must always go," Tourgée remarks of the lawyer, "before our
Christian civilization reduces him finally to his proper level of 'essential
inferiority.'"[48] In this single sentence, Tourgée adopts a view of the
Negro and the mulatto well beyond that of most of the liberal racial
thinkers of this day. The desire of the mixed-blood to participate in the
white man's world, Tourgée reveals, does not arise primarily from the
white blood in his veins, for blacks evidence the same yearnings. It
arises from the fact that this mulatto and other Afro-Americans are
excluded from the white world, although their juxtaposition to it makes it
natural that they should desire admittance. It is not the possession of
white blood itself, but being brought into proximity yet not into
membership in the white man's more desirable world that has caused
dissatisfaction among mulattoes and other Afro-Americans. Lawyer
Phelps is led to declare, clearly echoing the feelings Tourgée had
expressed earlier in *A Royal Gentleman*, that "slavery was but the
seeding; the harvest has just begun."[49]

Eva eventually, perhaps inevitably, resigns herself to her fate by
becoming a novitiate of a Catholic order and devoting herself to work
among Afro-Americans. As Lawyer Phelps explains, she saw "no other
way to avoid either deception or the confession of inferiority."[50] It is a
curious conclusion, for it seems to indicate an uncertainty on Tourgée's
part about just who the mulatto is and how important a role his white
blood plays in determining his attitudes and assumptions about himself
and his world. In both Toinette and Eva Collins, it is the white
attributes which Tourgée accentuated and which made the characters
appealing, if tragic, figures for his white reading public. In Eva Collins'
dilemma, though, he emphasized the problems facing all Afro-Americans,
both mulatto and black. Perhaps this paradoxical stance is evidence of
the confusion which haunted the vast majority of liberal whites (and, as
was indicated above, many Afro-Americans as well)--just how much was
the black man like the white? Was the mulatto, because of the

admixture of white blood, more like the white man than his darker brother? What role was the mixed-blood to play in the new racial system evolving in America in the late nineteenth century?

While Tourgée, like Cable, was able to make effective use of mixed-blood characters, only one writer was really able to step outside the traditional patterns of the supposedly tragic situation of the mulatto. In *An Imperative Duty* (1892), William Dean Howells demonstrated an unusual detachment in dealing with, what to other white writers of his day, was a melodramatically heart-rending situation.

The novel ostensibly follows the usual pattern of a beautiful, high-spirited young woman, Rhoda Aldgate, learning that her mother was really an "accomplished and beautiful" octoroon from New Orleans (although legally married to a physician from the North). The aunt who raised Rhoda has kept this knowledge from her, but when the young woman is about to marry a white man, the aunt feels compelled by her sense of duty to reveal to her the truth. This is contrary to the advice of her physician, Dr. Olney, the character from whose point of view the story is seen. He contends that in certain situations, expediency justifies at least a silent denial of the truth. Olney had been subtly prepared for the drama of racial tensions of which he was to become a part by observing the contrast between the Negroes and whites of the lower class in Boston. He reflected that the blacks wished to imitate the manners of the best among the white race, while the young whites tried to mimic the worst. Yet despite his sympathetic outlook, when the aunt gasps out, "My niece is of negro descent," he instinctively recoils from the words "in a turmoil of emotion for which there is no other term but disgust." It was an emotional response that was "profound and pervasive." His "race instinct expressed itself in a merciless rejection of her beauty, her innocence, her helplessness because of her race." Howells was trying to deal with the situation realistically, for he indicated that "the impulse had to have its course;" before Olney, or any white man, could feel pity, he felt repulsion. Soon Olney does master this feeling, though, "with an abiding compassion, and a sort of tender resignation."[51]

The news is, of course, a great shock to Rhoda, and true to form she immediately cancels her wedding plans. Meanwhile, Dr. Olney has become increasingly attached to Rhoda, and the story of her true racial background only seems to make her more appealing because of "the remote taint of her servile and savage origin."[52] When he proposes to her, she at first refuses to be his wife, despite the fact that she has grown to love him. As Everett Carter, a student of Howell's works, has noted, "the dictates of a Puritan civilization, which has carried the cult of personal conscience into an obsession with duty, impelled her to re-enter the Negro race, to try to educate them, and elevate them."[53] Would it not be cowardly to desert them, she cries to Olney, "and live happily apart from them, when--"   "When you might live so miserably with them?" Olney finishes for her. Through Olney, Howells sought to bring reason to a situation which other writers described as hopelessly tragic. "You would have some such duty toward them, perhaps," Olney tells the girl,

> if you had voluntarily chosen your part with them--if you had ever *consented* to be of their kind. Then it *would* be base and cowardly to desert them; it would be a treason of the vilest sort. But you never did that, or anything like it, and there is no more specific obligation upon you to give your life to their elevation than there is upon me. Besides, I doubt if that sort of specific devotion would do much good. The way to elevate them is to elevate *us*, to begin with. It will be an easier matter to deal with those simple-hearted folks after we've got the right way ourselves.[54]

Rhoda is at first unconvinced, but eventually her love "performed the effect of common-sense for them, and in its purple light they saw the every-day duties of life plain before them."[55]   They keep Rhoda's background a secret, marry, and soon move to Italy to live, where Olney must only occasionally combat Rhoda's Puritanical impulses towards self-sacrifice.

Unlike the authors of his age, then, Howells sought to deal with the question of what an individual who discovers himself to be possessed of Negro blood would actually do, given the circumstances of his world. To Howells, it was unreasonable to expect such a person to acknowledge publicly his racial heritage and then martyr himself to the race.   In taking such a position, however, Howells was making a subtle statement about the nature of American race relations.   In determining to pass, his heroine was admitting the injustices and unfavorable conditions under which the mass of Afro-Americans was forced to live.

Most writers who dealt with mixed-bloods as unfortunate victims of caste were unable to treat their characters in the rather cavalier manner of Howells.   Nevertheless, there was no unanimity in white portraits of the mulatto as a tragic figure.   Conservative authors tended to be overwhelmed by the hopelessness of the mulatto's plight, largely because they viewed black/white relations in static terms.   Because all Afro-Americans were doomed to an inferior status, the mixed-blood was forever prohibited from reaching the plane to which his white blood, and the race traits which it entailed, naturally led him to aspire.   Such characters consequently seemed to be disconsolately resigned to their fate.   More liberal writers, on the other hand, envisioned an eventually more equitable resolution of race relations.   As a result, they sometimes saw the mulatto's position as less forlorn.   At other times they used the mulatto's status to decry the injustices of the treatment accorded all Afro-Americans.

Albion Tourgée employed the title character of *Pactolus Prime* (1890) in just this fashion. By this time, Tourgée had lost much of the optimism which had underlain his earlier works on the struggles of Afro-Americans in the Reconstruction South. As Theodore L. Gross has said, *Pactolus Prime*

> in his least eloquent statement of racial problems; it is a novel of a bitter man, written in bitter language, a novel by a sensitive nationalist, who recognized the complacency of his fellow "citizen-kings" and who would not forget the unfulfilled pledges of the Northern politicians.[56]

The book's chief concern is a didactic plea for a program of national education for the Negro, yet it is also important for its reflections of a liberal's uncertainty about the role of the mulatto in America.

Tourgée set out three distinct philosophies which he felt mixed-bloods had developed concerning their status in a sharply biracial society. One, as noted above, was Eva Collins' resignation to her suddenly discovered Negro blood and the decision to become a martyr to the race. The other two are more complex. Pactolus Prime, the son of a slave mother and a white father, was white in appearance as a child and educated by his master. He was later deprived of his fiancée, May, by the same master, who desired her for himself. Prime left his South Carolina plantation to fight for the Union forces during the Civil War, passing as a white man. When he returned he found that May had been seduced by his master and had had a child by him. Prime took her and the boy to the North, but in escaping was shot by his old master and suffered the strange consequences of having his hair fall out and his skin become black. Later in Washington, D.C., he serves as a bootblack in a hotel and through shrewd investments amasses a fortune which provides for May and which he hopes will establish his daughter in white society. May's son Benny works for him as a bootblack, although he hopes one day to become a successful lawyer.

Benny exhibits a strong race-consciousness, accompanied by the desire to be a leader of the race which Tourgée felt characterized a portion of the mulatto population. Benny is optimistic about the contribution which he might make to the betterment of the race. Prime, having lived on both sides of the color line, urges a different course for Benny. The wise choice, Prime feels, is to be white and get rich, to think of himself first and then of the needs of his race. "Thank God you're as near white as you are," Prime tells Benny.

It may not do *you* much good, but your children may have a heap
better chance in this world, and an even show for the next because
of it. . . . There can't any colored man have an even chance in this
world nor a fair show of gettin' to the next. . . . you ought to look
things square in the face, do the best for yourself, an' get to be a
white man as fast as possible. . . . You can't help the rest of the
colored race by remaining a nigger, and you can do a good thing for
yourself and save your children from an inheritance of woe by
making yourself white.[57]

Benny idealistically charges that such would be an unmanly desertion of
the race, but Prime realistically forces him to consider whether it is not
better "to be a man and *white*, than to be the same man and black?" If
a man could be either (the situation facing light-skinned mulattoes like
Benny), "how could he count the most--enjoy the most--as a white man
or as a nigger?"[58] He counters Benny's youthful desires to help the
Negro race by noting that as a white man he could achieve the most
substantial results:

As a white man you could do more than a thousand
colored men.   It is *white* sentiment, white civilization, white
Christianity that needs to be modified. The colored race asks no
special privilege, no peculiar consideration, no distinctive favor. If
equality of right, privilege and opportunity is secured for them, they
desire nothing more. If this is not secured them they will, some
time, grow sullen, resentful and dangerous. In this coming warfare
of opinion you may be a much more important factor as a white
than as a colored man. At all events you have it in your power to
lift one family from the gulf of despair. If everyone could do as
much the race-problem would soon be solved.[59]

Benny was unable to refute Pactolus Prime effectively despite his
sincere concern for the future of the race. Tourgée apparently saw little
future for the mulatto who would align himself with the Negro race and
seek to become a race leader. However, other white writers believed that
the mulatto could make an important contribution in this manner.
Rebecca Harding Davis clearly perceived this as the proper course for
John Broderip in *Waiting for the Verdict* (1867). After considerable
inner struggle, Broderip finally realizes that his proper place is with "his
people" and he gives up his medical practice to lead a Negro regiment in
the Union army during the Civil War. "It is so seldom," Davis says
through one sympathetic white character

that God puts such a chance in the path of a man! . . . Not worldly
greatness, though that's included; but to be the leader of a great
people out of slavery; out of the ignorance in which they've been
bound!   No man's work is so high as that.[60]

Eventually Broderip's concern for the welfare and freedom of his race overwhelms all of his other thoughts. He becomes a new man through the dedication of his life to those ends, "Pure, strong and humble beyond belief of any who had known him in other days."[61] A similar dedication to the needs of the black race overcomes Philip Morrow, the hero of Edward Sheldon's play *"The Nigger"* (1910). He quickly recognizes his duty when he is informed of his black blood. "If I'm a niggah myself, that's all the mo' reason I should help the *othah* niggahs!" he announces as he vows to sign a much disputed prohibition bill into law.[62] "I've got to wo'k fo' the niggahs--shouldah t' shouldah--" he tells his fiancée, "b'cause I'm a niggah myself, an' b'cause they need me awful bad!"[63]

Even Tourgée portrayed one mulatto along the lines of a race leader. Eliab Hill, a crippled ex-slave in the Reconstruction novel *Bricks Without Straw* (1880), is a teacher among the freedmen, a voice of moderation and reason among a people in need of wise leadership. The brutalities to which he is subjected by hostile local whites lend him the image of a black Christ, an image that was to reappear in the character of Pactolus Prime ten years later.[64] Yet Tourgée, perhaps a wiser man by then, had Prime urge the enthusiastic young Benny to forego such a career. He emphasized the particular obloquy suffered by the mulatto in the white man's America. The mulatto cannot be a white man, regardless of what he does, Prime contends, because the white man will not accept him as such; yet

> the nearer white he is, the less use white folks will have for him. They can afford to be kind to a black nigger like me, you see, but one who is whiter than some white men, . . . such a one is an object of suspicion--as far as you can see him. He's got no chance to be anything more or less than a nigger.[65]

To Prime, there can be no advantage to aligning oneself with the Negro race, so that the only viable course for the light mulatto is to escape the subordinate status of the Negro by passing for white. Indeed, the cynical Prime insists that there are thousands of blacks who "would gladly lie down and be flayed alive, if they might rise up white--the peers of white men and equal heirs of right and privilege with white Christians!"[66]

Passing seemed the logical course to a number of other sympathetic white writers as well. In *The Southerner* (1909), Walter Hines Page obviously condones the decision of a light-skinned mulatto woman to pass. In the North she has become the wife of a wealthy white man and to all appearances indistinguishable from a refined woman of pure white blood.[67] John Marshall, the man who discovers he has a small amount of black blood in Payne Erskine's novel *When the Gates Lift Up Their Heads* (1901), concludes to pass for white, with the knowledge and encouragement of his white fiancée. Toinette in Tourgée's *A Royal Gentleman* passes for white twice in the North, because she is aware of the discrimination she would suffer were her mixed blood known. She also lacks the personal devotion to the cause of race advancement that characterizes those mulattoes who opt for the role of race leader. Rhoda Aldgate in Howell's *An Imperative Duty* similarly is convinced of the expediency of passing for white, although she maintains something of "the sense of a guilty deceit" and is always unsure as to whether she should reveal her true racial background to people who become her friends.[68]

5

The thought that some individuals of mixed blood were surreptitiously passing over into the white race terrified white authors writing from a radical perspective. These extreme racists were contemptuous of the Negro's characteristics, disdainful of his aspirations, and endorsed policies of a severely repressive nature.[69] Their attitudes and actions evidenced a powerful hostility to Afro-Americans, as well as a pessimistic outlook about the future of race relations in America. To radicals, the essential notion was that of "retrogression"--the black man, freed from slavery, was reverting to a bestial state, and while he was not expected to survive the competition of the white race, his savage and animalistic tendencies posed a distinct threat to the physical and mental security of whites. Further, because the Negro was so grossly inferior to the white man, any mixing of the two races would inevitably be to the detriment of the dominant race.

Some radical writers could be surprisingly understanding about the tensions and difficulties encountered by refined mulattoes who bore little physical or cultural resemblance to the mass of darker Negroes. Thomas Dixon's treatment of the mulatto George Harris in *The Leopard's Spots* (1902) would seem to indicate that he grasped something of the problem of a mixed-blood bred and educated for a position which white America would not agree to grant him. In *The Call of the South* (1908), Robert Lee Durham introduced Hayward Graham, a light-skinned mulatto of fine white ancestry on his father's side, as an outstanding student and athlete at Harvard. Graham nevertheless suffers "the black humiliation" of being rejected by a select company of white volunteers for a war with Germany over the Venezuelan issue.[70] Durham was able to retain a sympathetic position towards Graham through much of the book, largely because of the mulatto's unstinting courage and patriotism.

Ultimately, however, all writers with the radical viewpoint saw the mulatto as a grave menace to white civilization, and the most important element of this fear was the notion that the mulatto represented the vanguard of the forces of racial amalgamation. Nowhere was this better revealed than in the works of Thomas Dixon, the archetypal radical writer and propagandist.

Dixon's views on the race question and the mulatto were clearly stated in his first fictional work, *The Leopard's Spots* (1902), and remained essentially unchanged for the rest of his life.[71] The book was the first volume of a trilogy which justified Southern resistance to Radical Reconstruction and told of the glorious role played by the Ku Klux Klan in saving Southern civilization from destruction at the hands of blacks and Northern reformers.[72] It was Dixon's belief that because of his fundamental racial traits, the Negro was inherently and unchangeably inferior to the white man and should therefore forever remain in a position of subordination to the white race.[73] The "Trilogy of Reconstruction," as it was called, was devoted to this idea--to the upholding of the purity of the white race against what Dixon felt were the dangers of black encroachment through equality and amalgamation. The mulatto was inextricably linked to this threat, for from Dixon's point of view, "One drop of Negro blood makes a Negro. It kinks the hair, flattens the nose, thickens the lips, puts out the light of intellect, and lights the fires of brutal passions."[74] The mulatto thus was no different from the pure black. In this short passage, Dixon captured the quintessence of contemporary white racial thought and the idea which adamantly relegated the mulatto and the status of a Negro.

The passions of which Dixon spoke were above all sexual in nature, driving the mulatto and his black brother to desire marriage with whites. To Dixon, the sexual impulse was an irrational and elemental force common to man and animal alike. It represented the "herd instinct" against which civilized man fought to assert his individual will in defense of home and family.[75] In the less civilized Negro, sensuality held far greater sway. The untamed animal desires caused by his black blood therefore made the mulatto a peculiar danger to family life, the cornerstone of the Anglo-Saxon's civilization and way of life. "The right to choose one's mate is the foundation of racial life and of civilization," Dixon said through his alter-ego in *The Leopard's Spots*, the Reverend John Durham.[76]

Dixon firmly held that ninety-nine of every one hundred Negroes passionately believed in and desired the assimilation of the races.[77] This was the point of his introduction of the mulatto George Harris to the story of *The Leopard's Spots*--to show the logical progression from recognition of the Afro-American as a political equal to the pressure he would exert for interracial marriage. Harris grows to love the daughter of Everett Lowell, the white Congressman from Boston who has befriended him. Lowell's many liberal preachments on the subject of Negro rights lead Harris to believe that Lowell is free from all racial prejudices, but when he asks permission to court Lowell's daughter he is sharply rebuffed. When Harris persists, Lowell argues with words that could have come from Dixon's own mouth (for indeed Dixon saw Lowell's response as the only one a sane white man could give):

> "Am I not a graduate of the same university as you? [Harris queries.] . . . am I not your equal in culture?"
> "Granted, [Lowell responds] nevertheless you are a Negro and I do not desire the infusion of your blood in my family."
> "But I have more white than Negro blood, sir."
> "So much the worse. It is the mark of shame."[78]

Lowell would rather see his daughter dead than married to a Negro.

> I happen to know the important fact that a man or woman of Negro ancestry, though a century removed, will suddenly breed back to a pure Negro child, thick-lipped, kinky-headed, flat-nosed, black skinned.[79]

In Dixon's mind, Harris' conduct was proof that blacks must be denied all forms of equality with whites. Rev. Durham expressed this sentiment with vigor:

> The beginning of Negro equality as a vital fact is the beginning of the end of this nation's life. There is enough negro blood here to make mulatto the whole Republic. . . . It's the one unsolvable riddle of the coming century. *Can you build, in a Democracy, a nation inside a nation of two hostile races?* We must do this or become mulatto, and that is death. Every inch in the approach of these races across the barriers that separate them is a movement toward death. You cannot seek the Negro vote without asking him to your home sooner or later. If you ask him to your house, he will break bread with you at last. And if you seat him at your table, he has the right to ask your daughter's hand in marriage.[80]

"Shall the future American be an Anglo-Saxon or a Mulatto?"[81] This was the question which haunted Dixon throughout *The Leopard's Spots* and his other fictional works dealing with the race problem. To him, the issue was clear, "The Republic can have no future if racial lines are broken and its proud citizenship sinks to the level of a mongrel breed of Mulattoes."[82] Further, the mongrel results of such mixing would be a far cry from the proud Anglo-Saxon:

> Amalgamation simply meant Africanisation. The big nostrils, flat nose, massive jaw, protruding lip and kinky hair will register their animal marks over the proudest intellect and rarest

beauty of any other race. The rule that had no exception was that one drop of Negro blood makes a Negro.[83]

In *The Clansman* (1905), the novel from which the motion picture *The Birth of a Nation* was drawn, Dixon emphasized a somewhat different aspect of what he felt to be the threat posed by the mulatto. Here he was concerned with the manner by which the mulatto woman imperiled the morals and wisdom of white men. Lydia Brown is the mistress of Austin Stoneman, an important Radical Republican senator patterned after Thaddeus Stevens. She is described as "a strange brown woman of sinister animal beauty and the restless eyes of a leopardess."[84] Indeed, Dixon repeatedly stressed her animal characteristics, for he wanted it to be clear that her haughty dignity and shrewd, civilized ways were merely a veneer overlaying the "she-devil" inside. As the Senator's power in Washington increases after Lincoln's assassination, Lydia Brown becomes "first lady" in the land, using her predatory charms and subtle ways to destroy both Stoneman and the nation. Not until he is dying does Stoneman recognize the mistakes of his personal and political life and the role played by his mistress:

> My will alone forged the chains of negro rule. Three forces moved me--party sucess, a vicious woman, and the quenchless desire for personal vengeance. When I first fell a victim to the wiles of the yellow vampire who kept my house, I dreamed of lifting her to my level. And when I felt myself sinking into the black abyss of animalism, I, . . . [He dies.][85]

The other mulatto character in *The Clansman* is Silas Lynch, Lydia Brown's other lover (further proof to Dixon of the mulatto's immoral nature). He is also described in animalistic terms:

> . . . a man of charming features for a mulatto, who had evidently inherited the full physical characteristics of the Aryan race, while his dark yellowish eyes beneath his heavy brows glowed with the brightness of the African jungle. It was impossible to look at his superb face, with its large, finely chiselled lips and massive nose, his big neck and broad shoulders, and watch his eyes gleam beneath the projecting forehead, without seeing pictures of the primeval forest. "The head of a Caesar and the eyes of the jungle" was the phrase coined by an artist who painted his portrait.
>
> His hair was black and glossy and stood in dishevelled profusion on his head between a kink and a curl.[86]

At Lydia's prompting, Stoneman becomes interested in Lynch and sends him to college. Lynch becomes a Methodist minister and a henchman of Stoneman, eventually being appointed Lieutenant-Governor of South

Carolina during Reconstruction.   He regards himself, and all other
Negroes, to be "as good as any pale-face who walks this earth."   Yet
Dixon emphasizes that his "sole aim of life was sensual," and his greatest
desire was to marry a white woman.[87]

In *The Clansman*, Dixon drew upon Abraham Lincoln to support
his contention that the two races could not hope to live in harmony in
America, so that eventually one would have to be excluded:

> We must assimilate or expel [he quotes Lincoln]. . . . I can conceive
> of no greater calamity than the assimilation of the negro into our
> social and political life as our equal. A mulatto citizenship would be
> too dear a price to pay even for emancipation.[88]

The cluster of ideas held by Dixon and other radical thinkers on
the mulatto and the threat of racial amalgamation in America all came
together in a lesser known work published in 1912 entitled *The Sins of
the Father*.   In this novel Dixon shifted away somewhat from his earlier
view that racial mixing was largely the result of the ill-thought actions of
white men to the notion that it was due primarily to the untamed sexual
passions of mulattoes and blacks.[89]   The book details the pursuit and
limited conquest of a noble Anglo-Saxon, Colonel Daniel Norton, by a
voluptuous, sensual mulatto named Cleo.   Throughout the novel Cleo is
described in highly animalistic terms, yet she retains a magnetic type of
beauty as well.   "Her skin was a delicate creamy yellow, almost white,
and her cheeks were tinged with the brownish red of ripe apple."[90]   Her
figure was shapely, her teeth perfect, her motions graceful and delicate.
Nevertheless, she struck Colonel Norton as a "willful, impudent, smiling
young animal."[91]

> As he looked into her eyes he fancied that he saw a young
> leopardess from an African jungle looking at him through the lithe,
> graceful form of a Southern woman. . . He couldn't shake off the
> impression that she was a sleek young animal, playful and
> irresponsible . . . every movement of her body [was] a throb of
> savage music from some strange seductive orchestra hidden in the
> deep woods![92]

When Cleo is hired by Norton's invalid wife ("the little mother"
as Dixon repeatedly referred to her) as a nurse for their child, Norton's
fate is sealed.

> The mere physical proximity to such a creature, vital, magnetic,
> unmoral, beautiful, and daring, could only mean one thing to a man
> of his age and inheritance--a temptation so fierce that yielding could
> only be a question of time and opportunity.[93]

Inevitably Norton does yield briefly to Cleo's charms. The knowledge of that fact eventually proves fatal to his wife. Norton's fall was explained by the same passions Dixon had referred to in *The Leopard's Spots*--sexual passions which civilized man struggled to suppress but which ran wild in the blood of mulattoes and blacks. Norton sought to explain his trials to his innocent wife:

> I fought as a wounded man, alone and unarmed, fights a beast in the jungle. With her sweet spiritual ideal of love [Dixon's norm for a white, middle-class woman], a sheltered, innocent woman can't remember that man is still an animal, with tooth and claw and unbridled passions, that when put to the test his religion and his civilization often are only a thin veneer, that if he becomes a civilized human being in his relations to women it is not by inheritance, for he is yet in the zoological period of development-- but that it is by the divine achievement of character through struggle. Try, dearest, if you can, to imagine such a struggle. This primeval man, in the shadows with desires inflamed by hunger, meets this free primeval woman who is unafraid, who laughs at the laws of Society because she has nothing to lose. Both are for the moment animals pure and simple. The universal in him finds its counterpart in the universal in her. And whether she be fair or dark, her face, her form, her body, her desires are his--and, above all, she is near--and in that moment with a nearness that overwhelms by its enfolding animal magnetism all powers of the mind to think or reflect. Two such beings are atoms tossed by a storm of forces beyond their control.[94]

White women, of course, were not subject to these desires, and this is what makes the mixed-blood like Cleo so dangerous--she looks like a white woman in her physical appearance, yet inside lurk the untamed passions of a savage animal. Consequently, she has the power to corrupt the morals of the white man and loose the animal urges within him, thereby endangering the stable and proper marriage and family life Dixon felt to be so crucial to white civilization.

Twenty years later, Norton has succeeded in mastering these inner drives,[95] but more important, he has come to recognize the curse represented by the presence of these sensual creatures with black blood and the concomitant necessity of maintaining absolute racial purity among whites. The issue becomes acutely pressing when Norton's son seeks to marry a girl whom Cleo has led Norton to believe is their illegitimate mulatto daughter. Norton tries desperately to convince his son that preserving racial purity is "God's first law of life,"[96] and that challenging that law would be the most dangerous threat to the future of America and mankind:

A pint of ink can make black gallons of water. The barriers once down, ten million negroes can poison the source of life and character for a hundred million whites. . . . No white man ever lived who desired to be a negro. Every negro longs to be a white man. No black man has ever added an iota to the knowledge of the world of any value to humanity. . . . The life of generations are bound up in you. . . . You are bound by the laws of heredity—laws that demand a nobler and not a baser race of men! Shall we improve the breed of horses and degrade our men? You have no right to damn a child to such a legacy![97]

The only solution to this dilemma, Norton contends, is total separation of the races, for if this were not achieved, the forces of democracy would eventually wear down every barrier between the two races and the result would be a "mongrel breed of a degraded nation."[98] In Norton's view, disfranchisement represents the essential first step in this process and he devotes himself to that end. Eventually, however, he must pay for his sins, and finally commits suicide because he cannot live with the thought of having fostered the evils which he so strongly condemns.

The Sins of the Father encompasses all of Dixon's fears about the mulatto and the threat of racial amalgamation in America. Cleo exhibits the primitive, animal tendencies lurking in all who possess black blood. As such, she is a threat to the white male, because his barely controlled inner urges can too easily break loose when confronted with such temptations. The mixing that would result would mean the degradation and mongrelization of the mighty Anglo-Saxon race. The only possible solution is to remove the source of this temptation; the races must be separated, probably by the forced emigration of blacks and mulattoes. Only through such means can the nation and the white race be saved.

Dixon was far from alone in his extreme racial views. Indeed, by the last years of the nineteenth century and into the first decade of the twentieth, radicalism was probably the dominant racial mentality in the South, and was making inroads into the North as well. During this period, a number of other authors echoed Dixon's warnings about the threat to whites posed by the presence of the mulatto. Joel Chandler Harris was for the most part a conservative apologist for the Old South and its paternal system of slavery. Yet in his only novel, *Gabriel Tolliver* (1902), he portrayed a mulatto woman in a manner quite similar to Dixon's later treatment of Cleo in *The Sins of the Father*. Edie Varner is a mulatto temptress, described as being "young, and bright, and handsome. She was almost white, and her face reminded you somehow of the old paintings of the Magdalene, with her large eyes and the melancholy droop of her mouth."[99] Although married to "a happy-go-lucky negro" (Harris' favorite kind), she is dissatisfied with her lot, always desiring material things and quick to seek out men who could satisfy her wants. Driven by "wild and untamed passions," she is particularly attracted to Hotchkiss, a white reformer from New England who almost falls prey to her seductive beauty: "A melancholy tenderness shone in her lustrous eyes, her rosy lips curved archly, and the glow of the peach-bloom was in her cheeks."[100] Unfortunately, Hotchkiss is shot by Edie's jealous husband before he surrenders to her allurements. Nevertheless, Harris succeeded in establishing a sharp contrast between the immoral sensuality of this mulatto woman and the modest, ladylike demeanor of his white heroine.

Norah Davis' novel *The Northerner* (1905) deals with a Southern white man living with the guilt of having become involved with a mulatto woman as a youth, although with less lurid detail than in Dixon's *The Sins of the Father*. "A boy of twenty, a summer in Dixie"-- what other result could be expected, given the South's "heritage of lust." Lesby, the mixed-blood, "was a warm, bright-colored creature, voluptuous and passionate, as all those women are," according to her victim, Hugh Watson.[101] She had seduced him and then abandoned their baby, Rosebud, to his care. Years later, Watson is haunted by the presence of Rosebud as the housemaid of his innocent fiancée, although Rosebud is ignorant as to the true identity of her father. Like other such characters, Rosebud is beautiful yet possesses sensual characteristics not seen in the descriptions of white women.

> The girl was well grown, though her strong, elastic figure retained the soft curves of childhood, which lingered, also, in the tints and contour of her face, as richly colored as a dusky rose. The dark olive of her complexion, coarsened by exposure, deepened upon her cheeks to an indefinite richness of tint which was not rose or scarlet, but a softened mingling of both; the lips of her wide, flexuous mouth were a clear scarlet, and her rich abundance of coarse, chestnut-tinted hair was parted simply above the brow, whose bold, intellectual development was evident at a glance. She had the straight features of the Caucasian ancestry, infused and vivified to a richer exuberance of nature by the warm blood of her mother's race.[102]

Because of her light color, Rosebud herself finds it difficult to adjust to her status as a Negro, and dislikes associating with blacks any more than necessary.[103] Yet Watson cannot bear the sight of her, largely because of the sin she represents. "I loathe her," he confides to a friend. "Every drop of blood in my body turns cold with disgust at the thought-- the sight of her!"[104] It is in discussing the matter with Rosebud, however, that Watson truly expresses the author's feelings about the relationship between a white man and the mixed-blood:

> Between you and this man [actually himself], Rosebud, though you
> are his daughter, and he is your father, there is the same wall of
> race--caste--color which has always been between the white race and
> the negro; which will always be there so long as the world stands
> and time is,--and which may not be passed. . . . That was a sin of
> the flesh, you know, and in the flesh will he repay.   But in the
> spirit, in all those things which belong to his higher nature, you can
> have no part. . . . He could not love you, cherish you; his very
> nature would recoil.   It is instinct, child, blood![105]

Rosebud has little choice but to concur meekly.

Throughout the book, Davis was concerned with emphasizing for her white readers the perils of crossing the color line. Miscegenation is alternately referred to as "The Curse of Dixie," "The Nameless Shame," "The Hidden Pain."   It was what came, Davis insisted, of "negro equality," and represented the very darkest, unspoken side of Southern life.[106]

Thomas Nelson Page, another conservative chronicler of the glories of the Old South, was more explicit in his denunciation of the mulatto curse during the short period that he swung over to a radical outlook. He seems to have been most concerned that the mulatto was a disruptive influence among the newly-freed blacks of the South.   In "How Andrew Carried the Precinct" (1894), Page told how Pettigrew, a vain mulatto, competed with an upstanding white Southerner for a local political office by arousing the emotions of the black voters.   Andrew, the white man's faithful black servant, nevertheless helps his former master to win out over the mulatto.[107]

Page was also aware of the animal passions so central to Thomas Dixon's radical fiction. Significant in this vein is Page's portrait of Moses the Trick-Doctor in *Red Rock*, a novel published in 1898.   Although a mixed-blood, Moses has inherited the grotesque appearance of his African forebears. He is "a yaller nigger" whose protruding lower jaw, deformed teeth, blue gums, villainously low forehead, and furtive, rolling eyes that "looked in quite different directions" clearly hint that he is very much the brute that his later behavior proves him to be. Moses is adept at swaying black audiences through his emotional appeals, and as a result is an important tool in the hands of unscrupulous radical politicians seeking to overthrow white rule in the Reconstruction South.   Moses is deeply convinced that he is "jest as good as any white man" and he is determined to prove it. His greatest goal, he says is "to marry a white 'ooman and meck white folks wait on me."[108]   Such notions lead him to attempt to rape an altruistic Northern white woman who had come South to start a school for the freedmen. Eventually he is run out of town by blacks who have remained loyal to their old masters, and it is later learned that he has been lynched for several crimes "sufficiently heinous to entitle him to be classed as one of the greatest scoundrels in the world."[109] In Moses, Page brought together the threatening image of the mulatto with that of the black brute rapist.

Next to Dixon, perhaps the most forceful statement of the radical view of the mulatto and the question of race mixture came in Robert Lee Durham's *The Call of the South*. Further, Durham's novel provides the clearest indication of the rationale underlying radical opposition to racial amalgamation. The story revolves around Hayward Graham, a mulatto of barely perceptible Negro blood, a man whose imposing physical appearance attracted the attention of all who saw him:

> He was broad of shoulder, full-chested, straight-backed, with a head magnificently set on; and had closely cropped black hair showing a decided tendency to curl, dark eyes, evenly set teeth as white as a fox-hound's, a clean-shaved face neither full nor lean, and pleasing to look upon, a complexion of noticeable darkness, yet all but white and without a trace of colour.[110]

Graham is acutely conscious of the rebuffs and discriminations he suffers because of his Negro blood, yet he remains highly patriotic, performing with conspicuous gallantry as a cavalryman in a war against Germany. He later becomes footman for a President who champions liberal democracy and recognition of the Negro's basic rights.[111] In this capacity, Graham is thrown into contact with the President's idealistic daughter, Helen. After rescuing her from a runaway horse and revealing to her his heroic past on the football field at Harvard and the battlefield in Venezuela, Graham wins her love and respect, "like a modern Othello."[112] They are then secretly married, although platonically, anticipating a public wedding once Graham receives a commission in the army.

Up to this point, Durham seems sympathetic to his character's abilities and dreams. But beneath his civilized veneer, there lurks in Graham a savage beast, fed by the spirit of Guinea Gumbo, his great-grandfather. Guinea Gumbo had been an African savage imported to Kentucky as a slave. There he was eventually killed for having kidnapped, raped, and murdered the daughter of his master in a primitive hut in the swamps. Similar brutal passions rise in Graham's blood as the fickle Helen's attentions turn to other men, until one day, waylaid by a storm, he and Helen are forced to seek refuge in an isolated hut. Helen repeatedly spurns his advances and denies his rights to her love. This only infuriates the beast in him more:

> In a flash of light she sees [his face] – distorted! With a shriek of terror she widely tries to push him from her; but the demon of the

blood of Guinea Gumbo is pitiless, and against the fury of it, as of
the storm, she fights and cries - in vain.[113]

The tragedy, of course, is played out to the end.   Helen is
delivered of a very dark child, explained by Durham as a "recession:"

> It was a negro baby: the colour that was of Ethiopia, the
> unmistakable nose, the hair that curled so tightly, the lips that were
> African, the large whites of the eyes.   Verily a negro baby: and yet
> in an indefinable way a likeness of Helen, a caricature of Helen, a
> horrible travesty of Helen's features in combination with whose?   Not
> Hayward Graham's.   But whose, then?   Helen's and whose? . . . Mr.
> Phillips could not answer his own question - he had never seen
> Guinea   Gumbo.[114]

The President soon dies of heart failure, even Graham, because of his
considerable white blood, disdains the child, and Helen goes mad.
     The lesson of the tale, Durham felt, was that granting any
degree of social equality of Afro-Americans necessarily meant racial
amalgamation and the "mongrelization of the superior breed."   This was
the crux of the issue as far as Durham and other radical writers and
thinkers were concerned--racial mixing inevitably produced a being
inferior to its white progenitor, so that mixing on a wide scale would
degrade and ultimately destroy the white race.

6

     Such thinking, of course, was central to the way most Americans
understood the meaning of race and racial differences in the late
nineteenth and early twentieth centuries.   Ideas about race as a socio-
biological phenomenon, about the distinctiveness and permanence of a
variety of racial traits and instincts, and about the inherent inferiority of
the Negro and his racial heritage were fundamental to all of these
fictional treatments of the subject of race mixing.   The white race, it was
believed, had developed a way of life and a social and cultural system
through thousands of years of civilization which put the race infinitely far
ahead of the African and his Negro brothers in America.   Any mixing of
the white race and the black would weaken the offspring's heritage of
white racial qualities because of the deleterious effects of inheriting the
savage instincts of his black parent.
     These notions are clearly evident in Durham's *The Call of the
South*.   In a speech denouncing President Phillips' social recognition of
two black leaders, Evans Rutledge, a young Senator from South Carolina,
based his arguments against social intermingling of the two races on this
understanding of race.[115]   Rutledge believed that even the most refined

Afro-American carried within him the blood of his savage African ancestors:[116]

> An occasional isolated negro may have broken the shackles of ignorance, measurably and admirably brought under control the half-savage passions of his nature, acquired palpable elegances of person and manner, and taken on largely the indefinable graces of culture; yet beneath all this creditable but thin veneer of civilization there slumber in his blood the primitive passions and propensities of his immediate ancestors, which are transmitted through him as latent forces to burst out in his children and grandchildren in answer to the call of the wild. A man is not made in one generation or two. Every man gets the few ruling passions of his life from the numberless endowments of a hundred progenitors, and these few show out, while scores of others run so deep in his blood that they never crop out in his deeds but pass quietly on as static forces of good or evil to his children and their children before rising to the surface as dynamics in life and character.[117]

Regardless of how cultured and accomplished a Negro might be, regardless of how much white blood might be infused into his veins, he remained the descendant of primitive, inferior black Africans,

> and in his blood who shall say what jungle passions [there are], predilections and impulses, nobly and hardly held in check, that hark back to the African wilds from which they are so lately transplanted.

> . . . the whole trend of his life may be set upward: but there is yet between his new purposes and the savagery of the primitive man in him a far thinner bulwark of heredity than protects a white man from the elemental brute and animal forces of his nature.[118]

This was the primary point that Durham meant to make through the story of Hayward Graham. Despite Graham's seemingly civilized exterior, inside were concealed the brutal, animal passions of Guinea Gumbo and his other forebears, waiting silently to leap to the fore when his jealousy and primitive sexual desires were aroused. Ultimately, this menace threatened all of white America, and necessitated the sharpest vigilance lest the Negro be inclined to think himself the equal of the white man and seek to amalgamate further with him. The issue was far too important to be taken lightly, for in the end the future of mankind was at stake. The Anglo-Saxon was the great civilizer of the world, but if he allowed his blood to become degraded by the infusion of inferior black blood,

> then the progression of civilization and of character must not only stop but must actually recede [from] a juncture with the black and backward race in the blood of a hybrid progeny. There the fine

edge would be taken off every laudable characteristic of the white man. There the splendid Anglo-Saxon spirit of leadership and initiative would be neutralized by the sluggish blood of the Ethiop race. There the Anglo-Saxon's fine energies and clear sensibilities would be deadened and muddled by the infusion of this soporific into his veins. There vile, unknown, ancestral impulses, the untamed passions of a barbarous blood, would be planted in the Anglo-Saxon's very heart.[119]

Since amalgamation would "beat back the white into the lagging footsteps and gross animalism of the black,"[120] it had to be prevented by whatever means were necessary. The only really sure means of doing so, Durham insisted, was "a social separation of the white and black races in America from the lowest to the highest," at least until the far-off day when the Negro will have come to approximate the white in racial excellence.[121]

Durham's strident appeal for racial purity based upon contemporary understanding of heredity and race was echoed by a large number of other white fictionists, including some well outside the radical camp. This seems an indication of the universality of the basic elements of the era's racial thought, especially regarding the inferiority of the Negro and the idea of a Lamarckian transmission of acquired racio-cultural traits. This pattern of thought is evident in fictional works by a variety of authors who were responding to what they perceived as the dangers inherent in racial amalgamation. The image of the mulatto inevitably suffered from this line of thinking, both because he was visible evidence to guilt-ridden whites that racial mixing had already taken place on an extensive scale, and because it was often felt that it was he who most desired further intermixing.

Thomas Dixon, of course, was one of the most outspoken critics of further amalgamation. In *The Leopard's Spots* (1902), he emphasized the hazards of granting Afro-Americans any sort of equality because it would lead to racial mixing and a mulatto America. His arguments were strongly tinged with the sort of ideas typical of the racial attitudes and theory of the period. To Dixon, the Negro was hopelessly inferior, closer to a jungle animal than to the civilized white man. Between the two races stretched an unbridgeable gulf of thousands of years of antithetical race history. The real tragedy of the Negro lay not in his experience in America as a slave, but in his race's "inheritance of six thousand years of savagery in the African jungle." During this long span of time, while the Anglo-Saxon was steadily advancing towards a more civilized and refined state, the black man remained sunk in barbarism. Further, the Negro could not progress in the evolutionary scale because he lacked the inner resources which Dixon's interpretation of Darwinism led him to believe were the measure of racial fitness.[122] With the Negro so inferior to the white man, mixing could only be to the detriment of the latter, and must therefore be prevented.

Dixon's *The Sins of the Father* evidenced an even stronger insistence upon maintaining racial purity. After his own fall, this is the cause to which Daniel Norton devotes his life, raising his son to abhor the idea of miscegenation and leading a newspaper campaign to achieve total racial segregation. In his arguments against mixing, the logic of contemporary popular racial thought is clearly manifested. Any significant interaction between the two races, Norton contends, means

> the gradual breaking down of racial barriers and the degradation of our people to a mongrel negroid level. . . . No such miracle of evolution can gloss over the meaning of such a tragedy. The Negro is the lowest of all human forms, four thousand years below the standard of the pioneer Aryan who discovered this continent and peopled it with a race of empire builders. The gradual mixture of our blood with his can only result in the extinction of National character--a calamity so appalling the mind of every patriot refuses to accept for a moment its possibility.[123]

The sensual Cleo, herself showing "growing marks of her negroid character" as she grew older, was to Dixon an insidious agent of the forces of racial amalagamation, just as in real life he felt Booker T. Washington was actually pressing for eventual amalgamation of the races.[124]

The core of popular white opposition to racial mixing involved the notion of each race possessing unique inner qualities which distinguished it from other racial groups. Indeed, while whites were obviously highly conscious of physical differences between whites and blacks, in racial theory the more significant differences were those which were internal, bound up with the concept of racial instincts or geniuses. It was in this realm that it was believed the Negro was most inferior. Logically, then, mixing such qualities with the superior impulses of the white race would markedly degrade the latter, ultimately to the detriment of world progress.

This line of thought, based upon the belief in distinct racial traits, was the foundation of the radical position vis-à-vis the Negro, but there is ample evidence that it extended well beyond the radical circle. Margaret Deland was essentially a conservative in her racial views, yet in her short story, "A Black Drop" (1908), it was intimated that the beautiful heroine Lily was of mixed blood because she displayed certain characteristics of temperament, of physique, and even of taste: "Until I stopped her," explains her white teacher, "she used a sort of heavy perfume. *They all do.*"[125] Because black blood imparted its own characteristics, intermarriage was simply unthinkable. "It is instinct,"

Deland declared. "The white man who marrries a negro pushes his race back; and if he doesn't feel the repulsion of it, there is something wrong with him!"[126]

Similar sentiments are apparent in Gertrude Atherton's *Senator North*, a novel published in 1900. One of the book's sub-plots involves Harriet Walker, the illegitimate child of an octoroon. Harriet attempts to pass for white with the grudging acquiescence of her half-sister, Betty Madison, having agreed to Betty's stipulation that she promise to reveal her true racial background before she marries. Harriet is already secretly married to Betty's cousin, however.   Although she is remarkably beautiful, displaying only Anglo-Saxon physical features, Harriet nevertheless cannot hide the tell-tale signs of her black ancestry: a religious frenzy in her singing, her blue fingernails which she keeps a bright pink, an occasional "fatuous grin of the negro,"[127] and the tragic reversion to type when she attends a Negro camp meeting. Under the religious fervor of this experience she tells her husband, a Southern gentleman, of her mixed blood. Aghast, he shoots himself as the only honorable solution, and Harriet conveniently drowns herself a few days later.

Atherton displays little sympathy for Harriet's plight. Indeed, it is as though her understanding of race and racial traits made Harriet's demise inevitable. Speaking through Senator North early in the book, she foreshadows Harriet's fate in terms clearly drawn from contemporary race theory:

> She is nearly all white [the Senator says of Harriet]; how much of racial lying, and slothfulness, barbarism, and general incapacity that black vein of hers contains will give you food for thought, for she certainly will reveal herself in the course of a year.[128]

Even liberals subscribed to this fundamental outlook. William Dean Howell's *An Imperative Duty* (1892) was tinged with a peculiar sort of primitivism, a point of view which involved a belief in the essential superiority of "primitive" characteristics supposedly unique to culturally backwards races and groups. Through Dr. Olney, Howells observed the spontaneity of Boston's Afro-Americans, a primitive characteristic which he contrasted to the somber ways of the white residents of the city. Similarly, Dr. Olney is attracted to Rhoda Aldgate for those aspects of her personality which her aunt would see as the effects of her savage ancestry--her "readiness for laughter," her carefree nature and obvious irresponsibility. Indeed, it is Olney's own animal nature which Rhoda is most successful in arousing in the first place, presumably because of her own sensual appeal and inner urges.[129]

Howells, of course, seemed to condone interracial marriage, at least that between whites and mulattoes with very weak ties to the black race. A similar attitude was implied in the fiction of George Washington Cable and Payne Erskine. All three writers were conspicuous for their liberal attitudes towards mulattoes and Afro-Americans in general. The vast majority of white authors, however (and the white public for whom they were writing), was adamantly opposed to racial amalgamation, regardless of the overall racial perspective of the individual fictionist. This is largely explained by the general agreement as to the Negro's inherent inferiority to the white man, and by the nearly universal adherance, whether consciously or not, to the basic precepts of contemporary racial theory. Radical writers like Thomas Dixon and Robert Lee Durham viewed the mulatto as a menace. He represented the vanguard of the forces of miscegenation, corrupting the morals and destroying the the family life of the noble Anglo-Saxon and thereby threatening the future of civilization itself. Conservatives like Margaret Deland or Matt Crim, while dreading further amalgamation, were aware of the tragic nature of the mulatto in a world dominated by race-conscious whites. Most liberals also sensed the tragedy in the mulatto's position, but because they were more optimistic than others about the future of race relations in America, they envisioned a positive role for the mixed-blood as a leader of the black race. Nevertheless, they were also aware that the mulatto, since he had often been closely exposed to the desirable world of white America, could easily become embittered when repeatedly rejected by whites despite his physical and cultural resemblance to them. Perhaps because they sensed what their own reactions would be to such continued discriminations, a number of liberal writers apparently sympathized with the decision of some light-skinned mulattoes to pass for white when given the opportunity.

7

The contradictions and disparities inherent in white America's perception of the mulatto reflected, more than anything else, an uneasiness about the existence of a mixed-blood class in an allegedly biracial society. The only white author during this period who truly sought to come to grips with the attitudes surrounding the mulatto was one whose own racial position tended to defy classification. Samuel Clemens, though born and raised a Southerner, was eventually able to discard most of the racial prejudices imbibed during his youth. Yet despite an intensive personal search for the meaning of the black man's presence in America, Clemens was never able to achieve an entirely satisfactory answer. While vociferously championing the Afro-American's rights and censuring those who would deny them, he remained unsure about the nature of the Negro and his relation to the white man. To this extent, he could not entirely escape the power of the basic patterns of contemporary racial thought. Nevertheless, Clemens did come to recognize the sense of guilt which overwhelmed the South--a guilt growing out of the abuse of power in slavery and miscegenation which, though highly evident, could not be admitted.

This guilt and its consequences are the focus of Mark Twain's *The Tragedy of Pudd'nhead Wilson* (1894), an often overlooked work which nonetheless offers one of Clemens last and most pessimistic assessments of the South and its people. Through the story of Roxana, the fair-skinned slave, and Tom, her degenerate son growing up as a white man, Twain demonstrated that the South's greatest crime was not miscegenation itself, "but the white Southerners' unwillingness to admit that mulattoes were, after all, the products of their own lust."[130] Since mulattoes by their very presence offered visible evidence of a covert bond between the two races, that bond had to be overtly denied at all costs. The result was a deceit and an intense discrimination which warped the lives of all.

Ultimately it was not the mulatto himself that the white American feared, but what the mulatto revealed about the forces which were lurking within the white man himself. Ironically, it was the most radical of white writers like the fictionist Thomas Dixon or the popularizers of race theory like William Benjamin Smith and Robert W. Shufeldt who came closest to recognizing this fact. Their solution was to deny staunchly the mulatto's ties to the white race and to urge total separation of the races to insure the purity of the superior white blood. To recognize and admit the mulatto's white blood would be to admit the white man's role in miscegenation and the undermining of the racial purity that most whites cherished so highly. Paradoxically, the shock and pathos less extreme white writers and readers associated with the figure of the tragic mulatto resulted from the fact that he *did* so resemble them. However, it was because they saw themselves and their own passions in the supposed sensuality of the mulatto that whites were forced to try to shut him out of their minds. The mulatto was so much like them, yet he could not be. He had to be black, for if he *were* like the white man, what did that reveal about the white man himself?

NOTES

[1]Hugh Gloster, *Negro Voices in American Fiction* (Chapel Hill: University of North Carolina Press, 1949), p. 12

[2]Robert E. Park, "Racial Assimilation in Secondary Groups, with Particular Reference to the Negro," *American Journal of Sociology*, XIX, 5 (March, 1914), 620.

[3]C. Vann Woodward develops these liberal and conservative positions as two of four dominant modes of racial thought in the South following Reconstruction in his *The Strange Career of Jim Crow* (2nd rev. ed.: London and New York: Oxford University Press, 1966). The other two positions are those of extreme racists and the agrarian reformers who sought unity across racial lines to further class interests. See pp. 31-109 for his discussion of these four basic perspectives. Idus A. Newby deals with a similar tripartite division of American racial thought in his *Jim Crow's Defense; Anti-Negro Thought in America, 1900-1930* (Baton Rouge: Louisiana State University Press, 1965). Although he is concerned with thte period from 1900 to 1930, Newby's interpretation seems applicable to the quarter-century after Reconstruction as well. For a fictional statement of the divisions in Southern racial attitudes, see Alexander Corkey, *The Testing Fire* (New York: H. K. Fly Company, 1911).

[4]Rebecca Harding Davis, *Waiting for the Verdict* (New York: Sheldon & Company, 1868 [1867]), p. 313.

[5]*Ibid.*, p. 300.

[6]Margaret Deland, "A Black Drop," in *R. J.'s Mother, and Some Other People* (New York: Harper & Brothers, 1908), pp. 217-272. "It's bigger than I am" is the plaintive explanation with which Lily's white lover leaves her.

[7][Walter Hines Page], *The Southerner, A Novel: Being the Autobiography of Nicholas Worth* (New York: Doubleday, Page & Company, 1909), p. 306.

[8]Thomas Dixon, *The Leopard's Spots: A Romance of the White Man's Burden--1865-1900* (New York: Doubleday, Page & Co., 1902). This is not to say that Dixon did not see sinister threats posed by the mulatto's presence in America. Such a view was even evident in his treatment of the character of George Harris. The character himself, incidentally, was plucked from the pages of Harriett Beecher Stowe's *Uncle Tom's Cabin*.

[9]George W. Cable, "'Tite Poulette," in *Old Creole Days* (New York: Charles Scribner's Sons, 1879), p. 213.

[10]*Ibid.*, p. 221.

[11]It seems significant to note that neither woman even considers the possibility of marrying another mulatto, much less a black.

[12]Penelope L. Bullock, "The Treatment of the Mulatto in American Fiction from 1826 to 1902" (unpublished M.A. thesis, Atlanta University, 1944), pp. 70-71.

[13]Cable, "Madame Delphine," in *Old Creole Days*, pp. 42-44.

[14]*Ibid.*, pp. 30-31.

[15]*Ibid.*, p. 63.

[16]See Bullock, "Treatment of Mulatto in American Fiction," pp. 72-73.

[17]George W. Cable, *The Grandissimes* (New York: Charles Scribner's Sons, 1880), p. 173.

[18]*Ibid.*, pp. 74-75.

[19]*Ibid.*, p. 89.

[20]*Ibid.*, p. 172.

[21]*Ibid.*, pp. 51-52.

[22]Sterling Brown, *The Negro in American Fiction*, Bronze Booklet No. 6 (Washington, D.C.: The Associates in Negro Folk Education, 1937), p. 65.

[23]Cable, *The Grandissimes*, pp. 255, 258.

[24]*Ibid.*, p. 73.

[25]*Ibid.*, pp. 184-185. Cable expressed similar sentiments through Kristian Koppig in "'Tite Poulette," p. 222, and through Père Jerome in "Madame Delphine," p. 21, both in *Old Creole Days*.

[26]Bullock notes Cable's innovation in using the *gens de couleur* of Louisiana, a previously unexploited subject. "In doing so," she comments, "he is the first novelist to reveal that during slavery there were Negroes who lived in freedom in the deep South without a continual fear that some overshadowing evil might suddenly snatch their liberty from them." Bullock, "Treatment of Mulatto in American Fiction," p. 77.

[27]Cable, *The Grandissimes*, p. 255.

[28]Payne Erskine, *When the Gates Lift Up Their Heads: A Story of the Seventies* (Boston: Little, Brown, and Company, 1901).

[29]Matt Crim, "Was This An Exceptional Case?" in *In Beaver Cove and Elsewhere* (New York: Charles L. Webster & Co., 1892), pp. 218-219.

[30]Grace Elizabeth King, "The Little Convent Girl," in *Balcony Stories* (New York: Century Co., 1893).

[31]Edward Sheldon, *"The Nigger": An American Play in Three Acts* (New York: Macmillan Company, 1910), p. 132.

[32]*Ibid.*, pp. 191-192.

[33]*Ibid.*, p. 255.

[34]This technique was employed by Mark Twain in *The Tragedy of Pudd'nhead Wilson, and the Comedy of those Extraordinary Twins* (Hartford, Conn.: American Publishing

Company, 1894), and by William Dean Howells in *An Imperative Duty* (New York: Harper & Brothers, 1892).

[35]Sheldon, *"The Nigger,"* p. 33 (emphasis in original).

[36]*Ibid.*, p. 245.

[37]As Chapter IV indicated, this was just the opposite of the attitudes usually expressed in Afro-American fiction of this period.

[38]Tourgée's long crusade for the rights of Afro-Americans is best detailed in Otto H. Olsen, *Carpetbagger's Crusade: The Life of Albion Winegar Tourgée* (Baltimore: Johns Hopkins University Press, 1965). The literary aspects of Tourgée's career are treated in Theodore L. Gross, *Albion W. Tourgée* (New York: Twayne Publishers, Inc., 1963), and Edmund Wilson, *Patriotic Gore: Studies in the Literature of the American Civil War* (London and New York: Oxford University Press 1962), pp. 529-548.

[39]Gross, *Tourgée*, p. 39.

[40]Albion W. Tourgée, *A Royal Gentleman* (New York: Fords, Howard, & Hulbert, 1881), pp. 377-378.

[41]*Ibid.*, p. 441.

[42]Published under the pseudonym of "Henry Churton" as *Toinette: A Tale of the South* (New York: J. B. Ford and Company, 1874).

[43]Olsen, *Carpetbagger's Crusade*, p. 215.

[44]Tourgée. *A Royal Gentleman*, p.v. "Do be reasonable, Toinette," Hunter exclaims when she refuses his offer of concubinage,

> "and lay aside your high notions. Wherever did you get them from? Freedom does not make you white any more than Lee's surrender made me black. You are not a lady, and need not try to act the part of one. The barrier which nature and the law has put between us matrimonially is insuperable. . . . You will find that Geoffrey Hunter will never demean himself by marrying a nigger! . . . Social equality will never prevail here [in the South]." (pp. 442-443)

[45]*Ibid.*, p. 79.

[46]*Ibid.*, pp. 432-433.

[47]Albion W. Tourgée, *Pactolus Prime* (New York: Cassell Publishing Company, 1890), pp. 205-206.

[48]*Ibid.*, p. 206.

[49]*Ibid.*, p. 264.

[50]*Ibid.*, p. 358.

[51]Howells, *An Imperative Duty*, p. 44.

[52] *Ibid.*, p. 133.

[53] Everett Carter, *Howells and the Age of Realism* (Philadelphia: J. B. Lippincott Company, 1950), p. 85. Carter's comments about *An Imperative Duty* and the works of other authors which preceded it are particularly perceptive. See pp. 79-87.

[54] Howells, *An Imperative Duty*, pp. 142-143.

[55] *Ibid.*, p. 146.

[56] Gross, *Tourgée*, p. 133.

[57] Tourgée, *Pactolus Prime*, pp. 38-41.

[58] *Ibid.*, p. 43.

[59] *Ibid.*, pp. 140-141.

[60] Davis, *Waiting for the Verdict*, p. 316.

[61] *Ibid.*, pp. 358-359.

[62] Sheldon, *"The Nigger,"* p. 175.

[63] *Ibid.*, p. 254.

[64] Albion W. Tourgée, *Bricks Without Straw* (New York: Fords, Howard, & Hulbert, 1880).

[65] *Ibid.*, pp. 59-60.

[66] *Ibid.*, p. 46.

[67] [Page], *The Southerner*, pp. 421-423.

[68] Howells, *An Imperative Duty*, p. 149.

[69] Newby, *Jim Crow's Defense*, p. ix.

[70] Robert Lee Durham, *The Call of the South* (Boston: L. C. Page & Company, 1908), pp. 7-8.

[71] Note the position expressed in Dixon's last novel, *The Flaming Sword* (Atlanta: Monarch Publishing Co., 1939). The book sought to describe the "Conflict of Color in America" from 1900 to 1938.

[72] The other two volumes in Dixon's trilogy were *The Clansman: An Historical Romance of the Ku Klux Klan* (New York: Doubleday, Page & Co., 1905). and *The Traitor: A Story of the Fall of the Invisible Empire* (New York: Doubleday, Page & Co., 1907).

[73] Max Frank Harris, "The Ideas of Thomas Dixon on Race Relations" (unpublished M.A. thesis, University of North Carolina at Chapel Hill, 1948), pp. 17-18.

[74] Dixon, *The Leopard's Spots*, p. 242.

[75] Maxwell Bloomfield, "Dixon's *The Leopard's Spots:* A Study in Popular Racism," *American Quarterly*, XVI, 3 (Fall, 1964), 397.

[76]Dixon, *The Leopard's Spots*, p. 333.

[77]Thomas Dixon, *The Play That Is Stirring The Nation: The Clansman* (New York: American News Company, 1905), p. 24. Dixon included W. E. B. Du Bois, Booker T. Washington, and Kelly Miller, a professor at Howard University and outspoken critic of Dixon's works, in this group. See Harris, "Ideas of Dixon on Race Relations," pp. 24-25.

[78]Dixon, *The Leopard's Spots*, p. 391.

[79]*Ibid.*, pp. 393-394.

[80]*Ibid.*, p. 242. As if to make the point even more forcefully, Dixon has George Harris tell Congressman Lowell essentially the same thing.   See pp. 391-393.

[81]*Ibid.*, p. 159.

[82]*Ibid.*, p. 198.

[83]*Ibid.*, p. 382.

[84]Dixon, *The Clansman*, p. 79.

[85]*Ibid.*, p. 371.

[86]*Ibid.*, p. 93.

[87]*Ibid.*, pp. 204, 274.   These same images of mulatto characters were subsequently translated into visual forms when *The Clansman* was made into the movie, *The Birth of a Nation.*   See Everett Carter, "Cultural History Written with Lightening: The Significance of *The Birth of a Nation*," *American Quarterly*, XII, 3 (Fall, 1960), 347-357.

[88]*Ibid.*, p. 46.

[89]In *The Leopard's Spots*, for instance, Dixon had explained racial mixing as "the result of surviving polygamous and lawless instincts of the white male," i.e., as a relic of the considerable abuses of power inherent in the slave system (p. 333).

[90]Thomas Dixon, *The Sins of the Father: A Romance of the South* (New York: D. Appleton and Co., 1912), p. 25.

[91]*Ibid.*, p. 78.

[92]*Ibid.*, pp. 25, 34, 79-80.

[93]*Ibid.*, p. 43. See also p. 123.

[94]*Ibid.*, pp. 152-153.

[95]Indeed, Norton also seems to have shifted much of the blame for his earlier weakness to Cleo. "She came into my life at last--" he tells his incredulous son, "a sensuous young animal with wide, bold eyes that knew everything and was not afraid." *Ibid.*, p. 443.

[96] *Ibid.*, p. 401.

[97] *Ibid.*, pp. 403, 402.

[98] *Ibid.*, p. 196.

[99] Joel Chandler Harris, *Gabriel Tolliver: A Story of Reconstruction* (New York: McClure, Phillips & Co., 1902), p. 293.

[100] *Ibid.*, p. 295.

[101] Norah Davis, *The Northerner* (New York: Century Co., 1905), p. 166.

[102] *Ibid.*, p. 124.

[103] *Ibid.*, pp. 121, 125, 198.

[104] *Ibid.*, p. 169.

[105] *Ibid.*, pp. 127-128.

[106] *Ibid.*, 182-183.

[107] Thomas Nelson Page, "How Andrew Carried the Precinct," in *Pastime Stories* (New York: Harper & Brothers, 1894), pp. 127-142.

[108] Thomas Nelson Page, *Red Rock, A Chronicle of Reconstruction* (New York: Charles Scribner's Sons, 1898), p. 291.

[109] *Ibid.*, p. 582.

[110] Durham, *Call of the South*, p. 7.

[111] This includes social intercourse with respectable Afro-Americans, as the President dines with two Negro leaders in an incident patterned after Theodore Roosevelt's much publicized luncheon with Booker T. Washington. President Phillips' liberal views are described in *ibid.*, pp. 129-134.

[112] Brown, *Negro in American Fiction*, p. 96.

[113] Durham, *Call of the South*, p. 290.

[114] *Ibid.*, p. 385.

[115] Curiously, Durham was less confident of the "race instinct" as a natural inhibitor of racial mixing. While other whites generally felt some security in at least the white race's natural aversion to intermixture with blacks, Durham was clearly uneasy about this issue. This explains his adamant insistence that social mingling be prohibited:

> When racial barriers are broken down and it is proper for negroes and whites to associate freely and intimately, when you--white men-- receive negroes on a plane of social equality, your women will marry them, your sons will take them to wife . . . No two races of people,

living together, have ever *intermingled socially* without amalgamating."

Ibid., pp. 176-177 (emphasis in original).

[116]Such a position necessarily involves the view that native Africans have always lived a savage, uncivilized life and continue to do so. Durham cites "scientists and explorers, missionaries and travellers" to support this picture. As was noted in Chapter II above, this was the popular view of Africa and black Africans in America in the late nineteenth and early twentieth centuries, a view which strongly served to reinforce the attitudes of white Americans about the nation's Afro-American population.

[117]Durham, *Call of the South*, p. 180.

[118]Ibid., p. 181.

[119]*Ibid.*, pp. 187-188.

[120]*Ibid.*, p. 188.

[121]*Ibid.*, P. 189.

[122]See Bloomfield, *"The Leopard's Spots:* Study in Popular Racism," 396. One drop of George Harris' blood "in my family could push it backward three thousand years of history," Congressman Lowell told the mulatto in a passage clearly reflective of contemporary ideas about race. Dixon, *The Leopard's Spots*, p. 394.

[123]Dixon, *Sins of the Father*, p. 201.

[124]In this regard, see Harris, "Ideas of Dixon on Race Relations," p. 51.

[125]Deland, "A Black Drop," in *R. J.'s Mother*, p. 266 (emphasis in original).

[126]*Ibid.*, p. 236.

[127]Gertrude Atherton, *Senator North* (New York and London: John Lane: The Bodley Head, 1901), p. 161.

[128]*Ibid.*, p. 123.

[129]For a fuller treatment of the primitivist aspects of Howells' *An Imperative Duty*, see Anne Ward Amacher, "The Genteel Primitivist and the Semi-Tragic Octoroon," *New England Quarterly*, XXIX, 2 (June, 1956), 216-227. The primitivist attitudes which later emerged during the 1920's in white America's perceptions of the Negro seem to have been something of an adjustment of prevailing beliefs in distinct racial traits, instincts, and "geniuses" to the sort of cultural relativist position espoused by Franz Boas and other more liberal thinkers within the scientific community. Howells' attitudes are somewhat in the same vein of thought.

[130]Arthur G. Pettit, *Mark Twain and the South* (Lexington: University of Kentucky Press, 1974), p. 154. Pettit's chapter on *The Tragedy of Pudd'nhead Wilson* offers numerous insights into Twain's attitudes towards mulattoes and racial amalgamation. Indeed, the entire book is the story of how one sensitive American white, perhaps more than anyone else in his generation, sought to come to grips with the questions surrounding black/white relations in this country. That Twain's efforts ended in

confusion and despair speaks to the magnitude of the problem that engulfed the nation then as well as now. See also James M. Cox, *Pudd'nhead Wilson*: The End of Mark Twain's American Dream," *South Atlantic Quarterly*, LVIII, (1959), 351-363.

CONCLUSION

The contact of two disparate races has everywhere resulted in race mixture, and the American experience has not differed from this traditional pattern. Yet the peculiarities of the American racial system have shaped this sexual interaction in a particularly painful way, so that both the black and white races have had considerable difficulty in adjusting to this basic fact of their coexistence. As a result, the position of the mulatto, the product of racial crossing, has been marked by a poignant anomalousness. His kinship disavowed by the dominant group, he has found himself thrust back into the Negro race, although physically and often culturally dissimilar to it. In his consequent marginality the mulatto offers a revealing reflection of the fundamental nature of race relations in this country and the insecurity in the mind of the white race regarding its connection with the black.

In the years between Reconstruction and the First World War, attitudes and images about mulattoes and the question of race mixing were an integral part of the manner in which Americans understood the meaning of race and racial differences. During the ante-bellum period, the mulatto population had grown steadily, but its position, while clearly subordinate to that of the white race, remained somewhat unsettled. By the end of the era, however, notions about the natural inferiority of the mulatto were crystallizing into distinct theories which would shape white attitudes in the succeeding half-century. Be hind these perceptions of the mulatto stood an intellectual pattern generated by an intersection of Darwinism, Lamarckianism, and polygenism. It emphasized the distinctiveness and permanence of racial traits and instincts and ultimately, therefore, the differences which separated races rather than the qualities which they shared. From this perspective, racial mixing was a grave mistake, for it mixed and jumbled these racial traits into a discordant combination in the mulatto. More important, though, was the belief that the permanence of these racial traits by definition made the mulatto something other than a white man. His black traits, the product of a long African heritage of savagery and sensuality, were too powerful to be erased by even the superior characteristics which he received through the blood of his white progenitors. "One drop of black blood makes a Negro" was the popular appraisal of the situation, and it summarized quite neatly the fundamental belief that regardless of how white a mulatto might appear and/or act, he nevertheless remained a Negro.

Attitudes about mulattoes and race mixing, sociologist Everett V. Stonequist has suggested, are important indices of the racial problems of a society and the direction in which its race relations are moving at a given time.[1]   In the late nineteenth and early twentieth centuries, the white and black races were clearly moving farther apart in the United States, and this estrangement was explained to a degree by the very nature of those attitudes and perceptions among whites.   It seems doubtful whether too many whites were greatly troubled by their second-class treatment of the Negro, considering their deep convictions regarding his essential inferiority.   However, many whites were notably uneasy about the presence and the status of the mulatto.   His existence on the importance of maintaining racial purity, and he threatened to blur the distinctions whites sought so diligently to draw between the races.

More significantly, though, the white man's obvious responsibility for miscegenation represented a challenge to his own inherent sense of superiority.   If the mulatto looked white and acted white and was yet a Negro, what was it that distinguished a white man? "The purity of blood" was a simple answer, but blood itself was a literal and figurative manifestation of fundamental inner racial characteristics and personality traits.   What sort of qualities were revealed by the white man's patent inability to restrain his own sexual desire enough to resist mating with the Negro?   From this perspective, was he really that different from the sensual, inferior black man he so contemned?

Perhaps in the white man's attempts to alleviate such haunting uneasiness there is a clue to why he was so determined to label the mulatto as black.   Given his sense of inherent superiority to the Negro, it was impossible for the white man to cope with the thought that in this most basic of human drives he had no more self-control than the lowly Negro.   Yet by insisting that the mulatto was in fact black, by disavowing any kinship with him, the white man effectively denied his own involvement in the mulatto's creation.   Only by blocking the true nature of the mulatto from his mind by refusing to recognize color differences among Afro-Americans could he maintain his self-perceptions of superiority.   That such deliberate misperceptions became endemic to the American racial system is indicative of just how determined the white man was to allieviate this mental turmoil.

BIBLIOGRAPHY

PRIMARY SOURCES

I. BOOKS

A. PUBLIC DOCUMENTS

The Acts and Resolves. Public and Private, of the Province of the Massachusetts Bay. 21 vols. Boston: Wright & Potter, 1869-1922.

Archives of Maryland. 69 vols. Baltimore: Maryland Historical Society, 1883-

Candler, Allen D., comp. *The Colonial Records of the State of Georgia.* 26 vols. Atlanta: C. P. Byrd, 1904-1916.

Catterall, Helen Tunnicliff, ed. *Judicial Cases Concerning American Slavery and the Negro.* 3 vols. Washington, D.C.: Carnegie Institution of Washington, 1926-1937.

A Century of Population Growth: From the First Census of the United States to the Twelfth, 1790-1900. Washington, D.C.: Government Printing Office, 1909.

Clark, Walter, ed. *The State Records of North Carolina.* 26 vols. Goldsboro, N.C.: Nash Brothers, Printers, 1886-1907.

Cooper, Thomas, and McCord, David J., eds. *Statutes at Large of South Carolina.* 10 vols. Columbia, S.C.: 1836-1841.

DeBow, J. D. B. *Statistical View of the United States . . . Being a Compendium of the Seventh Census.* Washington, D.C.: A. O. P. Nicholson, Public Printer, 1854.

Hening, William Waller, comp. *The Statutes at Large: Being a Collection of All the Laws of Virginia, from the First Session of the Legislature, in the Year 1619.* 13 vols. Richmond, New York and Philadelphia: 1819-1823.

Mitchell, James T., *et al. The Statutes at Large of Pennsylvania from 1682 to 1809.* 18 vols. Harrisburg, Pa.: C. M. Bush, 1896-1915.

Negro Population in the United States, 1790-1915. Washington, D.C.: Government Printing Office, 1918.

U. S. Department of Interior. Office of the Census. *Eleventh Census of the United States, 1890: Population.*

B. FICTION

Ashby, William M. *Redder Blood, a Novel.* New York: Cosmopolitan Press, 1915.

Atherton, Gertrude. *Senator North.* New York and London: John Lane: The Bodley Head, 1901.

Cable, George W. *The Grandissimes.* New York: Charles Scribner's Sons, 1880.

_____. *Old Creole Days.* New York: Charles Scibner's Sons, 1879.

Chesnutt, Charles W. *The House Behind the Cedars.* Boston: Houghton, Mifflin and Company, 1900.

_____. *The Marrow of Tradition.* Boston and New York: Houghton, Mifflin and Company, 1901.

_____. *The Short Fiction of Charles W. Chesnutt.* Edited and with an Introduction by Sylvia Lyons Render. Washington, D.C.: Howard University Press, 1974.

_____. *The Wife of His Youth, and Other Stories of the Color Line.* Boston and New York: Houghton, Mifflin and Company, 1899.

Chopin, Kate. *Bayou Folk.* Boston: Houghton, Mifflin and Company, 1894.

Corkey, Alexander. *The Testing Fire.* New York: H. K. Fly Company, 1911.

Crim, Matt. *In Beaver Cove and Elsewhere.* New York: Charles L. Webster & Co., 1892.

Davis, Norah. *The Northerner.* New York: Century Co., 1905.

Davis, Rebbeca Harding. *Waiting for the Verdict.* New York: Sheldon & Company, 1868 [1867].

Deland, Margaret. *R. J.'s Mother, and Some Other People.* New York: Harper & Brothers, 1908.

Dixon, Thomas. *The Clansman: An Historical Romance of the Ku Klux Klan.* New York: Doubleday, Page & Co., 1905.

_____. *The Flaming Sword.* Alanta: Monarch Publishing Co., 1939.

_____. *The Leopard's Spots: A Romance of the White Man's Burden--1865-1900.* New York: Doubleday, Page & Co., 1902.

_____. *The Sins of the Father: A Romance of the South.* New York: D. Appleton and Co., 1912.

_____. *The Traitor: A Story of the Fall of the Invisible Empire.* New York: Doubleday, Page and Co., 1907.

Downing, Henry F. *The American Cavalryman: A Liberian Romance*. New York: Neale Publishing Company, 1917.

Du Bois, W. E. Burghadt. *The Quest of the Silver Fleece, A Novel*. Chicago: A. C. McClurg & Co., 1911.

Dunbar, Paul Laurence. *The Sport of the Gods*. New York: Dodd, Mead and Company, 1902.

Durham, Robert Lee. *The Call of the South*. Boston: L. C. Page & Company, 1908.

Erskine, Payne. *When the Gates Lift Up Their Heads: A Story of the Seventies*. Boston: Little, Brown, and Company, 1901.

Fowler, Charles H. *Historical Romance of the American Negro*. Baltimore: Press of Thomas & Evans, 1902.

Gilmore, F. Grant. *The Problem, a Military Novel*. Rochester, N.Y.: Press of Henry Conolly Co., 1915.

Grant, John Wesley. *Out of the Darkness, or Diabolism and Destiny*. Nashville: National Baptist Publishing Board, 1909.

Griggs, Suton E. *The Hindered Hand: or, The Reign of the Repressionist*. Nashville: Orion Publishing Company, 1905.

————. *Imperium in Imperio*. Cincinnati: Editor Publishing Co., 1899.

————. *Overshadowed*. Nashville: Orion Publishing Company, 1901.

————. *Pointing the Way*. Nashville: Orion Publishing Company, 1908.

————. *Unfettered*. Nashville: Orion Publishing Company, 1902.

Harper, Frances E. W. *Lola Leroy, or Shadows Uplifted*. Philadelphia: Garrigues Brothers, 1892.

Harris, Joel Chandler. *Gabriel Tolliver: A Story of Reconstruction*. New York: McClure, Phillips & Co., 1902.

Holley, Marietta. *Samantha on the Race Problem*. New York: Dodd, Mead & Company, 1892.

Holmes, Charles Henry. *Ethiopia, The Land of Promise: A Book with a Purpose*. New York: Cosmopolitan Press, 1917.

Hopkins, Pauline E. *Contending Forces: A Romance Illustrative of Negro Life*. Boston: Colored Co-operative Publishing Company, 1900.

Howells, William Dean. *An Imperative Duty*. New York: Harper & Brothers, 1892.

[Johnson, James Weldon.] *The Autobiography of an Ex-Coloured Man*. Boston: Sherman, French and Company, 1912.

Jones, J. McHenry. *Hearts of Gold.* Wheeling, W. Va.: Daily Intelligence Steam Job Press, 1896.

King, Grace Elizabeth. *Balcony Stories.* New York: Century Co., 1893.

McClellan, George Marion. *Old Greenbottom Inn and Other Stories.* [Louisville]: George M. McClellan, 1906.

Micheaux, Oscar. *The Conquest: The Story of a Negro Pioneer.* Lincoln, Nebr.: Woodruff Press, 1913.

————. *The Forged Note: A Romance of the Darker Races.* Lincoln, Nebr.: Western Book Supply Company, 1915.

————. *The Homesteader, A Novel.* Sioux City, Iowa: Western Book Supply Company, 1917.

Page, Thomas Nelson. *Pastime Stories..* New York: Harper & Brothers, 1894.

————. *Red Rock, A Chronicle of Reconstruction.* New York: Charles Scribner's Sons, 1898.

[Page, Walter Hines.] *The Southerner, A Novel: Being the Autobiography of Nicholas Worth.* New York: Doubleday, Page & Company, 1909.

Pryor, G. Langhorne. *Neither Bond Nor Free (A Plea).* New York: J. S. Ogilvie Publishing Company, 1902.

Rogers, Joel Augustus. *From "Superman" to Man.* Chicago: M. A. Donohoe & Company, Printers, 1917.

Shackelford, Otis M. *Lillian Simmons, or The Conflict of Sections.* Kansas City, Mo.: Published by the Author by the Press of R. M. Rigby Printing Co., 1915.

Sheldon, Edward. *"The Nigger": An American Play in Three Acts.* New York: Macmillan Company, 1910.

Thorne, Jack [David Bryant Fulton]. *Hanover; or The Persecution of the Lowly, A Story of the Wilmington Massacre.* n.p.: M. C. L. Hill, 1900.

Tourgée, Albion W. *Bricks Without Straw.* New York: Fords, Howard & Hulbert, 1880.

————. *Pactolus Prime* New York: Cassell Publishing Company, 1890.

————. *A Royal Gentleman.* New York: Fords, Howard, & Hulbert, 1881.

Twain, Mark. *The Tragedy of Pudd'nhead Wilson, and The Comedy of Those Extraordinary Twins.* Hartford, Conn.: American Publishing Company, 1894.

Waring, Robert Lewis. *As We See It.* Washington, D.C.: C. F. Sudwarth, 1910.

C. NONFICTION

"Ariel" [Buckner H. Payne]. *The Negro: What is His Ethnological Status?* 2nd ed. Cincinnati: By the Author, 1867.

Bailey, Thomas Pierce. *Race Orthodoxy in the South, and Other Aspects of the Negro Question.* New York: Neale Publishing Company, 1914.

Baker, Ray Stannard. *Following the Color Line: American Negro Citizenship in the Progressive Era.* New York: Doubleday, Page & Company, 1908.

Barringer, Paul B. *The American Negro: His Past and Future.* 3rd. ed. Raleigh, N.C.: Edwards & Broughton, 1900.

Barrows, Isabel C., ed. *First Mohonk Conference on the Negro Question, Held at Lake Mohonk, Ulster County, New York, June 4, 5, 6, 1890.* Boston: George H. Ellis, 1890.

Baxter, J[edediah] H[yde]. *Statistics, Medical and Anthropological, of the Provost-Marshall-General's Bureau, derived from Records of the Examination for Military Service in the Armies of the United States During the Late War of the Rebellion, of Over a Million Recruits, Drafted Men, Substitutes, and Enrolled Men.* 2 vols. Washington, D.C.: Government Printing Office, 1875.

Blumenbach, Johann Friedrich. *The Anthropological Treatises of Johann Friedrich Blumenbach.* Edited by Thomas Bendyshe. London: Published for the Anthopological Society by Longman, Green, Longman, Roberts & Green, 1865.

Boas, Franz. *The Mind of Primitive Man.* New York: Macmillan Company, 1911.

Brace, Charles Loring. *The Races of the Old World: A Manual of Ethnology.* New York: Charles Scribner, 1863.

Brinton, Daniel G. *The Basis of Social Relations: A Study in Ethnic Psychology.* Edited by Livinston Farrand. New York and London: G. P. Putnam's Sons, 1902.

_____. *Negroes.* Philadelphia: J. B. Lippincott Company, 1891.

_____. *Races and Peoples: Lecures on the Science of Ethnography.* New York: N. D. C. Hodges, Publisher, 1890.

Broca, Paul. *On the Phenomena of Hybridity in the Genus Homo.* Translated and edited by C. Carter Blake. London: Published for the Anthropological Society by Longman, Green & Roberts, 1864.

Brooklyn Ethical Society. *Man and the State: Studies in Applied Sociology.* New York: D. Appleton and Company, 1892.

Bruce, Philip Alexander. *The Plantation Negro as a Freeman: Observations on his Character, Condition and Prospects in Virginia.* New York: G. P. Putnam's Sons, 1889.

Bruce, W. Cabell. *The Negro Problem.* Baltimore: John Murphy & Co., 1891.

Calhoun, William P. *The Caucasian and the Negro in the United States.* Columbia, S.C.: R. L. Bryan, 1902.

Carroll, Charles. *"The Negro A Beast," or "In the Image of God."* St. Louis: American Book and Bible House, 1900.

_____. *The Tempter of Eve; or, The Criminality of Man's Social, Political, and Religious Equality with the Negro, and the Amalgamation to which These Crimes Inevitably Lead.* St. Louis: Adamic Publishing Co., 1902.

"Caucasian" [William H. Campbell]. *Anthropology for the People, a Refutation of the Theory of the Adamic Origin of All Races.* Richmond: Everett Waddey Co., 1891.

Commons, John R. *Races and Immigrants in America.* New York: Macmillan Company, 1907.

Cope, Edward D. *The Origin of the Fittest: Essays on Evolution.* New York: D. Appleton and Company, 1887.

_____. *The Primary Factors of Organic Evolution.* Chicago: Open Court Publishing Company, 1896.

[Croly, David Goodman.] *Miscegenation: The Theory of the Blending of the Races, Applied to the American White Man and Negro.* New York: H. Dexter, Hamilton & Co., 1864.

Culp, D. W. *Twentieth Century Negro Literature, or A Cyclopedia of Thought on the Vital Topics Relating to the American Negro by One Hundred of America's Greatest Negroes.* Napierville, Ill. and Atlanta: J. L. Nichols & Co., 1902.

Dixon, Thomas. *The Play That Is Stirring the Nation: The Clansman.* New York: American News Company (Publisher's Agents), 1905.

Dowd, Jerome P. *The Negro Races: A Social Study.* New York: Macmillan Company, 1907.

Du Bois, W. E. Burghardt. *The Conservation of Races.* American Negro Academy, *Occasional Papers*, No. 2 Washington, D.C.: By the Academy, 1897.

_____. *The Souls of Black Folk: Essays and Sketches.* Chicago: A. C. McClurg & Co., 1903.

Eggleston, Edward. *The Ultimate Solution of the American Negro Problem.* Boston: Richard G. Badger, 1913.

Ferguson, George Oscar. *The Psychology of the Negro, An Experimental Study.* New York: Science Press, 1916.

Fulkerson, Horace Smith. *The Negro: As He Was; As He Is; As He Will Be.* Vicksburg, Miss.: Commerical Herald, Printers, 1887.

Gould, Benjamin Apthorp. *Investigations in the Military and Anthropological Statistics of American Soldiers.* New York. Published for the U. S. Sanitary Commission by Hurd and Houghton, 1869.

Grant, Madison. *The Passing of the Great Race, or The Racial Basis of European History.* New York: Charles Scribner's Sons, 1916.

Griggs, Sutton E. *Wisdom's Call.* Nashville: Orion Publishing Company, 1911.

Hart, Albert Bushnell. *The Southern South.* New York: D. Appleton and Company, 1910.

Herder, Johann Gottfried von. *Reflections on the Philosophy of the History of Mankind.* Abridged, and with an Introduction, by Frank E. Manuel. Chicago: University of Chicago Press, 1968.

Hoffman, Frederick L. *Race Traits and Tendencies of the American Negro.* New York: Published for the American Economic Association by the Macmillan Company, 1896.

Hogan, William Ransom and Davis, Edwin Adams, eds. *William Johnson's Nachez: The Antebellum Diary of a Free Negro.* Baton Rouge: Louisiana State University Press, 1957.

[Holland, Edwin Clifford.] *A South Carolinian, A Refutation of the Calumnies Circulated against the Southern and Western States, Respecting the Existence of Slavery among Them, to Which is Added a Minute and Particular Account of the Actual Condition of Their Negro Population.* Charleston: A. E. Miller, 1822.

Holm, John James. *Holm's Race Assimilation, or The Fading Leopard's Spots.* Napierville, Ill.: J. L. Nichols & Company, 1910.

Hughes, Henry. *Treatise on Sociology, Theoretical and Practical.* Philadelphia: Lippincott, Grambo & Co., 1854.

Humphrey, Seth K. *Mankind: Racial Values and the Racial Prospect.* New York: Charles Scribner's Sons, 1917.

McCord, Charles H. *The American Negro as a Dependent, Defective and Delinquent.* [Nashville: Press of Benson Printing Company], 1914.

Marshall, Charles K. *The Colored Race Weighed in the Balance.* Nashville: Southern Methodist Publishing House, 1883.

Mayo, Marion J. *The Mental Capacity of the American Negro.* New York: Science Press, 1913.

Mecklin, John Moffatt. *Democracy and Race Friction: A Study in Social Ethics.* New York: Macmillan Company, 1914.

Murphy, Edgar Dadner. *Problems of the Present South.* New York: Macmillan Company, 1904.

Nott, Josiah C., and Gliddon, George R. *Types of Mankind: or, Ethnological Researches, Based upon the Ancient Monuments, Paintings, Sculptures, and Crania of Races, and Upon Their Natural, Geographical, Philological, Biblical History.* London: Trubner & Co., 1854.

Odum, Howard W. *Social and Mental Traits of the Negro: A Study of Race Traits, Tendencies and Prospects.* Columbia University Studies in History, Economics and Public Law, XXXVII, 3. New York: Columbia University Press, 1910.

Page, Thomas Nelson. *The Negro: The Southerner's Problem.* New York: Charles Scribner's Sons, 1904.

Paxton, John D. *Letters on Slavery: Addressed to the Cumberland Congregation, Virginia.* Lexington, Ky.: Abraham T. Skillman, 1833.

Price, John Ambrose. *The Negro: Past, Present, and Future.* New York and Washington, D.C.: Neale Publishing Company, 1907.

Randle, Edwin Henderson. *Characteristics of the Southern Negro.* New York and Washington, D.C.: Neale Publishing Company, 1910.

Reuter, Edward Byron. *The Mulatto in the United States, including a Study of the Role of Mixed-Blood Races Throughout the World.* Boston: Richard G. Badger, 1918.

Shaler, Nathaniel S. *The Citizen: A Sudy of the Individual and the Government.* New York: Barnes & Co., 1904.

_____. *The Individual: A Study of Life and Death.* New York: D. Appleton and Company, 1900.

Shannon, Alexander Harvey. *Racial Integrity and Other Features of the Negro Problem.* Nashville: Printed for the Author by the Publishing House of the M. E. Church, South, 1907.

Shufeldt, Robert W. *America's Greatest Problem: The Negro.* Philadelphia: F. A. Davis Company, 1915.

_____. *The Negro: A Menace to American Civilization.* Boston: Richard G. Badger, 1907.

Smith, William Benjamin. *The Color Line: A Brief in Behalf of the Unborn.* New York: McClure, Phillips & Co., 1905.

Southern Society for the Promotion of the Study of Race Conditions and Problems in the South. *Race Problems in the South: Proceedings of the First Annual Conference . . . at Montgomery, Alabama.* Richmond; B. F. Johnson Publishing Company, 1900.

Spencer, Herbert. *The Principles of Sociology.* 3 vols. New York: D. Appleton and Company, 1876-1897.

Stone, Alfred Holt. *Studies in the American Race Problem*. With an Introduction and three papers by Walter F. Willcox. New York: Doubleday, Page & Company, 1908.

Talbot, Eugene S. *Degeneracy: Its Causes, Signs and Results*. New York: Charles Scribner's Sons, 1904.

Thomas, William Hannibal. *The American Negro: What He Was, What He Is, and What He May Become*. New York: Macmillan Company, 1901.

Thomas, William I. *Source Book for Social Origins*. Chicago: University of Chicago Press, 1909.

Tillinghast, Joseph Alexander. *The Negro in Africa and America*. Publications of the American Economic Association, 3rd. ser., III, 2. New York: Macmillan Company, 1902.

[Van Evrie, John H.] *Subgenation: The Theory of the Normal Relation of the Races; an Answer to "Miscegenation."* New York: John Bradburn, 1864.

_____. *White Supremacy and Negro Subordination; or, Negroes a Subordinate Race, and (So-called) Slavery Its Normal Condition*. New York: Van Evrie, Horton & Co., 1868.

II. ARTICLES

A. FICTION

Allen, Sarah A. [Pauline E. Hopkins.] *Hagar's Daughter, A Story of Southern Caste Prejudice*. Serialized in *Colored American Magazine*, beginning II, 5 (March, 1901), 337.

Deekun, A. Gude. "A Georgia Episode." *Colored American Magazine*, III, 1 (May, 1901), 3-8.

Hopkins, Pauline E. "A Dash for Liberty." *Colored American Magazine*, III, 4 (August, 1901), 243-247.

_____. *Winona, A Tale of Negro Life in the South and Southwest*. Serialized in *Colored American Magazine*, beginning V, 1 (May, 1902), 29.

B. NONFICTION

Bardin, James. "The Psychologial Factor in Southern Race Problems." *Popular Science Monthly*, LXXXIII (October, 1913), 368-374.

Belin, H. E. "A Southern View of Slavery." *American Journal of Sociology*, XIII, 4 (January, 1908), 513-522.

Bean, Robert Bennett. "The Negro Brain." *Century Magazine*. LXXII, 5 (September, 1906), 778-784.

_____. "Some Racial Peculiarities of the Negro Brain." *American Journal of Anatomy*, V, 4 (September, 1906), 353-432.

Benet, W. C. "Is the Negro a Failure?" Reprinted from the Augusta *Chronicle*, April, 1886.

Boas, Franz. "Human Faculty as Determined by Race." *Proceedings of the American Association for the Advancement of Science*, XLIII (1894), 301-327.

Boughton, Willis. "The Negro's Place in History." *Arena*, XVI (September, 1896), 612-621.

Bruce, Philip Alexander. "The Negro Population of the South." *Conservative Review*, II, 2 (November, 1899), 262-280.

Chesnutt, Charles W. "Post-Bellum--Pre-Harlem." *The Crisis*, XXXVIII, 6 (June, 1931), 194.

Cope, Edward D. "The African in America." *Open Court*, IV, 21 (July 17, 1890), 2399-2400.

_____. "The Developmental Significance of Human Physiognomy." *American Naturalist*, XVII, 6 (June, 1883), 618-627.

_____. "Evolution and Its Consequences." *Penn Monthly*, III, (May, 1872), 230-238.

_____. "On the Hypothesis of Evolution, Physical and Metaphysical." *Lippincott's Magazine*, VI (July, 1870), 29-41.

_____. "The Return of the Negroes to Africa." *Open Court*, IV, 16 (June 12, 1890), 2331.

_____. "Two Perils of the Indo-European." *Open Court*, III, 48 (January 23, 1890), 2052-2054.

Curry, Jabez L. M. "The Negro Question." *Popular Science Monthly*, LV (June, 1899), 173-180.

Dixon, W. A. "The Morbid Proclivities and Retrogressive Tendencies in the Offspring of Mulattoes." *Journal of the American Medical Association*, XX, 1 (January 7, 1893), 1-2.

Dudley, Thomas Underwood. "How Shall We Help the Negro?" *Century Magazine*, XXX, 2 (June, 1885), 273-280.

Ellis, George W. "The Psychology of American Race Prejudice." *Journal of Race Development*, V, 3 (January, 1915), 297-315.

Ellwood, Charles A. "Review of *The Color Line: A Brief in Behalf of the Unborn* by William Benjamin Smith." *American Journal of Sociology*, XI, 4 (January, 1906), 570-575.

_____. "Review of *The Negro Races* by Jerome P. Dowd." *American Journal of Sociology*, XIII, 6 (May, 1908). 855-858.

_____. "The Theory of Imitation in Social Psychology." *American Journal of Sociology*, VI, 6 (May, 1901), 721-741.

Ferguson, George Oscar. "The Mental Status of the American Negro." *Science Monthly*, *XII (June, 1921), 533-543.*

Freeman, M. H. "The Educational Wants of the Free Colored People." *Anglo-African Magazine*, I, 4 (April, 1859), 115-119.

Grady, Henry W. "In Plain Black and White (A Reply to Mr. Cable)." *Century Magazine*, XXIX, 6 (April, 1885), 909-917.

Hall, G. Stanley. "The Negro in Africa and America." *Pedagogical Seminary*, XII, 3 (September, 1905), 350-368.

Harris, Mrs. L. H. "A Southern Woman's View." *Independent*, LI (May 18, 1899), 1354-1355.

Hill, Walter B. "Uncle Tom Without A Cabin." *Century Magazine*, XXVII, 6 (April, 1884), 859-864.

Hoggan, Francis. "The American Negro and Race Blending." *Sociological Review*, II, 4 (October, 1909), 349-360.

Hunt, Sanford, B. "The Negro as a Soldier." *Anthropological Review*, VII, 1 (January, 1869), 40-54.

Jordan, H. E. "The Biological Status and Social Worth of the Mulatto." *Popular Science Monthly*, LXXXII (June, 1913), 573-582.

_____. "The Inheritance of Skin Color." *Science*, N.S., XXXVI (August 2, 1912), 151-152.

Kelsey, Carl. Discussion of an article by D. Collin Wells, "Social Darwinism." *American Journal of Sociology*, XII, 5 (March, 1907), 711.

_____. "The Evolution of Negro Labor." *Annals of the American Academy of Political and Social Science*, XXI, 1 (January, 1903), 55-76.

LeConte, Joseph. "The Effect of Mixture of Races on Human Progress." *Berkeley Quarterly*, I, 1 (April, 1880), 83-102.

_____. "The Genesis of Sex." *Popular Science Monthly*, XVI (December, 1879), 167-179.

McCurley, W. S. "Impossibility of Race Amalgamation." *Arena*, XXI, 4 (April, 1899), 446-455.

McGee, W. J. "The Trend of Human Progress." *American Anthropologist*, N. S., I, 3 (July, 1899), 401-447.

Mecklin, John Moffatt. "The Philosophy of the Color Line." *American Journal of Sociology*, XIX, 3 (November, 1913), 343-357.

Morgan, John T. "Shall Negro Majorities Rule?" *Forum Extra*, I, 1 (March, 1890), 15-28.

Murphy, Edgar Gardner. "The Task of the Leader: A Discussion of Some of the Conditions of Public Leadership in Our Southern States." *Sewanee Review*, XV, 1 (January, 1907), 1-30.

Nott, Josiah C. "The Mulatto a Hybrid--Probable Extermination of the Two Races If the Whites and Blacks are Allowed to Intermarry." *American Journal of the Medicial Sciences*, VI (1843), 252-256.

_____. "The Negro Race." *Anthropological Review*, IV, 3 (July, 1866), 103-116.

Osborn, Henry, Fairfield. "The Present Problem of Heredity." *Atlantic Monthly*, LXVII (March, 1891), 353-364.

Park, Robert E. "Racial Assimilation in Secondary Groups, with Particular Reference to the Negro." *American Journal of Sociology*, XIX, 5 (March, 1914), 608-623.

Reinsch, Paul S. "The Negro Race and European Civilization." *American Journal of Sociology*, XI, 2 (September, 1905), 145-167.

Reuter, Edward Byron. "The Superiority of the Mulatto." *American Journal of Sociology*, XXIII, 1 (July, 1917), 83-106.

Ross, Edward A. "The Causes of Race Superiority." *Annals of the American Academy of Political and Social Science: America's Race Problems*, XVIII (July, 1901), 67-89.

Shaler, Nathaniel S.. "The African Element in America." *Arena*, II (November, 1890), 660-673.

_____. "An Ex-Southerner in South Carolina." *Atlantic Monthly*, XXVI (July, 1870), 53-61.

————. "Nature and Man in America." *Scribner's Magazine*, VIII, 3 (September, 1890), 360-367.

————. "The Nature of the Negro." *Arena*, III (December, 1890), 23-35.

————. "The Negro Problem." *Atlantic Monthly*, LIV (November, 1884), 696-709.

————. "The Negro Since the Civil War." *Popular Science Monthly*, LVII (May, 1900), 29-39.

————. "Science and the African Problem." *Atlantic Monthly*, LXVI (July, 1890), 36-45.

Spencer, Herbert. "Comparative Psychology of Man." *Popular Science Monthly*, VII. (January, 1876), 257-269.

Thomas, William I. "The Psychology of Race Prejudice." *American Journal of Sociology*, IX, 5 (March, 1904), 593-611.

————. "Race Psychology: Standpoint and Questionnaire, with Particular Reference to the Immigrant and the Negro." *American Journal of Sociology*, XVII, 6 (May, 1912), 725-775.

Wake, C. Staniland. "The Race Question." *Open Court*, IV, 18 (June 28, 1890), 2353-2355.

Wallis, Wilson D. "Moral and Racial Prejudice." *Journal of Race Development*, V, 2 (October, 1914), 212-229.

Watson, Thomas E. "The Negro Question in the South." *Arena*, VI (October, 1892), 540-550.

Weatherly, Ulysses G. "Race and Marriage." *American Journal of Sociology*, XV, 4 (January, 1910), 433-453.

————. "A World-Wide Color Line." *Popular Science Monthly*, LXXIX (November, 1911), 474-485.

"When Is A Caucasian Not A Caucasian?" *Independent*, LXX (March 2, 1911), 478-479.

Winston, George T. "The Relation of the Whites to the Negroes." *Annals of the American Academy of Political and Social Science: America's Race Problems*, XVIII (July, 1901), 103-118.

Woodworth, Robert S. "Racial Differences in Mental Traits." *Science*, N.S., XXXI (February 4, 1910), 171-186.

SECONDARY SOURCES

L BOOKS

Aptheker, Herbert. *Annotated Bibliography of the Published Writings of W. E. B. Du Bois.* Millwood, N.Y.: Kraus-Thomson Organization Limited, 1973.

Barton, Rebecca Chalmers. *Race Consciousness and the American Negro: A Study of the Correlation Between the Group Experience and the Fiction of 1900-1930.* Copenhagen: Arnold Busck, 1934.

Berlin, Ira. *Slaves Without Masters: The Free Negro in the Antebellum South.* Vintage Books. New York: Random House, Inc., 1974.

Blassingame, John W. *Black New Orleans, 1860-1880.* Chicago: University of Chicago Press, 1973.

Bloch, J. M. *Miscegenation, Melaleukation, and Mr. Lincoln's Dog.* New York: Schaum Publishing Co., 1958.

Boller, Paul F., Jr. *American Thought in Transition: The Impact of Evolutionary Nauralism, 1865-1900.* Chicago: Rand McNally, 1969.

Bone, Robert. *The Negro Novel in America.* Rev. ed. New Haven: Yale University Press, 1965.

Brackett, Jeffrey R. *The Negro in Maryland: A Study of the Institution of Slavery.* Johns Hopkins University Studies in History and Political Science, Extra Volume VI. Baltimore: N. Murray, Publication Agent, Johns Hopkins University, 1889.

Brown, Letitia Woods. *Free Negroes in the District of Columbia, 1790-1846.* New York: Oxford University Press, 1972.

Brown, Sterling. *The Negro in American Fiction.* Bronze Booklet Number 6. Washington, D.C.: The Associates in Negro Folk Education, 1937.

Burrow, John W. *Evolution and Society: A Study in Victorian Social Theory.* Cambridge: University Press, 1966.

Carmichael, A. C. *Domestic Manners and Social Condition of the White, Coloured, and Negro Population of the West Indies.* London: Whittaker, Treacher, and Co., 1833.

Chesnutt, Helen. *Charles W. Chesnutt, Pioneer of the Color Line.* Chapel Hill: University of North Carolina Press, 1952.

Clamorgan, Cyprian. *The Colored Aristocracy of St. Louis.* St. Louis: 1858.

Coody, Archibald, IV. *"The Race Question" From The White Chief: A Story of the Life and Times of James K. Vardaman.* n.p.: 1944.

Cope, Robert S. *Carry Me Back: Slavery and Servitude in Seventheenth Century Virginia.* Pikeville, Ky.: Pikeville College Press of the Appalachian Studies Center, 1973.

Daniels, John. *In Freedom's Birth-Place.* Boston: Houghton, Mifflin Co., 1914.

Degler, Carl N. *Neither Black Nor White: Slavery and Race in Brazil and the United States.* New York: Macmillan Company, 1971.

Du Bois, W. E. Burghardt. *The Philadelphia Negro: A Social Study.* Publications of the University of Pennsylvania Series in Economy and Public Law, No. 14. Philadelphia: Univeristy of Pennsylvania Press, 1899.

Faris, Robert E. L. *Chicago Sociology, 1920-1932.* San Francisco: Chandler Publishing Co., 1967.

Filene, Peter Gabriel. *Him/Her/Self: Sex Roles in Modern America.* New York: Harcourt Brace Jovanovich, Inc., 1974.

Fischer, Roger A. *The Segregation Struggle in Louisiana, 1862-1877.* Urbana: University of Illinois Press, 1974.

Frazier, E. Franklin. *The Negro Family in the United States.* Chicago: University of Chicago Press, 1939.

————. *The Negro in the United States.* Rev. ed. New York: Macmillan Company, 1957.

Frederickson, George M. *The Black Image in the White Mind: The Debate on Afro-American Character and Destiny, 1817-1914.* New York: Harper & Row, Publishers, 1971.

Friedman, Lawrence J. *The White Savage: Racial Fantasies in the Postbellum South.* Englewood Cliffs, N.J.: Prentice-Hall, Inc., 1970.

Genovese, Eugene D. *Roll, Jordan, Roll: The World the Slaves Made.* New York: Pantheon Books, 1974.

Gloster, Hugh. *Negro Voices in American Fiction.* Chapel Hill: University of North Carolina Press, 1948.

Gossett, Thomas F. *Race: The History of an Idea in America.* New York: Schocken Books, 1965.

Green, Constance McLaughlin. *The Secret City: A History of Race Relations in the Nation's Capital.* Princeton, N.J.: Princeton University Press, 1967.

Greene, John C. *The Death of Adam: Evolution and Its Impact on Western Thought.* Ames, Iowa: Iowa State University Press, 1959.

Gross, Seymour L., and Hardy, John Edward, eds. *Images of the Negro in American Literature.* Chicago: University of Chicago Press, 1966.

Gross, Theodore L.   *Albion W. Tourgée.*   New York: Twayne Publishers, Inc., 1963.

Haller, John S., Jr.   *Outcasts From Evolution: Scientific Attitudes of Racial Inferiority, 1859-1900.*   Urbana: University of Illinois Press, 1971.

Haller, Mark H.   *Eugenics: Hereditarian Attitudes in American Thought.*   New Brunswick, N.J.:   Rutgers University Press, 1963.

Harris, Marvin.   *Patterns of Race in the Americas.* New York: Walker and Company, 1964.

Herskovits, Melville J.   *The American Negro: A Study in Racial Crossing.*   New York: Alfred A. Knopf, Inc., 1928.

Hinkle, Roscoe C., and Hinkle, Gisela J.   *The Development of Modern Sociology, Its Nature and Growth in the United States.*   New York: Random House, 1954.

Hoetink, Harry.   *The Two Variants in Caribbean Race Relations: A Contribution to the Sociology of Segmented Societies.*   Translated by Eva M. Hooykaas.   London and New York: Published for the Institute of Race Relations by Oxford University Press, 1967.

Hofstadter, Richard M.   *Social Darwinism in American Thought.*   Rev. ed., Boston: Beacon Press, 1955.

Hogan, William Ransom, and Davis, Edwin Adams.   *The Barber of Natchez.*   Baton Rouge: Louisiana State University Press, 1954.

Holmes, William F.   *The White Chief: James Kimble Vardaman.*   Baton Rouge: Louisiana State University Press, 1970.

Hubbell, Jay B.   *The South in American Literature, 1607-1900.*   Durham, N.C.:   Duke University Press, 1954.

Jackson, Luther Porter.   *Free Negro Labor and Property Holding in Virginia, 1830-1860.* New York: D. Appleton-Century Co., Inc.

_____.   *Negro Office-Holders in Virginia, 1865-1895.*   Norfolk, Va.:   Guide Quality Press, 1945, [c. 1946].

James, D. Clayton.   *Antebellum Natchez.*   Baton Rouge: Louisiana State University Press, 1968.

Johnsen, Julia E., comp.   *Selected Articles on The Negro Problem.*   New York: H. W. Wilson Company, 1921.

Johnston, James Hugo.   *Race Relations in Virginia and Miscegenation in the South.* Amherst: University of Massachusetts Press, 1970.

Jordan, Winthrop D.   *White Over Black: American Attitudes Toward the Negro, 1550-1812.*   Chapel Hill: University of North Carolina Press, 1968.

Kemble, Frances Ann. *Journal of a Residence on a Georgia Plantation in 1838-1839.* New York: Harper & Brothers, 1863.

Kennedy, David M. *Birth Control in America: The Career of Margaret Sanger.* New Haven: Yale University Press, 1970.

Klineberg, Otto. *Characteristics of the American Negro.* New York: Harper & Brothers, 1944.

Kolchin, Peter. *First Freedom: The Responses of Alabama's Blacks to Emancipation and Reconstruction.* Westport, Conn.: Greenwood Press, 1972.

Levy, Eugene. *James Weldon Johnson: Black Leader, Black Voice.* Chicago: University of Chicago Press, 1973.

Litwack, Leon F. *North of Slavery: The Negro in the Free States, 1790-1860.* Chicago: University of Chicago Press, 1961.

Logan, Rayford W. *The Betrayal of the Negro from Rutherford B. Hayes to Woodrow Wilson.* London: Collier-Macmillan, 1965.

Loggins, Vernon. *The Negro Author: His Development in America to 1900.* New York: Columbia University Press, 1931.

Lovejoy, Arthur O. *The Great Chain of Being: A Study of the History of an Idea.* Cambridge: Harvard University Press, 1936.

Madge, John Hylton. *The Origins of Scientific Sociology.* New York: Free Press of Glencoe, 1962.

Mangum, Charles S., Jr. *The Legal Status of the Negro.* Chapel Hill: University of North Carolina Press, 1940.

Meier, August. *Negro Thought in America, 1880-1915: Racial Ideologies in the Age of Booker T. Washington.* Ann Arbor: University of Michigan Press, 1963.

_____, and Rudwick, Elliott M. *From Plantatiion to Ghetto: An Interpretive History of American Negroes.* New York: Hill and Wang, 1966.

Nash, Gary B. *Red, White and Black: The Peoples of Early America.* Englewood Cliffs, N.J.: Prentice-Hall, Inc., 1974.

Newby, Idus A. *Challenge to the Court: Social Scientists and the Defense of Segregation, 1954-1966.* Rev. ed. Baton Rouge: Louisiana State University Press, 1969.

_____. *Jim Crow's Defense: Anti-Negro Thought in America, 1900-1930.* Baton Rouge: Louisiana State University Press, 1965.

Nolen, Claude H. *The Negro's Image in the South: The Anatomy of White Supremacy.* Lexington: University of Kentucky Press, 1967.

Okoye, Felix N. *The American Image of Africa: Myth and Reality.* Buffalo: Black Academy Press, Inc., 1971.

Olmsted, Frederick Law. *A Journey in the Seaboard Slave States, with Remarks on Their Economy.* New York: Dix & Edwards, 1856.

Olsen, Otto H. *Carpetbagger's Crusade: The Life of Albion Winegar Tourgee.* Baltimore: Johns Hopkins University Press, 1965.

Osborn, Henry F.. *Cope: Master Naturalist.* Princeton, N.J.: Princeton University Press, 1931.

Park, Robert Ezra.. *Race and Culture.* Glencoe, Ill.: The Free Press, 1950.

Perdue, Robert E. *The Negro in Savannah, 1865-1900.* Jericho, N.Y.: Exposition Press, 1973.

Pettigrew, Thomas F. *A Profile of the American Negro.* Princeton, N.J.: D. Van Norstrand Company, Inc., 1964.

Pettit, Arthur G. *Mark Twain and the South.* Lexington: University of Kentucky Press, 1974.

Reuter, Edward Byron. *The American Race Problem: A Study of the Negro.* New York: Thomas Y. Crowell Company, 1927.

_____. *Race Mixture: Studies in Intermarriage and Miscegnation.* New York: Whittlesey House of McGraw-Hill Book Company, Inc., 1931.

Rice, Lawrence D. *The Negro in Texas, 1874-1900.* Baton Rouge: Louisiana State University Press, 1971.

Sellers, James Benson. *Slavery in Alabama.* University: University of Alabama Press, 1950.

Smith, Samuel Denny. *The Negro in Congress, 1870-1901.* Chapel Hill: University of North Carolina Press, 1940.

Stampp, Kenneth M. *The Peculiar Institution: Slavery in the Ante-Bellum South.* Vintage Books. New York: Random House, 1956.

Stanton, William. *The Leopard's Spots: Scientific Attitudes toward Race in America, 1815-1859.* Chicago: University of Chicago Press, 1960.

Starke, Catherine Juanita. *Black Portraiture in American Fiction: Stock Characters, Archetypes and Individuals.* New York: Basic Books, Inc., 1971.

Sterkx, H. E. *The Free Negro in Ante-Bellum Louisiana.* Rutherford, N.J.: Fairleigh Dickinson University Press, 1972.

Stocking, George W. *Race, Culture, and Evolution: Essays in the History of Anthropology..* New York: The Free Press, 1968.

Stonequist, Everett V. *The Marginal Man: A Study in Personality and Culture Conflict.* New York: Charles Scribner's Sons, 1937.

Taylor, Orville W. *Negro Slavery in Arkansas.* Durham, N.C.: Duke University Press, 1958.

Tindall, George B. *South Carolina Negroes, 1877-1900.* Columbia: University of South Carolina Press, 1952.

Tischler, Nancy M *Black Masks: Negro Characters In Modern Southern Fiction.* University Park: Pennsylvania State University Press, 1969.

Tucker, David M. *Black Pastors and Leaders: Memmphis, 1819-1972.* Memphis: Memphis State Univeristy Press, 1975.

Tuttle, William M., Jr., ed. *W. E. B. Du Bois.* Great Lives Observed. Englewood Cliffs, N.J.: Prentice-Hall, Inc., 1973.

Vogeli, Jacque. *Free But Not Equal: The Midwest and the Negro During the Civil War.* Chicago: University of Chicago Press, 1967.

Washington, Booker T. *The Future of the American Negro.* Boston: Small, Maynard & Company, 1900.

Whiteman, Maxwell. *A Century of Fiction by American Negroes, 1853-1952: A Descriptive Bibliography.* Philadelphia: By the Author, 1955.

Wikramanayake, Marine. *A World in Shadow: The Free Black in Antebellum South Carolina.* Columbia: University of South Carolina Press, 1973.

Williamson, Joel. *After Slavery: The Negro in South Carolina During Reconstruction, 1861-1877.* Chapel Hill: University of North Carolina Press, 1965.

[Wilson, Joseph W.] *Sketches of the Higher Classes of Colored Society in Philadelphia.* Philadelphia: 1841.

Wood, Forrest G. *Black Scare: The Racist Response to Emancipation and Reconstruction.* Berkeley: University of California Press, 1968.

Wood, Peter H. *Black Majority: Negroes in Colonial South Carolina From 1670 through the Stono Rebellion.* New York: Alfred A. Knopf, Inc., 1974.

Woodson, Carter G. *Free Negro Heads of Families in the United Sates in 1830.* Washington, D.C.: Association for the Study of Negro Life and History, Inc., 1925.

Woodward, C. Vann. *The Strange Career of Jim Crow.* 2nd. rev. ed. New York: Oxford University Press, 1966.

Wynes, Charles E. *Race Relations in Virginia, 1870-1902.* Charlottesville: University of Virginia, 1961.

II. ARTICLES

Amacher, Anne Ward. "The Genteel Primitivist and the Semi-Tragic Octoroon." *New England Quarterly,* XXIX, 2 (June, 1956), 216-227.

Barr, Ruth B., and Hargis, Modeste. "The Voluntary Exile of Free Negroes of Pensacola." *Florida Historical Quarterly*, XVII, 1 (July, 1938), 1-14.

Benjamin, Marcus. "Edward Drinker Cope." *Leading American Men of Science.* Edited by David Starr Jordan. New York: Henry Holt and Company, 1910.

Berry, Mary F. "Negro Troops in Blue and Gray: The Louisiana Native Guard, 1861-1863." *Louisiana History*, VIII, 2 (Spring, 1967), 165-190.

Blakely, Allison. "Richard T. Greener and the 'Talented Tenth's' Dilemma." *Journal of Negro History*, LIX, 4 (October, 1974), 305-321.

Bloomfield, Maxwell. "Dixon's *The Leopard's Spots*: A Study in Popular Racism." *American Quarterly*, XVI, 3 (Fall, 1964), 387-401.

Brown, Sterling A. "Alas the Poor Mulatto." *Opportunity*, XI, 3 (March, 1933), 91.

————. "A Century of Negro Portraiture in American Literature." *Massachusetts Review*, VII, 1 (Winter, 1966), 73-96.

————. "Negro Characters as Seen by White Authors." *Journal of Negro Education*, II, 2 (April, 1933), 179-203.

Browning, James B. "The Beginnings of Insurance Enterprise Among Negroes." *Journal of Negro History*, XXII, 4 (October, 1937), 417-432.

Bullock, Penelope L. "The Mulatto in American Fiction." *Phylon*, VI, 1 (Spring, 1945), 78-82.

Carter, Everett. "Cultural History Written with Lightening: The Significance of *The Birth of a Nation*." *American Quarterly*, XII, 3 (Fall, 1960), 347-357.

Collier, Eugenia. "The Endless Journey of an Ex-Coloured Man." *Phylon*, XXXII, 4 (Winter, 1971), 365-374.

Cox, James M. "*Pudd'nhead Wilson*: The End of Mark Twain's American Dream." *South Atlantic Quarterly*, LVIII (1959), 351-363.

Daykin, Walter L. "Negro Types in American White Fiction." *Sociology and Social Research*, XXII, 1 (September-October, 1937), 45-52.

Diggs, Irene. "Color in Colonial Spanish America." *Journal of Negro History*, XXXVIII, 4 (October, 1953), 403-427.

Du Bois, W. E. Burghardt. "Postscript: Chesnutt." *The Crisis*, XL, 1 (January, 1933), 20.

Duncan, John D. "Slave Emancipation in Colonial South Carolina." *American Chronicle, A Magazine of History*, I, 1 (January, 1972), 59-70.

Everett, Donald E. "Free Persons of Color in Colonial Louisiana." *Louisiana History*, VII, 1 (Winter, 1966), 21-50.

Fitchett, E. Horace. "The Origin and Growth of the Free Negro Population of Charleston, South Carolina." *Journal of Negro History*, XXVI, 4 (October, 1941), 421-437.

_____. "The Traditions of the Free Negro in Charleston, South Carolina." *Journal of Negro History*, XXV, 2 (April, 1940), 139-152.

Fleming, Robert E. "Sutton E. Griggs: Militant Black Novelist." *Phylon*, XXXIV, 1 (Spring, 1973), 73-77.

Foner, Laura. "The Free People of Color in Louisiana and St. Domingue: A Comparative Portrait of Two Three-Caste Slave Societies." *Journal of Social History*, III, 4 (Summer, 1970), 406-430.

Ford, Thomas W. "The Miscegenation Theme in *Pudd'nhead Wilson*." *Mark Twain Journal*, X, 1 (1955), 13-14.

Garvin, Russell. "The Free Negro in Florida Before the Civil War." *Florida Historical Quarterly*, XLVI, 1 (July, 1967), 1-17.

Gloster, Hugh. "Sutton Griggs, Novelist of the New Negro." *Phylon*, IV, 4 (1943), 335-345.

Haller, John S., Jr. "Civil War Anthropometry: The Making of a Racial Ideology." *Civil War History*, XVI, 4 (December, 1970), 309-324.

_____. "Race and the Concept of Progress in Nineteenth Century American Ethnology." *American Anthropologist*, LXXIII, 3 (June, 1971), 710-724.

_____. "Race, Mortality, and Life Insurance: Negro Vital Statistics in the Late Nineteenth Century." *Journal of the History of Medicine and Allied Sciences*, XXV, 3 (July, 1970), 247-261.

_____. "The Species Problem: Nineteenth-Century Concepts of Racial Inferiority in the Origin of Man Controversy." *American Anthropologist*, LXXII, 6 (December, 1970), 1319-1329.

Herskovits, Melville J. "A Critical Discussion of the 'Mulatto Hypothesis.'" *Journal of Negro Education*, III, 3 (July, 1934), 389-402.

Hoetink, Harry. "Race Relations in Caraçao and Surinam." *Slavery in the New World: A Reader in Comparative History*. Edited by Laura Foner and Eugene D. Genovese. Englewood Cliffs, N. J.: Prentice-Hall, Inc., 1969.

Horowitz, Donald L. "Color Differentiation in the American System of Slavery." *Journal of Interdisciplinary History*, III, 3 (Winter, 1973), 509-543.

Jenks, Albert Ernest. "The Legal Status of Negro-White Amalgamation in the United States." *American Journal of Sociology*, XXI, 5 (March, 1916), 666-678.

Johnson, Charles S., and Bond, Horace M. "The Investigation of Racial Differences Prior to 1910." *Journal of Negro Education*, III, 3 (July, 1934), 328-339.

Johnson, Guion Griffis. "The Ideology of White Supremacy, 1876-1910." *Essays in Southern History*. Edited by Fletcher Melvin Green. James Sprunt Studies in History and Politican Science, Vol. 31. Chapel Hill: University of North Carolina Press, 1949.

Jordan, Winthrop D. "American Chiaroscuro: The Status and Definition of Mulattoes in the British Colonies." *William and Mary Quarterly*, 3rd ser., XIX, 2 (April, 1962), 183-200.

Klein, Herbert S. "The Colored Freedmen in Brazilian Slave Society." *Journal of Social History*, III, 1 (Fall, 1969), 30-52.

Lamplugh, George R. "The Image of the Negro in Popular Magazine Fiction, 1875-1900." *Journal of Negro History*, LVII, 2 (April, 1972), 177-189.

Larson, Charles R. "The Novels of Paul Laurence Dunbar." *Phylon*, XXIX, 3 (Fall, 1968), 257-271.

Levy, David W. "Racial Stereotypes in Antislavery Fiction." *Phylon*, XXXI, 3 (Fall, 1970), 265-279.

Meier, August. "Negro Class Structure and Ideology in the Age of Booker T. Washington." *Phylon*, XXIII, 3 (Fall, 1962), 258-266.

Montagu, M. F. Ashley. "The Myth of Blood." *Psychiatry*, VI, 1 (February, 1943), 15-19.

The Nation, I, 11 (September 14, 1865), 332.

Noxen, Frank W. "College Professors Who Are Men of Letters." *The Critic*, XLII, 2 (February, 1903), 124-135.

Odum, Herbert H. "Generalizations on Race in Nineteenth-Century Physical Anthropology." *Isis*, LVIII, 1 (Spring, 1967), 5-18.

Park, Robert E. "Mentality of Racial Hybrids." *American Journal of Sociology*, XXXVI, 4 (January, 1931), 534-551.

Pekkala, Salme; Hamilton, Marian B.; and Alford, Wiley, comps. "Some Words and Terms Designating, or Relating to, Racially Mixed Persons or Groups." *Race: Individual and Collective Behavior*. Edited by Edgar T. Thompson and Everett C. Hughes. Glencoe, Ill.: The Free Press, 1958.

Perry, Louis Clausiel. "Studies in the Religious Life of the Negroes of Nashville, Tennessee." *Vanderbilt University Quarterly*, IV, 2 (April, 1904), 80-97.

Pfeifer, Edward J. "The Genesis of American Neo-Lamarckism." *Isis*, LVI, 2 (Summer, 1965), 156-167.

Reuter, Edward Byron. "Racial Theory." *American Journal of Sociology*, L, 6 (May, 1945), 452-461.

Shockley, Ann Allen. "Pauline Elizabeth Hopkins: A Biographical Excursion Into Obscurity." *Phylon*, XXXIII 1 (Spring, 1972), 22-26.

Simkins, Francis Butler. "Ben Tillman's View of the Negro." *Journal of Southern History*, III, 2 (May, 1937), 161-174.

Stonequist, Everett V. "The Problem of the Marginal Man." *American Journal of Sociology*, XLI, 1 (July, 1935), 1-12.

_____. "Race Mixture and the Mulatto." *Race Relations and the Race Problem: A Definition and an Analysis*. Edited by Edgar T. Thompson. Durham, N.C.: Duke University Press, 1939.

Sydnor Charles S. "The Free Negro in Mississippi Before the Civil War." *American Historical Review*, XXXII, 4 (July, 1927), 769-788.

Thomas, David Y. "The Free Negro in Florida Before 1865." *South Atlantic Quarterly*, X, 4 (October, 1911), 333-345.

Tregle, Joseph G., Jr. "Early New Orleans Society: A Reappraisal." *Journal of Southern History*, XVIII, 1 (February, 1952), 20-36.

Vitales, Morris S. "The Mental Status of the Negro." *Annals of tthe American Academy of Political and Social Science: The American Negro*, CXL (November, 1928), 166-177.

Welter, Barbara. "The Cult of True Womanhood, 1820-1860." *American Quarterly*, XVIII, 2 (Summer, 1966), 151-174.

Woodson, Carter G.. "The Beginnings of Miscegenation of Whites and Blacks." *Journal of Negro History*, III, 4 (October, 1918), 335-353.

Zanger, Jules. "The 'Tragic Octoroon' in Pre-Civil War Fiction." *American Quarterly*, XVIII, 1 1(Spring, 1966), 63-70.

Zelinsky, Wilbur. "The Population Geography of the Free Negro in *Ante-Bellum America*." *Population Studies*, III, 4 (March, 1950), 386-401.

III. UNPUBLISHED MATERIALS

Bullock, Penelope L. "The Treatment of the Mulatto in American Fiction from 1826 to 1902." Unpublished M.A. thesis, Atlanta University, 1944.

Boucher, Morris Raymond. "The Free Negro in Alabama Prior to 1860." Unpublished Ph.D. dissertation, State University of Iowa, 1950.

Burton, O. Vernon. "The Slave Community in Edgefield, South Carolina, 1850-1880." Unpublished Ph.D. dissertation, Princeton University, 1975.

Darnell, Regna. "Daniel Garrison Brinton: An Intellectual Biography." Unpublished M.A. thesis, Univeristy of Pennsylvania, 1967.

Fitchett, E. Horace. "The Origins and Growth of the Free Negro Population of Charleston, South Carolina." Unpublished Ph.D. dissertation, University of Chicago, 1950.

Flewelling, Roy Stanley, Jr. "Three Voices on Race: Thomas Dixon, Marcus Garvey and Lothrop Stoddard on the Future of the American Stock." Unpublished M.A. thesis, University of North Carolina at Chapel Hill, 1971.

Ford, Nick Aaron. "The Negro Author's Use of Propaganda in Imaginative Literature." Unpublished Ph.D. dissertation, State University of Iowa, 1945.

Harris, Max Frank. "The Ideas of Thomas Dixon on Race Relations." Unpublished M.A. thesis, University of North Carolina at Chapel Hill, 1948.

Holt, Thomas. "The Emergence of Negro Political Leadership in South Carolina During Reconstruction." Unpublished Ph.D. dissertation, Yale University, 1973.

Peterson, Margaret Frances. "Suspended Animation: Race Relations in the Literature of Charles Waddell Chesnutt, David Bryant Fulton and James Ephraim McGirt." Unpublished M.A. thesis, University of North Carolina at Chapel Hill, 1972.

Piper, Ada. "Activities of Negroes in the Territorial Government of the District of Columbia, 1871-1874." Unpublished M.A. thesis, Howard University, 1943.

Ramsey, William McCrea. "Character Stereotypes in the Novels of Charles Waddell Chesnutt." Unpublished M.A. thesis, University of North Carolina at Chapel Hill, 1969.

Smith, Helena M. "Negro Characterization in the American Novel: A Historical Survey of Work by White Authors." Unpublished Ph.D. dissertation, Pennsylvania State University, 1959.

Stocking, George Ward, Jr. "American Social Scientists and Race Theory: 1890-1915." Unpublished Ph.D. dissertation, University of Pennsylvania, 1960.

Sweat, Edward F. "The Free Negro in Ante-Bellum Georgia." Unpublished Ph.D. dissertation, Indiana University, 1957.

INDEX

83031

E
185.62
M46

MENCKE, JOHN
    MULATTOES AND RACE MIXTURE.